Emmett Till and the Mississippi Press

Emmett Till and the Mississippi Press

Davis W. Houck and Matthew A. Grindy

Foreword by
Keith A. Beauchamp

University Press of Mississippi
Jackson

www.upress.state.ms.us

The University Press of Mississippi is a member of
the Association of American University Presses.

Copyright © 2008 by University Press of Mississippi
All rights reserved
Manufactured in the United States of America

∞

Library of Congress Cataloging-in-Publication Data

Houck, Davis W.
Emmett Till and the Mississippi press / Davis W. Houck and Matthew A. Grindy ;
foreword by Keith A. Beauchamp.
p. cm.
Includes bibliographical references and index.
ISBN-13: 978-1-934110-15-7 (cloth : alk. paper)
ISBN-10: 1-934110-15-9 (cloth : alk. paper) 1. Mississippi—Race relations—
Press coverage. 2. Till, Emmett, 1941–1955—Death and burial—Press
coverage. 3. African Americans—Crimes against—Mississippi—Press
coverage. 4. Trials (Murder)—Mississippi—Sumner—Press coverage. 5. African
Americans—Civil rights—Mississippi—Press coverage. 6. Journalism—Political
aspects—Mississippi—History—20th century. 7. Rhetoric—Political aspects—
Mississippi—History—20th century. 8. Racism—Mississippi—History—20th
century. 9. Mississippi—Race relations—History—20th century. 10. Public
opinion—Mississippi—History—20th century. I. Grindy, Matthew A. II. Title.
E185.93.M6H59 2008
364.1′34—dc22

2007014910

British Library Cataloging-in-Publication Data available

To Emmett, of course,
===

and Javorius Allen, Shawn Bryan, Franklin Mitchell,
Willie Holloway, Akeila Pleas, Deon'Shaye Lilly,
Antonio Jenkins, Marquise Jenkins, Theodus Holloway,
and Kwamen Battle—Emmett's heirs at the
Miccosukee Carrie Wilson Boys and Girls Club
and also
to the Northwest ghost town hunter who sparked my
fascination with history—my father, Scott Grindy

Contents

Foreword   *ix*

Acknowledgments   *xiii*

Introduction   *3*

One
"Sowing Seeds of Hatred"
(August 28–September 1)   *12*

Two
"Comely Carolyn"
(September 2–September 6)   *26*

Three
"Resentful of the Slant"
(September 7–September 9)   *44*

Four
"The World Is Watching"
(September 10–September 18)   *58*

Five
"Every Last Anglo-Saxon One of You"
(September 19–September 23)   *72*

Six
"Forgotten as Quickly as Possible"?
(September 24–September 30)   *107*

Seven
"Like Father—Like Son"
(October 1955–January 1956)   *126*

Eight
Retrospective Prospects   *153*

Notes   *167*

Works Cited   *189*

Index   *207*

Foreword

> The events which transpired five thousand years ago; five years ago or five minutes ago, have determined what will happen five minutes from now; five years from now or five thousand years from now. All history is a current event.
>
> —Dr. John Henrik Clarke

Knowledge is power and nowhere is that truer than in the investigative information acquired during my twelve years of research on the Emmett Till case. Armed with the right facts one can change the way history is written and encourage a nation to reevaluate that history. We must remember that initiating a cleansing dialogue is crucial in the process of racial reconciliation.

My journey with Emmett Louis Till began when I was just ten years of age growing up in Baton Rouge, Louisiana. Very inquisitive and a lover of reading, I can remember rumbling through some old magazines my parents kept in our study. Standing out very conspicuously, I noticed an old *Jet Magazine* and decided to take a look. After turning a few pages, I accidentally came across a photo of the disfigured face of Emmett Till. As I remember, on one page a gray Fedora graced his head, a round but friendly light-skinned face that looked angelic. But illuminated from the page of the cover story and on another page was the horrific, disfigured face that his mother, the late Mrs. Mamie Till-Mobley, would describe as the face of hate. From that day to present, I have not been able to get that image out of my mind. It is as if this was the Creator's way of introducing me to what has become a most influential memory in my life. How did this little boy end up like this? Since 1995, that's a question that permeates most of my waking moments.

The Emmett Till case quickly became an educational tool used in my household to teach me about the racism that still lurks in America. Young Emmett Till has become what Anne Frank is to many in the Jewish community—a name, a face, and a lesson forever etched in the consciousness of Black America.

On May 10, 2004, forty-nine years after the murder of Emmett Till, my dream finally came to fruition when it was announced that the United States Justice Department was reopening this infamous murder case, citing my research and film both as a major factor and as a starting point for its investigation. Words can't express the pride I felt knowing that I was able to fulfill

Foreword

a promise that I made to Emmett's mother before she passed away on January 6, 2003.

It has taken decades to finally come closer to the truth surrounding the murder of Emmett Louis Till, a fourteen-year-old Black Chicago youth slain near Money, Mississippi, August 28, 1955. Till was a mere boy when he visited his southern relatives and lost his life in the stifling landscape of the Mississippi Delta; it was a part of the world infamous for its unrelenting caste system. In a letter to a northern friend written in the fall of 1965, one of the Delta's most fearless leaders, Mrs. Fannie Lou Hamer, wrote, "it's like waiting for a dangerous beast to come out. You [know] he is there but you just can't do anything but wait." That beast devoured the cocky young boy friends and relatives called Bobo. He never had the chance to grow up to face life's challenges and become a productive citizen. His innocence was taken for the simple act of a whistle, a whistle that can still be heard more than fifty years later.

One hundred days after the murder of Emmett Louis Till, a fearless seamstress, Mrs. Rosa Parks, heard Till's whistle, and when she was asked what was going through her mind when she refused to get up from her seat on a city bus in Montgomery, Alabama, Mrs. Parks replied, "I thought of Emmett Till, and I just couldn't go back." Till's whistle would also be heard through the ears of a Baptist minister, Dr. Martin Luther King Jr., who would lead the Montgomery Bus Boycott at twenty-six years of age and later lead a nation into a movement for "change." Dr. King stated, that the "Till case served as an intimidation tactic to keep Black people away from the voting polls."

This infamous murder would continue to haunt the American psyche, inspiring some of the most important activists of our day. Muhammad Ali, James Baldwin, Toni Morrison, and a generation of civil rights activists have credited Emmett Till's murder as a major influence on their lives.

The Till case was undeniably a pivotal factor in mobilizing what would become the American Civil Rights Movement. To many, the murder was just a senseless act, committed by two white men with total disregard for the life of a black boy. For those who have been touched by his legacy, his murder has proven to be a catalyst for change; it continues to serve as a milestone of this country's dark civil rights past, which transcends generations, cultures, and color lines.

If it weren't for the gruesome image of Emmett Till, there would likely not be a Keith A. Beauchamp, filmmaker, today. So, too, perhaps with the overall media coverage of the Till case, which many believe contributed to the mass movement that became the Black Freedom Movement.

I first met Davis Houck and Matt Grindy back in February 2006, when I

Foreword

spoke at Florida State University's thirty-first annual Film and Literature Conference held in Tallahassee. At a panel presentation on how the Mississippi press wrote about the murder and trial, I was fascinated by what Houck and Grindy call the rhetorical dynamics of the journalists' coverage of the case. While we were using a different lexicon and a different medium, it was clear that we shared a common concern for the many injustices committed on August 28, 1955, and afterward. Over a memorable lunch at Carlos's Cuban Cafe, we quickly became far more than individuals interested in an old civil rights case; we discovered, in the way that friends do, that our backgrounds and sensibilities led us in very similar directions. We promised to stay in touch. We did—and we have.

Readers of Houck and Grindy's revealing and amazing journey through the Mississippi press will come away with a new appreciation for what blacks faced in the Jim Crow Deep South circa 1955. It is clear that far more was at stake than the murder of a northern black boy; rather, the case quickly embodied all of the South's post-*Brown* fears: miscegenation, the threat of a domestic communist conspiracy, the end of its Way of Life, an unrelenting hatred and suspicion of the North. But Houck and Grindy also show us many heretofore unknown aspects of the Till case: how the police issued a warrant for Carolyn Bryant's arrest; how the Till family initially was received positively; how Roy Wilkins and the NAACP's involvement changed the dynamics in Mississippi; how and why Sheriff H. C. Strider contradicted his grand jury and trial testimony; the likelihood that the defense planned a defense of justifiable homicide. In sum, Houck and Grindy reveal many details about the case that helped acquit J. W. Milam and Roy Bryant. And convicted Mississippi. Theirs is a fascinating history, of interest to those of us who grew up with Emmett Till, and to the many who are only just now learning about a boy, a whistle, and a murder.

Keith A. Beauchamp
Brooklyn, NY

Acknowledgments

In researching and writing on the Emmett Till case over the past several years, we have incurred many debts, perhaps none greater than to Hugh Stephen Whitaker for pioneering work done back in 1962. As a master's degree student at Florida State University, Steve risked a great deal in getting many Mississippians to talk openly about the murder, trial, and aftermath. Forty-five years later, this native son of Tallahatchie County remains a unique and important source on the case, a critical reader and a good listener. He is also a friend and neighbor. We also received great encouragement and feedback from Keith Beauchamp, another son of the South devoted to seeking justice for the killing of Emmett Till. When Keith could have easily played the role of prima donna filmmaker and *60 Minutes* subject on a visit to Tallahassee, instead he eagerly shared resources and offered expert counsel, and he always followed through. If Emmett Till and his family one day get justice, it will be in no small part because of Keith's fearless and indefatigable work.

Sometimes racist organizations inadvertently contribute to salubrious ends; such is the case in this project. Not long ago Reverend Edwin King of Jackson, Mississippi, was bequeathed a gift from a former secretary of a local white Citizens' Council: a trove of local and national newspaper articles on the Till murder, trial, and aftermath. Reverend King, who is without peer when it comes to sharing primary and secondary source material on a movement he helped lead, generously loaned us the council's stash of documents. We are also grateful to the former Tougaloo chaplain for carefully reading and commenting on an earlier draft of this manuscript. We also received important documents from Devery Anderson, whose website—www.emmetttillmurder.com—is a terrific resource for anyone looking to research the case. Devery also offered valuable suggestions for tracking down missing names, dates, and places. We look forward to reading his book on Emmett Till in the near future.

This project could not have been conducted with any degree of completeness without the treasures of the Mississippi Department of Archives and History in Jackson. To the organization and its hard-working staff, go thanks for helping us tell a painful and personal story about a state much maligned for its racial past. Certainly no other state has stared as unblinkingly at its past as has Mississippi—and done something about it. Part of that reconciliation

Acknowledgments

project resides in Cleveland, Mississippi, under the auspices of the Delta Center for Culture and Learning and its generous director, Luther Brown. Luther and Dr. Henry Outlaw hosted a class of Florida State University students and one anxious professor in the fall of 2004; in the process they made civil-rights history come alive to a group weaned on books and articles. We will never forget the haunted beauty of the long-abandoned Bryant Grocery and Meat Market—or the lunch that followed it.

Our home university, Florida State, provided many resources as this project moved through its various stages. Perhaps the most valuable resource of all came in the form of seven talented, hard-working, and early rising undergraduates. We thank Jennifer Santoro, Nicole Maestri, Mary Hice, Beth Walker, Jason Parker, Shelly Sobol, and Kate Ficarrotta for enduring a semester of painstaking microfilm work on our behalf. Thanks also go to the good folks at Strozier Library's interlibrary loan department and its intrepid director, Velma Smith, for making sure our many Mississippi orders got filled.

Several people read and commented on earlier drafts of this book, none more thoroughly than Dave Dixon of Saint Joseph's College and Mark Mulligan of Florida State University. Thanks also go to Bill Lawson, Beth Walker, Ulla Bunz, Ingrid Hatten, Chuck Morris, Marty Medhurst, Stephen J. Whitfield, Denise Bostdorff, Colm McAindru, and Kate Ficarrotta for providing helpful feedback as the project unfolded.

We offer a special thank you to Charles McLaurin of Indianola, Mississippi, and the Student Nonviolent Coordinating Committee. "Mr. Mac," as he is known in his adopted hometown, gave two strangers several hours of riveting oral history about what it meant to grow up young and black and ambitious in Jim Crow Mississippi. You are right, Mr. Mac: that visage of Frederick Douglass becomes you.

The staff at the University Press of Mississippi has encouraged and nurtured this project from day one. To Seetha Srinivasan and Walter Biggins, in particular, go our thanks for having faith in the project, acting promptly on that faith, and providing sage counsel as we moved through the often difficult process of publication. We understand so much better now why this press remains a leading light among university presses, especially in its commitment to the complicated and often painful subjects of race and social justice.

Finally, to our friends and families who have lived with this project and probably know more about Emmett Till and civil rights than they had ever hoped, we give our thanks and love. Davis wishes to thank Ingrid Hatten for her critical eye, her willing ear, and for giving up her summer to make sure

Acknowledgments

that this book made it to print. Matt is especially thankful for the assistance of his brilliant and supportive spouse, Amber Bell, who provided insightful editing; and the in-depth discussions during walks around Lake Ella were critical to the creative flow. When Matt's participation in this project was threatened by a series of unexpected life events, she lifted him quite literally back into the academic saddle. He is eternally grateful for her encouragement to pursue his passion.

Emmett Till and the Mississippi Press

Introduction

> For two days the river keeps you down
> Then you rise to the light without a sound
> Past the playgrounds and empty switching yards
> The turtles eat the skin from your eyes so they lay open to the stars.
> Your clothes give way to the current and river stone
> Till every trace of who you ever were is gone
> And the things of the earth they make their claim
> That the things of heaven may do the same.
>
> Bruce Springsteen, *Matamoros Banks*

When we first listened to the mournful lament of *Matamoros Banks*, the final song of Bruce Springsteen's haunting meditation on living and dying, *Devils and Dust*, we could not help but ask the question: Was this Emmett Till he was singing about? Even though later verses depict a Mexican's fatal journey to the U.S. border, how curious that Springsteen got so many of the details right. It was on the third day that the fourteen-year-old Chicago boy's lifeless and naked corpse finally broke the surface of the muddy Tallahatchie River, his legs raised by an eddy in the current, his torso anchored with barbwire to a muddy bottom by the heavy blast wheel of a cotton gin fan. The catfish and turtles had feasted on his terribly mutilated body. In fact, the body was so bloated and disfigured that even his great-uncle Moses Wright could not immediately identify him; it would take a ring to finally coax Wright to believe that his great-nephew lay lifeless in front of him. And what of the corporeal violence of a Jim Crow world which set into motion the justice and grace of the eternal? The zero-sum cosmology ensured that the "big talking" boy they called Bobo would make out on the other side—and in our collective consciousness.

But in addition to the factual details, what are we to make of Springsteen's line 6? Was the musician, whose scrupulous attention to lyrical detail is legendary, trying to show us his cards a bit more conspicuously? Even if it is an abbreviation, beginning a line with "Till" in a song with this many striking parallels to a case about crossing a different sort of border, perhaps Springsteen is attempting to get us to see racial and ethnic mobility anew. And the irony is somewhat jarring: even though "every trace" of bodily identity is gone, still there is a successful identification; somehow the dead can still speak. That Springsteen might even develop narrative parallels between the Till case and illegal immigration also tells us something quite profound about a boy and an event that defined civil rights for a generation of activists.

Something about that boy and his murder in 1955 continues to resonate with us more than fifty years after the awful desecration. The story has migrated a long way in the interim: from a small-town disappearance worthy of three brief paragraphs in the local paper to a story on the front pages of international newspapers and a wedge issue in the cold war; something about the Emmett Till story captivated us. Was it the archetypal quality of the story? Were the villains so villainous and the saints so virtuous that any moral vexation expressed about the case was just another manifestation of racism? Was it part of the story of America, a nation struggling, in Dr. King's words, "to live out the true meaning of its creed?" Had Emmett Till become America's Anne Frank, a photograph substituted for a diary? Or was this simply an interracial drama about sex and murder in the Deep South, though cast in compelling ways and staged without a clear ending? Perhaps it was all of them. But where did this all start? And why? And how? We think answers can be found in Mississippi.

Even as his lye-packed corpse headed north on the Illinois Central railroad, Emmett Louis Till would never really leave the state of Mississippi. More than fifty years after the kidnap-murder, the black fourteen-year-old Chicago boy has even become part of the physical landscape. In the summer of 2005, Mississippi unveiled the Emmett Till Memorial Highway, a thirty-two-mile stretch of Highway 49E that connects Tutwiler and Greenwood. While the highway's rechristening was featured prominently in the Mississippi press, little commented upon was a historically apropos junction: in a small Delta town, the Emmett Till Memorial Highway intersects with the H. C. "Clarence" Strider Highway. In the town of Webb, the burly sheriff who actually testified for the defense crosses paths with the supposed "big talking, wolf whistler." That small town is also the birthplace of none other than Till's mother, Mamie. A busy and memorable intersection, for certain.

While Mississippi lawmakers might not have been fully aware of the rhetorical significance of the memorial, nor yet its memorable crossroads, it is an altogether fitting part of the Delta landscape: the road begins in Leflore County, not far from the tiny hamlet of Money, where Emmett was abducted, crosses into Tallahatchie County, where his badly beaten body was recovered, and skirts the county seat of Sumner, where the murder trial took place. And yet the Till memorialization project does not end, literally, in Tutwiler. Even today, plans are in place for a Till memorial at the courthouse

Introduction

in Leflore County and a memorial path that leads from Money to Sumner. There is even talk of possible memorial status for the long-abandoned Bryant Grocery and Meat Market in Money.

Do all Mississippi roads lead inevitably back to Emmett Till? In *Sons of Mississippi: A Story of Race and Its Legacy*, Paul Hendrickson uses a slightly different metaphor: nearly every Mississippi story touches, in "some spiritual, homing way," on the Till case and its accompanying geography. The ironies of the memorialization project abound: Till was from Chicago and spoke memorably to Carolyn Bryant in a "northern brogue"; following the trial, opinion leaders in Mississippi hoped that the murder and trial would simply be forgotten; a conservative Mississippi legislature created the highway bill with almost as much haste as the Tallahatchie jurymen brought in their not guilty verdict; and, a body, once rumored to be a plant of the National Association for the Advancement of Colored People (NAACP), now occupies uncontested symbolic space.[1]

But the question is still begged: Why all the fuss? Why all the public handwringing over the death of one young black boy murdered by supposedly two local white men? Should public comment not have ceased with the supposed confession of the murderers in a January 1956 issue of *Look* magazine? In contemplating this important question, we would do well to note that all memorials perform a re-membering function; that is, public memorials stitch together a preferred and political visage, a new body. In Mississippi's case, no doubt the Till memorial enthusiasm is bound up with re-membering Emmett, whose body was so memorably dismembered. A body that was never correctly identified, it seems, is remembered instead in perpetuity.

And yet the Emmett Till case does not belong exclusively to Mississippi. Beginning with the television documentary *Eyes on the Prize* and Stephen J. Whitfield's book *A Death in the Delta*, scholars, playwrights, poets, songwriters, filmmakers—even Hollywood producers—remain riveted by it. Ebay customers can even buy Emmett Till "55" Jerseys. An advanced Google search on "Emmett Till" reveals 308,000 hits as of January 2007. Researchers and activists are even having loud, public fights over who got what first. Motivating much of this fixation is Keith Beauchamp's highly publicized and acclaimed documentary *The Untold Story of Emmett Louis Till*. In conducting interviews and research for that documentary, Beauchamp uncovered more than a dozen people who were involved, to varying degrees and in various capacities, with Till's murder. So compelling was his evidence that the Justice Department, with the cooperation of the Federal Bureau of Investigation (FBI), announced in May 2004 that the case would be reopened. This

Introduction

has catapulted Beauchamp into such prominent places as CBS's *60 Minutes* and Emmett Till back into national headlines.[2]

With all the public discourse on the case, why yet another book? Our project begins with a rather simple premise: predominantly white Mississippi newspapers significantly influenced public opinion in the state about the murder, trial, and aftermath. On the surface, our aim is also rather simple: documenting how that public opinion got formed and re-formed based on a careful reading of Mississippi newspaper articles, editorials, photographs, and letters to the editor. But as we will demonstrate in the chapters that follow, the "Till case," as it has come to be known, is not a simple story of two white defendants, a black victim, and the search for justice. The case became so much more so quickly that, more than fifty years later, it is little wonder that the case is central to Mississippi history, politics, and memory. The Till case quickly grew to encompass North-South relations; the role of Citizens' Councils and pro-civil-rights groups after *Brown v. Board of Education*; federalism versus localism; an increasingly hot cold war; the complicated roles of white women, black men, and social equality; imperiled white masculinity—and always the news media.

Perhaps more than any other theme, the Till case threw into dramatic relief the contested role of newspapers in adjudicating justice. Mamie Till often commented on the irony that one of the last pictures of her son was taken as he leaned against a television set; the new medium would indeed play a pivotal role in the nascent civil-rights movement. But far more important in 1955 was the role of newspapers and how the medium itself became a key battleground in the nation's racial consciousness. Some of the most important battles were fought early and in Mississippi, and, while Emmett Till provided a point of entry, the case quickly became far bigger than a black boy, an untoward whistle, and two insulted white half-brothers.[3]

So much bigger: in fact, for several months the Emmett Till case was nothing if not a high-stakes game of rhetorical criticism. That is, in editorial pages around the state, Mississippi journalists attempted to persuade their readers of the extent to which "outsiders" generally and northern newsmen particularly propagandized on behalf of a liberal Supreme Court, the NAACP, and Communists. In other words, any attack on the part of northern journalists related to the trial quickly became an attack on the state, its people, and its segregated way of life. Thus was the South fighting a proxy war, one whose opening fusillade came from a unanimous Supreme Court ruling on May 17, 1954. Thrust on the defensive by the federal government, the Mississippi press counterattacked as if in fact a way of life was at stake. And so one of many ironies: without such a fierce and often shrill and always loquacious

Introduction

defense of his murderers, Emmett Till might be just a peripheral footnote in civil-rights history. Martyrdom always needs prolix scribes.

We would also emphasize that, contrary to popular representations, the Mississippi media was not a monolith; there was indeed some diversity of opinion on the case. More important, though, was what we term the discursive trajectory of the newspaper coverage; that is, as we demonstrate in our first chapter, the first several days of newspaper coverage reveal a sympathetic treatment of Emmett Till: he was not the "wolf-whistling," "husky," "northern Negro rapist" out to assault white southern womanhood but a misguided "Negro youth" on a "vacation" who happened upon a vengeful wife on the lam from local police. This treatment changed literally overnight with angry comments made by the NAACP's executive secretary (later renamed executive director), Roy Wilkins, and by the murdered boy's grieving mother, Mamie Till. The point speaks to our emphasis throughout the project: public discourse about the case not only reflected opinion but formed and transformed it as well.

In many ways our treatment of the Till case is in keeping with the currents of civil-rights historiography: what became the civil-rights movement might be better conceptualized as the movements. While *Brown*, Rosa Parks, Dr. Martin Luther King, Jr., the Montgomery bus boycott, the Little Rock school integration crisis, the sit-ins, the Freedom Rides, the integration of Ole Miss, the Birmingham campaign, the March on Washington, Freedom Summer, and the Selma voting rights project rightfully occupy an important place in civil-rights scholarship, John Dittmer's "local people" are finally getting their much-deserved due—and with interest. Similarly, in critical circles, emphasis has been placed on what Steven Goldzwig deems "critical localism," a critical examination of discourse emanating from the unknown orator, the small-town weekly newspaper, and the unpublished letter. While eloquent and well-known texts such as King's "I Have a Dream," "Letter from Birmingham Jail," and "I've Been to the Mountaintop," and Malcolm X's "The Ballot or the Bullet" have come in for much critical comment, local and largely unknown speakers and writers also moved audiences—and on all sides of the racial divide.[4]

In a smaller-scale version of this project, we used nine predominantly white Mississippi newspapers to generalize about the entire state. Time and space constraints made that choice an unwelcome though necessary one. But in this project, we have aimed for as large a sample as possible. We have carefully examined nearly seventy Mississippi newspapers, from the *Aberdeen News* to the *Yazoo City Herald*. While some newspapers, especially in key Delta locales, remained elusive, most surviving papers have been carefully consulted. A majority of the papers were small-circulation weeklies. Many never printed a word on the disappearance, murder, trial, or aftermath, and so for some white and black Mississippians, the name Emmett Till might not have signified at all. But for the great majority of Mississippians, Till, Sheriff Strider, Mamie Till, Roy and Carolyn Bryant, J. W. Milam, Charles H. Diggs, Gerald Chatham, Sidney Carlton, Moses Wright, Willie Reed, Leroy "Too Tight" Collins, T. R. M. Howard, and Roy Wilkins became household names in an unfolding racial drama, especially in larger media markets such as Biloxi, Hattiesburg, Natchez, Vicksburg, Jackson, Greenville, Meridian, Greenwood, Tupelo, and Clarksdale.[5]

We have also included one black commercial newspaper in our analysis, Percy Greene's *Jackson Advocate*. Julius Thompson documents that there were five black commercial newspapers publishing in Mississippi in the 1950s—the *Greenville Delta Leader*, the *Jackson Advocate*, the *Jackson Mississippi Enterprise*, the *New Albany Community Citizen*, and the *Jackson Eagle Eye*—only the last was not a prosegregation, conservative paper. We have included Greene's *Advocate* not only because of its relatively large circulation but also because the black weekly published regularly and a microfilm record has survived. Much as we would have liked to include Arrington H. High's *Eagle Eye* in our analysis, copies of the mimeographed sheet are very elusive.[6]

Beyond our choice of specific newspapers, we read the Till coverage inclusively; hard news stories, editorials, letters to the editor, and photographs provide the mosaic from which we construct our story. As we attempt to illustrate throughout, editorializing was inevitable in each of the aforementioned areas, even in Associated Press (AP) and United Press (UP) wire reports. Editors were particularly keen to slant their news by editing wire stories in specific ways, whether through headlines or paragraphs being reordered or even omitted altogether; priority was made manifest in the placement of stories. The photographs of the case have a history all their own, beginning with the infamous postmortem image and extending through to the glamour shots of Carolyn Bryant and her photogenic family. While flattering photographs of the Till family existed, they quickly disappeared from public view and were substituted with far less endearing visual evidences. As we hope to illustrate, the visual played a profoundly important role in conveying and creating public opinion about the principals involved in the case. Carolyn Bryant, Mississippians quickly learned, was not homely. That said, the Mississippi press never published the pictures of Till's mutilated body nor yet the even gorier crime-scene photograph of Till's naked corpse that, despite being entered into official evidence, has never surfaced. Whether those photographs would have engendered pathos or provocation among white Mississippians, we know that they changed the lives of many black Americans.[7]

Introduction

We would emphasize from the outset that our analytic method is rhetorical, and, as rhetoricians, we focus principally on that which seeks for influence. While rhetoric has an ancient and complex history, praxis, and theoretical elaboration, spanning well over two millennia, we take many of our critical cues from Kenneth Burke, whose emphasis on naming, symbolic action, motive, and perspective inform our reading of the Mississippi press. Burke wrote famously that humans seek for vocabularies that offer "a faithful reflection of reality. To this end, they must develop vocabularies that are selections of reality. And any selection of reality must, in certain circumstances, function as a deflection of reality." In brief, language of necessity is always partial, concealing even while revealing, masking even when uncovering. Further, to name something or someone functions, to borrow from Burke, as a "terministic screen," a linguistic filter that shapes what we see and how we see it.[8]

Two brief examples should suffice. Almost universally the white Mississippi press described Carolyn Bryant as "a pretty 21-year-old married mother of two." Innocuous, certainly, on the surface, but rather insidious when paired with Mamie Till, "a somewhat plump 33-year-old divorced mother." We do not need Burke to remind us that the rhetorical stakes of such naming are very high. That same press initially depicted Emmett Till as "a 14-year-old Negro from Chicago visiting relatives." That description is very different from a "wolf-whistling and stuttering rapist."

The rhetorical tradition also encourages us to take something of the long and inclusive view; a snapshot of the press coverage—say from August 28 to September 1 or September 19 to 23—would lead to very partial (and misleading) conclusions about rhetorical patterns and tendencies. As would selecting from a small handful of Mississippi newspapers. Instead, we have scoured as many Mississippi newspapers for which microfilm copies exist, and our coverage extends into 1956. We have also opted to move across these myriad texts chronologically in order to better compare and contrast press coverage between and among the newspapers. Our aim is not to insinuate a unity (claiming, for example, that "the Mississippi press depicted Mamie Till as . . .") but instead to draw out revealing differences even as patterns emerge. In journalism parlance, such an approach encourages us to take note of "horizontal diversity," even if that diversity is rather singular. Furthermore, to ignore the progressive editor simply because his or her voice was a solitary one would be to overdetermine our conclusions before we even started.

We begin our examination of the press coverage on August 28, 1955, the day that Emmett Till was taken from the Wright home near Money. Perhaps not surprisingly, there was a great deal of sympathy expressed for the

Introduction

young boy and his family. Moreover, according to the police, a careful investigation was being conducted and the arrests of J. W. Milam and Roy Bryant were loudly declared. Police were also looking for Carolyn Bryant as well as an unnamed third man. News of the body's discovery on August 31 further catalyzed local and state officials' efforts to get justice for the badly mutilated youth. But things changed on September 1: with their very public condemnation of Mississippi and Mississippians, the NAACP's Roy Wilkins and Mamie Till drastically altered the discursive landscape.

Our second chapter traces the fallout between September 2 and 6 from this condemnation, including Sheriff Strider's overnight change of mind as to the identity of the corpse dredged out of the Tallahatchie. We also carefully examine the editorializing that followed the Wilkins and Till pronouncements; the *Jackson Daily News*, in particular, identified a new enemy in the increasingly publicized case—and it was not the two men under the protection of the National Guard in the Leflore County jail. As public sentiment closed ranks, Mississippians also glimpsed for the first time the aggrieved "victim" of the wolf-whistler, the "pretty, 21-year-old mother of two, Carolyn Bryant." Her looks would prove to be an important axis upon which public opinion would pivot in the weeks to come.

By the second week of September, editorializing focused less on the specifics of the case and more on what northern newspapers were saying about it. In chapter 3, we pay close attention to how the rural Mississippi press commented on the goings-on in Leflore and Tallahatchie Counties. Many of the weeklies borrowed from their metropolitan colleagues in editorializing while others still remained sanguine that justice might be done. Even so, by September 10, most of the press agreed that the Till kidnap-murder was the most sensational race case the state had ever witnessed.

Between September 10 and September 18, Mississippi public opinion continued to catalyze around the innocence of J. W. Milam and Roy Bryant, or at least the reasonable doubt of the prosecution's admittedly circumstantial evidence. Their innocence, we argue in chapter 4, was vouchsafed less by evidence bearing on the case and far more by unwarranted northern press intrusions into the state. The increasingly shrill and unreasoning Mississippi press tried to argue its case at the level of analogy: black on white crime was more prevalent in the north, and yet the northern press drew little attention to it; Mississippi was unfairly being singled out. Their proof of the state's interracial harmony was the heroic actions of one Dianne Kearney, a nine-year-old local white girl who had saved her black nurse from drowning—in the Tallahatchie River of all places.

Chapter 5 focuses on the complex and fascinating legal and rhetorical dy-

Introduction

namics that took hold between September 19 and September 23. In the tiny western county seat of Sumner, the press descended en masse to see exactly what Mississippi justice looked like, sounded like, and felt like. In its treatment of key trial participants, the Mississippi press was generally eager to see an acquittal—despite the eyewitness testimony of Willie Reed and the bodily identifications of Moses Wright and Mamie Till. The press literally framed the two men and their "attractive" wives in the context of family by surrounding them with their young boys. We also carefully examine the legal strategies of both prosecution and defense and the likelihood that the defense initially angled for a justifiable homicide defense.

We take the measure of Mississippi editorial opinion following the sixty-seven-minute not-guilty verdict in chapter 6. Most writers registered their approval of the verdict, citing the fairness of circuit judge Curtis Swango and the impression that their northern colleagues also thought the trial fair. But the hoped-for response on the part of the northern press was not forthcoming: editorialists had confused method with outcome. We also map the extent to which the Till story rapidly migrated to other race-related stories, including one from the small Delta town of Tchula involving Providence Farms, an interracial farming cooperative rumored to host events such as interracial swimming. Sheriff Strider also garnered more headlines with his claim that Emmett Till was still alive, touching off a new wave of headlines and rumors. Exactly where Till was the outgoing sheriff did not know.

Our final chapter on the Mississippi press moves across four months, from October 1955 through January 1956, and four major stories. The first involves the sensational story of Emmett Till's father, Private Louis Till, who had been hanged in Italy for raping two white women and murdering a third. Fallout from that story seemed to clearly influence the Leflore County Grand Jury convened to hear evidence bearing on the kidnapping charges. Nearly one month later, J. W. Milam's close friend Elmer Kimball shot and killed black gas station attendant Clinton Melton; thus began a new volley of interracial news stories influenced by the Till case. Finally, we close the chapter by examining another sensational story, that of Milam and Bryant's confession to William Bradford Huie—a confession nearly seamless with the initial defense strategy of justifiable homicide.

Our final chapter moves us to the present, demonstrating how the history of the Till case and specifically its legal outcome in 1955 continues to influence various commemorative acts and memorialization projects. Much of the memorial impulse is bound up with attempts at racial reconciliation, we argue, a present-day coming-to-terms rhetorically with a fractured past.

One

"Sowing Seeds of Hatred"
(August 28–September 1)

When he got off the Illinois Central train on Sunday, August 21, 1955, martyrdom did not have designs on Emmett Till. Even though history and memory have conspired to make him a most prominent martyr for the cause of civil rights, we ought to remember that civil rights and the larger freedom movement came to Till only after his heart stopped beating sometime in the early morning hours of August 28, 1955; his was a retrospective transformation—from a jocular black teen to the symbol of unbridled white Mississippi racism. In this transformation Till never had a say—at least not directly. And it almost did not happen. The secular might assign Till's death and transformation to the vicissitudes of fate; for the religious—and his mother, Mamie Till, quickly translated it thus—it was part of God's sometimes awful will made manifest, an Isaac-like sacrifice in which God did not pull his punch.

Unlike his niece, Moses Wright publicly ruminated on both interpretations; in the immediate days after Emmett was kidnapped from his and his wife Elizabeth's six-room house—the Mississippi press typically labeled it a cotton-field "shack"—the voluble and petite man locals called "Preacher" wrestled with his role in the burgeoning racial maelstrom. He had not yet given his great-nephew's life over to a divine telos, even as Emmett might well have been in church on Wednesday, August 24. To Clark Porteous of the *Memphis Press-Scimitar*, Wright blamed his son Maurice: "He took us to church Wednesday night, the East Money Church of God in Christ, in our car. He was supposed to be at a store near the church, but they went into Money without permission. Maurice doesn't have a driver's license and isn't supposed to drive in town."[1]

Moses Wright's anguish and second-guessing are clearly evident even today: Why didn't I drive? Why didn't I take the keys from Maurice? Why did we have to go to church at all on a Wednesday night? Why was my son so willing to disobey me? These questions mask the larger and inevitable metaphysical ones—ones that would remain forever private: Why didn't I get Emmett out of Mississippi? Why didn't I fight for my great-nephew's life?

13
"Sowing Seeds of Hatred" (August 28–September 1)

How could I freely let those white men enter my home in the middle of the night?

Less than three weeks after the Porteous interview, on the eve of the trial, Wright was still contemplating the secular possibilities. Instead of Maurice's teenage disobedience, though, Wright backed up to Chicago on August 13: What if Emmett had missed the 63rd Street train that he barely met? What if I hadn't been in Chicago and encouraged his mother to allow him to come for a visit? Chance, it seems, came cruelly to Moses Wright. But did the cumulative force of chance reveal a divine hand at work? In a November 1955 speech before a Phoenix, Arizona, audience, God had finally made evidentiary inroads into the case for Wright: "His clothes had been stripped off. But he was wearin' his father's ring. Seems like when you try to cover up things, God sees that. He sees all things."[2] God had also given Wright the strength to stay in Mississippi and testify—twice—he recounted to his Western listeners.

But we are getting ahead of ourselves. On Wednesday evening, August 24, history, memory, and God had not yet entered the public discourse over a slightly overweight black kid from Chicago's south side, whom friends and family playfully called "Bobo." From nearly all accounts, Emmett did not much care for cotton picking in the sweltering August heat; by week's end he would have only four dollars to show for his efforts. Neither did Emmett much care for Mississippi racial mores.

While accounts of what actually happened inside of the Bryant Grocery and Meat Market are hopelessly conflicting, some details have emerged in the haze of that hot August evening. With seven or eight of Emmett's cousins and neighbors, the 1946 Ford arrived at the store around 7:30 P.M. Some local black people played checkers outside the entrance. At one point, as the conversation turned to women, Emmett apparently pulled out his billfold and bragged of his white girlfriend back in Chicago. Somebody challenged Bobo: "If you are so heedless of the color line, let's see you get a date with the white woman in the store." And so with friends and family watching and with his "big-talking" reputation on the line, Emmett entered the store by himself.

Tending the store that evening was twenty-one-year-old Carolyn (née Holloway) Bryant, a high school dropout from nearby Indianola in Sunflower County. Later described memorably by a French newspaper as a "crossroads Marilyn Monroe," Carolyn Bryant had won a few local beauty pageants. In the sex- and beauty-obsessed rural South, her looks had won her several admirers, too.[3] On this evening, her twenty-four-year-old husband, Roy, was on the road in Texas hauling shrimp; their two young sons were being watched

14
"Sowing Seeds of Hatred" (August 28–September 1)

by twenty-seven-year-old sister-in-law Juanita Milam, married to Roy's older half-brother, John (J. W.). Some accounts have Juanita upstairs where the Bryants lived; others claim she was at her home in Glendora.

We do not know exactly what happened that evening when Emmett Till encountered Carolyn Bryant. In her rather salacious account delivered in court but out of range of the jury, Bryant claimed that a "black man" with a "northern brogue" grabbed her hand as she held it out to receive his money. As she fled to the back of the store, he met her at the counter's end and clasped her waist in his hands and spoke "obscenely" of having been with white women before. At this point, one of Emmett's cousins quickly entered the store and pulled him out. As he crossed the threshold onto the porch area, Emmett let out a loud, two-note "wolf whistle." Maurice yelled, "Boy you know better than that." Carolyn Bryant headed outside; some thought she was headed to a nearby parked car to grab a handgun. Maurice Wright quickly fired up the '46 Ford, and the gaggle of black youths jumped in. As they fled for the Wright house 2.8 miles away, they spotted behind them a rapidly approaching car. Maurice quickly pulled over on the dirt road, and the occupants fled into the dusky cotton fields. The car quickly passed, but the Mississippians in the Wright car knew that the events at the Bryant store would not. Neighbor and witness Rutha Mae Crawford would later warn that they "hadn't heard the last" of it.[4]

Whether Carolyn Bryant kept the events of August 24 to herself and her sister-in-law or she later told her husband we do not know. But even as some urged the Wright family to get Emmett out of town, Wednesday passed into Thursday, Thursday into Friday, and Friday into Saturday, and the memory of Emmett's interracial transgression dimmed. At some point, Moses Wright and his wife, Elizabeth, found out about it. We do not know what version of the story they heard or what their reaction was. Suffice it to say that Emmett's two-week vacation was not cut short, nor did word get back to Emmett's mother in Chicago.

As Saturday night turned into Sunday morning, things were quite festive at the Wright household. Finally, at 1 A.M., the merriment waned and everyone headed to bed. Emmett, as he had all week, doubled up with his twelve-year-old cousin Simeon ("Simmy"). Just after 2 A.M., a car with its headlights turned off stopped in the Wrights' gravel driveway. Moses Wright was awakened by these words: "Preacher, preacher, this is Mr. Bryant and I want to talk to you and the boy." Wright opened the door to find Bryant and the hulking J. W. Milam, who had a flashlight in his left hand and a Colt .45 in his right. Milam asked if Wright had two boys from Chicago staying with him. Wright replied that he did. "I want that boy that did the talk at

15
"Sowing Seeds of Hatred" (August 28–September 1)

Money," Milam demanded. Not far away, Elizabeth Wright could hear the threatening dialogue. She ran to Emmett's room, thinking to hide him outside amid the endless landscape of white cotton bolls. Milam saw her and bellowed, "Get back in that bed and I want to hear them springs." "Listen," she pleaded, "we'll pay you whatever you want to charge, we'll pay you if you release him." Elizabeth did not understand that this was not about money—not yet anyway.[5]

Entering the room in which Emmett was sleeping, Milam barked, "You the nigger who did the talkin'?" "Yeah," Emmett replied. "Don't say 'yeah' to me nigger," Milam retorted, "or I'll knock hell out of you. Get your clothes on." After putting on his shirt and white pants, Emmett reached for his socks. "Just the shoes," Milam ordered impatiently. As Emmett put on his socks and thick crepe-soled shoes, Preacher Wright begged the men not to take the boy. Why don't they just give him a good whipping and leave it at that? he may have argued. On their way out of the darkened house, Milam stated, "If this isn't the right boy, we'll bring him back and put him to bed." And to Wright more pointedly, he feigned a question: "Preacher, how old are you?" "Sixty-four," came the reply. "Well, if you know any of us, you won't live to see sixty-five," Milam warned.

Wright followed the two men—or was there a third standing outside?—as far as his screened porch. As the men reached the parked car, he heard, "Is this the right boy?" Another answered, "Yes." Wright could not be sure whether this was a woman's voice, but he was certain it was "lighter" than a man's. And with that, the lightless car headed west, back toward Money. Terrified and unable to sleep, "Simmy" and his cousin Wheeler Parker watched Moses Wright pace the house, shake his head, and mutter, "mmm, mmm, mmm."

With dawn frantic phone calls were made from a neighbor's house to relative Crosby Smith and, with much dread, to Emmett's mother in Chicago. Leflore County sheriff George Smith and his deputy sheriff John Ed Cothran quickly apprehended Roy Bryant and J. W. Milam based on their ready admission to having abducted Emmett; clearly Moses Wright had not heeded Milam's warning. Both men insisted that they had let the boy go once they learned he was "the wrong one." Smith was not buying; he knew both men, especially Bryant, all too well. To local newsmen, Smith confessed that he feared "foul play." Moses Wright also sensed the worst: with neighbors he began searching under local bridges for his grand-nephew's remains. In Chicago, a panicked Mamie Till fled as fast as her car could carry her to her mother's place; it would be but an ephemeral refuge from what was coming.[6]

16
"Sowing Seeds of Hatred" (August 28–September 1)

On Wednesday morning, August 31, seventeen-year-old Floyd Hodges was checking his trotlines in the muddy Tallahatchie River near Pecan Point, not far from the town of Philipp in Tallahatchie County. The young fisherman noticed what looked to be a pair of bare legs elevated above the water's surface. Several men removed the badly beaten and bloated body from a drift it had gotten hung up on, put it in a small boat, and moved it to shore. The body had been weighted down with a seventy-four-pound blast wheel from a cotton gin fan barbwired to the neck. Deputy Cothran later noted that a sizeable chunk of the crushed skull fell off in the boat. Later that morning, and with his neighbor Johnny Crawford, Moses Wright attempted to identify the body. It was Emmett, Wright later claimed. The silver signet ring with the initials "L. T."—for Louis Till, Emmett's father—was the only clear proof Wright had that the body belonged to his great-nephew. Crawford claimed that Emmett had been castrated.[7]

Thus begins the story of Emmett Till. We mention these details here not to shed any new light on the facts of the kidnapping and murder but to situate the reader at the beginning of what would become one of the most important media events of the civil-rights movement. To dwell solely at the outset on the week of events in late August in Leflore and Tallahatchie Counties would mask a larger context pivotal to understanding Mississippi racial politics circa 1955. Many scholars have attributed an emboldened racial activism among Mississippi blacks to the U.S. Supreme Court's May 17, 1954, unanimous verdict that segregation in America's public schools was inherently unequal. That verdict struck as a concussive blow to white southerners weaned on the demeaning and occasionally savage ways of Jim Crow. The specter that haunted the entire Southland—that of black male-white female sex—would now take solid form thanks to nine berobed justices intent, as it may have seemed to some southerners, on mongrelizing the Anglo-Saxon race. *Brown* bestirred a complacent white South—no lynchings had been recorded in years—and the immediate manifestation of their agitation was the kudzulike organization of white Citizens' Councils or what some have termed the "up-town Klan." Beginning with a meeting in Carolyn Bryant's hometown of Indianola, Citizens' Councils quickly formed in tiny hamlets and large cities alike: white womanhood, they felt, simply had to be protected against the fabled sexual appetites of black men. Blacks with the audacity to register their children at previously all-white public schools were met with swift retribution: loans were called in, mortgages were revoked, necessary products could not be purchased, workers were fired and kicked off plantations, and stores were boycotted. And these were the publicly sanctioned forms of violence.

17
"Sowing Seeds of Hatred" (August 28–September 1)

While southern blacks were no doubt emboldened by *Brown*, John Dittmer and others argue that the experiences of World War II formed a generation of black veterans: fighting and dying abroad for an American promise of freedom and equality vouchsafed a new and embodied racial consciousness in ways that a textualized Supreme Court verdict never could. Fighting for a cause mattered.[8]

Beginning with small-scale voter registration efforts, black Mississippi veterans began to organize under the aegis of the Mississippi Progressive Voters' League, the Mississippi State Democratic Organization, and local branches of the NAACP. Perhaps most influential, though, in the budding postwar movement for equal rights was an organization founded in late 1951 in the Delta town of Cleveland, the Regional Council of Negro Leadership (RCNL). Founded by the charismatic physician and entrepreneur Dr. Theodore Roosevelt Mason (T. R. M.) Howard—who would play a very influential role in the Till murder trial—of the all-black Delta community of Mound Bayou, the RCNL promoted voter registration, campaigned against police brutality, and even organized local boycotts against white storeowners for not providing equal facilities.

By 1955, black activism in the Delta combined with the heated rhetorical climate of Citizens' Council propaganda to form a volatile racial mix. On May 7, RCNL vice president and voting-rights advocate fifty-one-year-old Reverend George W. Lee was sprayed with buckshot fired by a passing car in his hometown of Belzoni. The blast tore off the lower left side of Lee's face; he died en route to the hospital. Remarkably, Lee's hometown newspaper, the *Belzoni Banner*, never mentioned the murder. Other papers claimed that Lee's demise was caused by a jealous paramour who ran him off the road. The buckshot?—this was merely dental fillings loosened in the crash. A grand jury was never convened to hear the evidence of the Belzoni murder. Up north, Mamie Till's hometown newspaper, the *Chicago Defender*, ran a shocking postmortem of Lee's stitched-together face. News of Mississippi's racial violence was migrating north.

One week before Emmett Till boarded the Illinois Central bound for the Delta, Brookhaven activist sixty-three-year-old Lamar (Ditney) Smith was shot in broad daylight on the courthouse lawn. Police estimated that a Saturday morning crowd of thirty to forty people had to have witnessed the murder. And yet at a grand jury hearing the indictments against three white men, not a single witness came forward to testify. Lee and Smith were older black men committed to the cause of advancing black civil rights. Their murders evoked very little by way of comment from the white Mississippi press. But with his disappearance and the eventual discovery of Emmett Till's nude,

18
"Sowing Seeds of Hatred" (August 28–September 1)

murdered corpse, the white Mississippi press had a potentially important story to report. This was not about civil rights, school desegregation, or the threat of interracial sex—not yet anyway. And, as long as the story was not about such volatile, "racial" topics, Emmett Till had a positive run of news. It would last exactly five days.

In the August 28 afternoon edition of the *Greenwood Commonwealth*, Emmett Till first entered into the public discourse of Mississippi. In a small, page-one headline, race, age, and geography were foregrounded; the three themes persist to this day. "Chicago Negro Youth Abducted by Three White Men at Money," the headline read. In the brief article lacking a byline, Sheriff Smith reported that Till had "made some 'ugly remarks' to Bryant's wife" and that three white men had abducted him from the Wright "home." Moses Wright would clearly not be silenced by J. W. Milam: he claimed that "he heard the men ask a woman in the car if Till was the right boy." While Milam and Bryant had been identified and jailed for their involvement in the "abduction," neither the third "white" man nor the "woman" were identified; but only the unidentified man was being "sought in the affair." Absent in the small article were details about when the "ugly remarks" had occurred and what they might have contained.[9]

Mississippians began to learn more on the twenty-ninth, as the story quickly moved from being a local Delta story to a statewide one. While news of Milam's arrest had not yet made it to Hattiesburg, the local paper there carried the AP wire story featuring Sheriff Smith's search for the third man and the supposedly "ugly remarks" made at the "Bryant store at Money." The state's largest-circulation paper, the *Jackson Daily News* (the morning version was the *Clarion-Ledger*) reported on its front page the identical information as the *Greenwood Commonwealth* did. In the south Delta town of Greenville, the *Delta Democrat-Times*, published by the relatively progressive Hodding Carter, mentioned in its UP story that only two white men were involved in the kidnapping. In its page-two story, no mention was made of the identity-confirming "woman" nor the supposedly "ugly remarks"; rather, "Till, of Chicago, apparently said something to offend Bryant's wife in a small store Saturday night." The missing boy's whereabouts remained "the 64-dollar question," the paper reported Smith as stating.[10]

Within twenty-four hours, Sheriff Smith's somewhat playful "question" had become a fear of "foul play." He held out hope that Till's family was either hiding him or had spirited him home to Chicago, but the ominous remarks received wide play in dailies from Grenada, Meridian, and Biloxi, which had just picked up the story. Curiously, though, even as it carried the story for the first time and on its front page, the *Meridian Star* made no men-

"Sowing Seeds of Hatred" (August 28–September 1)

tion of race—either of the victim or the perpetrators; instead of "two white men," the *Star* led with "two state men." While some newspapers continued to report that a third man was still being sought, the *Delta Democrat-Times* carried a new and important angle: Sheriff Smith reported his plans to question Roy Bryant's wife in the "mysterious disappearance." The *Democrat-Times* also reported the first suggestion of an interracial flirtation as it claimed that "the Bryants were said to have become offended when young Till waved to the woman and said 'goodbye' when he left the store." Thus had the "ugly remarks" become something far more provocative—and perhaps deadly. Instead of inflaming the increasingly tense racial situation, the black *Jackson Advocate* closed its first short article on the story by noting the "strong possibility that relatives were hiding the boy for fear of his safety, or had sent him back to Chicago, the home of his parents."[11]

On Wednesday, August 31, Sheriff Smith's fears were confirmed: Emmett Till's body had been discovered floating in the Tallahatchie River, and papers throughout the state were not bashful about announcing the grisly discovery. While several papers claimed that Till died from a "blow on the head," the *Greenwood Commonwealth* specified that death may have come from "a bullet hole in his head"; this was also one of the few papers to make mention of the fact that Moses Wright had identified the body. In other words, the identity of the corpse at this point was not in question. But that identity—stable as it was on Wednesday—would grow increasingly less certain as "outside interference" in the form of NAACP press releases appeared in Mississippi newspapers; doubt was proportional to discourse about it. But it was clear that whoever had killed Emmett Till—and many papers reported that "three white men and a woman took the boy from his uncle's [*sic*] home early Sunday"—had killed the wrong boy: even as his decaying body was shipped to a local morgue for hasty burial, the *Clarksdale Press Register*, the *Biloxi Daily Herald*, and the *Meridian Star* each reported that William Henry Huff, an NAACP lawyer from Chicago, was publicly calling on Attorney General Herbert Brownell to have the Justice Department and the FBI intervene in the case, as well as the Mississippi attorney general. Despite the shock and grief over losing her only child, it is clear that Mamie Till was announcing, however tentatively, that she (and some high-powered lawyers) were looking very carefully over the shoulder of Mississippi officials. But it was also clear—or so it seemed—to any and all newspaper readers that this was an open-shut kidnap-murder case—with at least two of the suspects jailed and the arrest of two more imminent.[12]

Perhaps the most positive press Emmett Till would ever receive in Mississippi occurred on September 1; thereafter he would be transformed into

20
"Sowing Seeds of Hatred" (August 28–September 1)

someone and something very insidious to the white South. Readers of the *Jackson Daily News* were greeted in the morning with the first pictures of the murdered youth; the *News* ran on its back pages a 1954 Christmas photo of Emmett, no longer the faceless or "merely" brutalized and naked corpse, and his mother. Pictured neatly in a striped tie and pressed white shirt, his well-dressed and attractive mother with her right arm proudly around her only son, the murdered youth and his grieving mother were presented with a profound pathos in the flattering photograph. These were not poor local blacks bereft of money, looks, and manners; rather, even minus a father or father figure, the photograph humanized the Tills, perhaps even making them safe—however briefly—for white Mississippians. The *News* was not the only Mississippi newspaper to run the holiday picture; on its front page, above the fold, the *Vicksburg Evening Post* featured the same AP photograph. The *Post*'s readers, like the *News*'s, had a sympathetic image instead of just the words "weighted body."[13]

But in addition to giving Emmett Till flattering two-dimensional form, sixteen-year-old Maurice Wright fleshed out his murdered cousin in the *Clarksdale Press Register*: "He had polio when he was three, and he couldn't talk plain. You could hardly understand him." Editorialists at the paper quickly ramified—erroneously—Wright's portrayal: "Those who kidnapped and murdered 14-year-old Emmett Till, a crippled and retarded child, have dealt the reputation of the South and Mississippi a savage blow." The legal and moral onus was clearly on Mississippi for killing the physically and mentally handicapped youth—factors that even at this point eclipsed Emmett Till's pigmentation: "If conviction with the maximum penalty of the law cannot be secured in this heinous crime, then Mississippi may as well burn all its law books and close its courts, for we cannot then stand before the nation and the world as a self-governing state capable of making and enforcing its own laws and punishing thus [*sic*] who most grievously offend those laws." The editor, though, did not advocate a court shutdown nor yet a public book burning in a very different September 26 editorial.[14]

While the first editorial on the case was stridently pro-Till, downstate in the notoriously racist town of McComb, prominent local physician-surgeon Dr. Robert H. Brumfield's letter to the editor received front-page, above-the-fold treatment in the *McComb Enterprise-Journal*. In it, Brumfield articulated what the *Press Register* only hinted at: "Now is the time for every citizen who loves the state of Mississippi to 'Stand up and be counted' before hoodlum white trash brings us to destruction." Local white "peckerwoods," though, were also in cahoots with the "better" white citizens, according to Brumfield. "The trouble in Mississippi," he continued, "is not the Negro, but it

"Sowing Seeds of Hatred" (August 28–September 1)

is the white trash who, because they can vote, are given a pat on the back and a wink of the eye by our political leaders." Without naming any names, Brumfield lumped together the murders of Reverend George Lee, Lamar Smith, and the "negro boy in Money" and laid their deaths in the "hands of the Citizens' Councils, and officials who go about making speeches and writing books that are sowing seeds of hatred in this state." For the first time press coverage of the Till case spoke to a broader set of concerns than just the principals involved; something far bigger, more complicated, and politicized was at stake than "just" another murder. By laying the blame on local poor whites who were being manipulated by elected officials and on those actively involved in the Citizens' Councils, Dr. Brumfield, perhaps with publisher Oliver Emmerich's blessing, had stitched together an explosive racial mosaic.[15]

Meanwhile, Henry Huff's call for broader intervention had been heeded—or so it seemed. In a page-one story, James Featherston of the *Jackson Daily News* led thus: "Gov. Hugh White today called for a complete investigation in the kidnap-slaying of a tongue-tied Chicago Negro boy whose death has appalled Mississippi and caused national repercussions." Governor White went a step further and released to the press a wire he had sent to the national office of the NAACP: "Parties charged with the murder are in jail. I have every reason to believe that the court will do their duty in prosecution. Mississippi does not condone such conduct."

Leading that investigation in Tallahatchie County was Sheriff H. C. "Clarence" Strider. A local plantation owner on his way out as sheriff, Strider ended up leading the investigation by virtue of where the body was discovered. While the kidnapping had occurred in Leflore County, Till's corpse had been pulled from the Tallahatchie County side of the Tallahatchie River. And, while Sheriff Strider has received no small ignominy and calumny for his role in the investigation and trial, his initial loyalties were rather clearly aligned with a seemingly burgeoning pro-Till contingent. First off, Strider expressed his belief that the corpse was in fact Till's and that he had been "cut up pretty badly like an axe was used." Strider added, "We found a bullet hole one inch above his right ear. The left side of his face had been cut up or beat up, plump into the skull." This rather gruesome description of Till's corpse implies that Strider had recoiled from the savage beating that preceded Till's death. Furthermore, based on his examination of the body, Strider claimed it "appeared to have 'been in the water about two days.'" Not only had the Tallahatchie sheriff made a positive identification of the body—later made plain by a death certificate he signed and shipped to Mamie Till—but he was eagerly pursuing justice: several newspapers reported that

22
"Sowing Seeds of Hatred" (August 28–September 1)

"a warrant charging kidnapping had been issued for Mrs. Bryant, the storekeeper's wife, but that she could not be found at her home." That the warrant was issued in Tallahatchie County and pursued by Strider strongly suggests that Carolyn Bryant was actively being sought as a potential murder and kidnapping suspect. Perhaps ironically, Leflore County Sheriff George Smith said that he was "continuing the search for the woman but said his chances appear slim since [Moses] Wright didn't see the woman." So while Strider sought to question if not arrest Mrs. Bryant, Smith was not even willing to conjecture about the identity of the "woman" in question. With the possibility of convening a grand jury as early as Monday, September 5, Sheriff Strider promised a "speedy prosecution."[16]

Meanwhile, as for the body itself, readers of the *Clarion-Ledger* learned that "Till was buried this afternoon [Thursday, September 1] at Money. His body 'was in such bad shape it couldn't be shipped' to Chicago for burial, a funeral home attendant said." Some have argued that Strider wanted the corpse buried quickly so as to hide from the family—and the world—the horribly disfigured body. Perhaps, but given Strider's initial earnest and eager pursuit of justice, it seems far more likely that the prompt burial in Money was simply a reflex action to get a rotting and bloated corpse, rapidly decaying from the heat and water, into the ground. Perhaps the Wright family, too, did not have the resources to have Emmett's body embalmed. But at this point, everyone still agreed that the body was indeed Emmett's. Even as a shallow grave was dug and Moses Wright contemplated a fitting eulogy, Mamie Till ordered her son's body shipped north. And despite the three-thousand-dollar bill charged by undertaker A. A. Rayner of Chicago, her uncle, Crosby Smith, agreed to accompany the body north—on the same Illinois Central line that had brought Emmett to the Delta just eleven days prior.[17]

Yet another Mississippi voice entered the increasingly congested and complex fray on September 1. From Indianola, Robert "Tut" Patterson, founder and executive secretary of the Association of Citizens' Councils—"groups organized to keep segregation in all walks of life"—stated that Till's death was "regrettable." And while it is improbable that Patterson had read Brumfield's public letter blaming the councils for Mississippi's racial violence, Patterson emphatically claimed that "one of the primary reasons for our organization is to prevent acts of violence." To charge them with fomenting a climate that led to Till's death was simply illogical, according to Patterson, akin to attributing his death "to the church he belonged to."[18]

Our analysis of the press coverage on September 1 suggests that new details related to the case were being revealed very quickly, and many news-

"Sowing Seeds of Hatred" (August 28–September 1)

papers were getting simple factual details wrong in their zeal to print the latest developments: J. W. "Nilan" was not forty years old, nor was Roy Bryant thirty; "Emmet Lewis Till" was not fifteen, nor was he retarded, though he did suffer from a slight polio-induced speech impediment; his body had not been buried in Money; a group of young black men had not gone to the Bryant Grocery and Meat Market on Saturday night; and the blast wheel weighing down Till's corpse did not weigh 125 pounds. But far more important and influential than several factual errors were the reported statements coming out of New York and Chicago that afternoon. NAACP Executive Secretary Roy Wilkins and to a lesser extent Mamie Till hastened the burial of positive representations of Emmett Till; any hopes of a legal victory also died that afternoon.

The *Clarion-Ledger's* page-one headline blared, "NAACP Officials Launch Bitter Attack on State." The article quoted in full "Ray Winkins'" incendiary statement: "It would appear from this lynching that the State of Mississippi has decided to maintain white supremacy by murdering children. The killers of the boy felt free to lynch him because there is in the entire state no restraining influence of decency, not in the state capital, among the daily newspapers, the clergy nor any segment of the so-called better citizens." Even though qualified ("it would appear"), the rhetorical force of Wilkins's statement was devastating: all of white Mississippi stood indicted in the eyes of the NAACP. It was an intemperate statement, made worse by its awful timing. In addition, Wilkins had invoked the dreaded word *lynching* and the entire specter of Mississippi's "rope-and-faggot" past. He also made Mississippi's transgression plural: it was not a "child" but "children." And of course with his reference to "better citizens," like Dr. Brumfield, Wilkins aimed his sights not at redneck vigilantism but at monied Citizens' Councils; the former were merely taking their violent cues from the latter.[19]

Wilkins' comments put white Mississippians on the defensive: Hadn't the state actually treated the Till family with a modicum of cross-racial respect and sympathy? Hadn't the governor gone to no small effort to reassure the NAACP that justice would prevail? Hadn't a few citizens spoken out loudly and in prominent places against such barbaric action? Wasn't Sheriff Strider vigorously working the case? It is clear that, even as he indicted them collectively, Roy Wilkins had not been reading any Mississippi newspapers. Certainly he had not seen the flattering photograph in the *Jackson Daily News*. Rhetorically speaking, Wilkins had given no self-respecting white person any space from which to respond; Mississippi's complicity in the racial murder was total. If Emmett Till could have turned over in his grave, he would have; his killers had just been granted a pardon by the state.

24
"Sowing Seeds of Hatred" (August 28–September 1)

And yet tucked away in a small file in the J. P. Coleman Papers in Jackson is a most interesting telegram. Sent to Governor White on August 31 at 4:38 P.M. from New York City, Wilkins was infinitely more qualified and diplomatic: the NAACP was calling on the governor "to use all the powers of your office to see that the lynchers of 14-year old Emmett Louis Till are brought to justice. We cannot believe that responsible officials of the state of Mississippi condone the murdering of children of any provocation." The telegram seemed to flatly contradict some of Wilkins's sentiments reported by the Mississippi press. Whether Wilkins's incredulities—"We cannot believe"—could have been so drastically mitigated in less than twenty-four hours is also improbable. But if anything, public diplomacy should have, at this point, triumphed over private expressions of juridical optimism. Perhaps the more interesting point is this: Why did White not release the more measured Wilkins statement to the press? Or, if he did, why did they not report it? Was Mississippi looking for a fight?[20]

In the same *Clarion-Ledger* story that carried Wilkins's statement, Mamie Till was quoted as saying, "Someone is going to pay for this. The entire state of Mississippi is going to pay for this?" But the *Delta Democrat-Times* quoted slightly differently: "The State of Mississippi will have to pay for this." As Hugh Stephen Whitaker has argued, she was merely referring to the financial implications of what had transpired. With a pending $3,300 burial bill to pay, little wonder that the grieving mother was not speaking figuratively. But in a smaller story on the same page of the newspaper, Till was reported as saying, "It's like walking into a den of snakes. They will do these things with hardly any provocation—they don't even need provocation." While "it" and "they" and "things" were without clear referents, she promised to "fight to the end to see that justice is done."[21]

Without naming any names or organizations, the *Jackson State Times* offered a gentle rejoinder to Wilkins and Mamie Till in one of the very early editorials bearing on the case: "Mississippians are shocked at the abduction and brutal slaying of a Negro boy near Greenwood. Murder finds no condonation [sic] in this state, and an increasing number of voices are being raised against violence of any kind in the handling of internal problems." The editorial expressed optimism that swift justice would be forthcoming, both from a grand jury and in the circuit court. And, the best answer to the "unreasoning criticism" coming from "some individuals and organizations" was for Mississippians to render it "meaningless by calmly and unhesitatingly going about the business of seeing that justice is sought through legal means." The measured tone of the *State Times*'s editorial would prove to be a hallmark of their coverage and comment on the case.[22]

25
"Sowing Seeds of Hatred" (August 28–September 1)

Meanwhile, the *Hattiesburg American* was accurate in labeling the Wilkins/Till statements as "inflammatory." Given all that would come in the days, weeks, and years following September 1, it is hard not to speculate about what might have happened had the statements not been released in the press. Would Strider have finally located Carolyn Bryant? Would white Mississippians have still rallied around Milam, Bryant, and their families? Would Emmett Till have gotten justice even in a Jim Crow courtroom where blacks rarely if ever served on juries and women were not allowed? And if he had, what would have happened to the civil-rights movement his death and trial supposedly sparked? Does Rosa Parks get up and move?

But as Hernando District Attorney Gerald Chatham prepared to impanel a grand jury for early the following week, the tenor and tone of the case would change dramatically. Already a few papers had found their alliterative hook: the "wolf-whistle" case had been joined, and far more was now at stake than the death of a northern black kid with a stutter.

Two

"Comely Carolyn"
(September 2–September 6)

As Emmett Till's pine-box coffin headed north on Friday, September 2—public viewing surely was out of the question—the discursive landscape in Mississippi was changing dramatically. Important definitions and traditions were at stake, as was that most prized Mississippi commodity: white female beauty. Many rural Mississippians were also reading the name Emmett Till for the first time as their weekly newspapers were often delivered on Fridays; as a consequence, most of them would never see the relatively positive run of news. And not surprisingly, Mississippians quickly closed ranks as Wilkins's vituperations circulated freely and loudly around the state.

Even as the memory of Emmett and Mamie's photograph faded quickly from memory, a new visage was on the horizon. The *McComb Enterprise-Journal*, along with several other daily newspapers, had a new and profoundly important description of the woman still "being sought" by police. In its front-page story, the *Enterprise-Journal* reported that "Emmitt [sic] Louis Till met death by gunshot and possibly by ax blow for whistling at the comely 27-year-old [sic] wife of a Delta white storekeeper." Thus did white female Mississippi beauty enter the public fray; it would be at the rhetorical epicenter of this case for several weeks. Emmett Till had not "leered and whistled at" a slatternly and pock-mocked hag nor yet a plain-looking bachelorette. No, Carolyn Bryant, readers learned for the first time, was beautiful, young, white, and married. Retrospectively, we can see that this was a deadly combination.[1]

But just how or where did the *Enterprise-Journal* and the other newspapers get wind of Mrs. Bryant's good looks? Pictures of her were still four days away. Had a local stringer for the AP wire story gotten a glimpse of her? Was her portfolio of beauty pictures from high school circulating among a voyeuristic press? Was her hometown paper, the *Indianola Enterprise-Tocsin*, floating the pictures it had on file, and had Mrs. Bryant not yet granted permissions to release them? Or, would her as yet unpublished beauty somehow correspond with Roy Wilkins's untimely fusillade?

White female beauty mattered to Mississippians in the summer of 1955—

27
"Comely Carolyn" (September 2–September 6)

as it had for years. In our extensive searching of the state's newspapers, we were struck by many cultural artifacts that appear exotic in the new millennium but most notably the sheer quantity of beauty photographs that ran on any and all pages of small and large Mississippi newspapers. Whether it was an international "beauty" or a local high school winner of the town's seasonal pageant, "beautiful" women and "girls" were frequently spotlighted in various states of undress. This was no buttoned-up and corseted Victorianism served up with June Cleaver sartorial frump. No, the daily depictions of white female beauty left little to the imagination: whether it was a come-hither prone shot, a titillating from-below peek, a claustrophobic décolletage glimpse, or even a spread-eagled cheerleading jump, Mississippi newspapers reveled in exposing beautiful white womanhood.

As a rule black women were never shown in a revealing beauty pose—if they were shown at all. A very rare "hot," "sultry," or "sizzling" Latina was as far as Mississippi would go. Mamie Till's appearance in part 2, page 12 of the *Jackson Daily News* was an exception to the general rule: black women were not to be seen, unless there was a tragic or perhaps criminal context to the photograph. And yet the gendered and racial dynamics of Mississippi beauty force us to question some of the common wisdom. That is, "racial looking" across the color line is more complex than the popular account would have it. Black men in the Jim Crow South could look upon, leer at, linger over, whistle at, and lewdly talk to any white female beauty they wanted—as long as it was done either in private, away from whites, or out of earshot; white publishers and editors, after all, openly encouraged them to. Whether featuring so many photographs of white female beauty was meant as a taunt or not, black men were encouraged to look at and even appreciate privately what might get them beaten and/or lynched done in public. It was all part of knowing one's "place." White female beauty was only a taboo for black men (and boys) in certain spaces. That Carolyn Bryant was now rendered "comely" spoke with renewed intensity about the threshold Emmett Till had crossed at the Bryant Grocery and Meat Market. White Mississippians could and would relish anew its beauty queens—and punish those who would transgress the private/public divide. Sex, and its many complexities and contingencies, had entered the story.

And so had the editorialists: "Winkins's" denigration of the whole state did not go without comment for long. In a lengthy editorial in the *Jackson Daily News*, the paper adopted a strategy it would pursue for months: fight back with counterexamples. The paper played up the death of one Willard Menter, a "New York City Negro factory worker" murdered by four white boys nearly a year previously. "No one called the killings anything other than

"Comely Carolyn" (September 2–September 6)

useless, senseless acts of savagery. No one believed they were lynchings," the *News* pointed out, not even the NAACP. While attempting to redefine the Till murder as "a stupid, horrible crime," the *News* tried to isolate the incident from the explosive issue of race, blaming it on "the sick mind[s] of men who should be removed from society by due course of law." It was not a manifestation of pathological racism, the *News* argued, but simply a sadistic act, much as in the Menter killing. At this point, the *News* was still very much on Emmett Till's side: "The boy was a polio victim and seems to have had a speech impediment which might have caused the whistle. He was also said to have been 'feeble minded.'" Furthermore, given the ready actions of Sheriff George Smith, Governor Hugh White, and the denunciations by Citizens' Council officials, "every responsible citizen in the state of Mississippi . . . deplored this evil act"; the crime merited "not one iota of sympathy for the killers." "[A] depraved mind or minds" had brutally taken the boy's life; it was an individual symptom not a cultural contagion, according to the *News*.[2]

Similarly, Governor White was quick to issue a statement, contra Wilkins, that Till's death was "not a lynching" but a "straight out murder." The editor at the *Laurel Leader-Call* castigated Wilkins for his "trashy talk" and expressed confidence that "public sentiment will not support the murderers in so brutal and devilish on [*sic*] act"; "the courts can be counted on to do their obvious duty." Likewise, the *Delta Democrat-Times* observed that "we must pursue this case with a grim determination as a demonstration that Mississippians, . . . do not indeed condone such action against anyone, white or black." The "best response" to Wilkins and the NAACP was for the "state to take the same legal revenge against these kidnapers and murderers as they would against any others. We feel confident that this will be done." The *Greenwood Commonwealth* moved its editorial on the case to a featured spot on its front page, stating, "This deplorable incident has made our section the target of unjustifiable criticisms, thoughtless accusations, and avenging threats." Like the *Leader-Call*, the *Commonwealth* believed that "the guilty parties shall be punished to the full extent of the law and that justice shall be administered irrespective of the color of the victim or the criminals," adding that the NAACP needed to "cease throwing stones" and "cease using the case as manufactured evidence to wage war against segregation."[3]

The *Commonwealth* also borrowed a rhetorical strategy from the *Jackson Daily News*: instead of a black New Yorker murdered by white youths, though, they alluded to a local story that would get a broad airing in the coming weeks. Not far from the very spot where Till's corpse was discovered, "a ten year old white girl . . . risked her life in the same river, . . . to save the life of

"Comely Carolyn" (September 2–September 6)

a negro woman who was drowning." While not yet named, Dianne Kearney, also from Money in Leflore County, had heroically saved her black nurse who had fallen into the Tallahatchie River. The *News* raised questions in Mississippians' minds: Why hadn't the NAACP taken this act as representative of race relations in the deep south? Wasn't theirs a very selective condemnation?[4]

Sadly, Roy Wilkins never retracted his incendiary statement nor apologized for his sweeping indictment. But back in Chicago, before she "hysterically sobbed" at the sight of her son's pine-box coffin, Mamie Till sought to temper her own inflammatory comments. On the front page of the *Meridian Star*, the grieving mother recounted some Jim Crow lessons to her son: "I told him, 'even if you have to get on your knees and bow when they (white person) pass, do so willingly.'" Even so, she along with Chicago mayor Richard Daley urged President Eisenhower "to act in the boy's Mississippi kidnap-slaying." Illinois governor William Stratton also encouraged the Mississippi attorney general "to make a complete investigation."[5]

Slowly though, almost imperceptibly, public opinion in Mississippi was moving away from the murdered son and grieving mother. Even as the *McComb Enterprise-Journal* again ran the Brumfield letter and as Sheriff Strider affirmed his belief that an ax had been used to kill Till—"it went too deep to be anything else"—the *Clarion-Ledger* published its first pictures of the accused kidnapper-murderers. Rather than a police mug shot, the paper featured J. W. Milam and Roy Bryant in separate side-by-side photographs—in military dress. The smiling men looked nothing like racist thugs, nor yet the "sick" and "depraved" criminals of the *Jackson Daily News*'s editorial; rather, the accused looked like avuncular and likeable smiling patriots proud to represent America abroad. The patriotic photographs would circulate widely in the days and weeks to come, transforming the exclusively verbal accusations against the two men into a more complex and perhaps contradictory visual field. Surely such happy patriots had served their country for the express purpose of ensuring freedom abroad—and at home. The *West Point Daily Times Leader* followed the lead of the *Clarion-Ledger*: the two men "being held without bail" were described as "Roy Bryant, a 27-year old [*sic*] ex-paratrooper, and his half-brother, 36-year-old J. W. Milam, an Army lieutenant in World War II."[6]

But to complete the transformation, the paratrooper (Bryant) and the Army lieutenant (Milam) needed a family and an advocate. In a widely printed article, their mother, Mrs. Eula Lee Bryant of Sharkey, Mississippi, came to the defense of her two boys. While the story ran on page 1 of the *Grenada Daily Sentinel-Star*, the *Jackson Daily News* featured it on page 14. The bold headline declared, "Mother of Pair Accused in Delta Slaying 'Will Stand

"Comely Carolyn" (September 2–September 6)

By Them.'" Mrs. Bryant claimed that her boys "'were never into any meanness' in their lives"; after all, they'd had a good role model: "Racial feeling had never been a characteristic of the men of her family. She said her children all 'worshipped' their father and 'all the Negroes at Glendora liked him like a father.'" While many slave owners had said much the same, the elderly Mrs. Bryant was rhetorically savvy about how best to represent her boys to a still-angry white Mississippi public: "'Roy, he's spent three years in the paratroops,' she said. 'J. W. was a lieutenant in the Army. He served in Germany during World War II. He started as a private and got his commission the hard way.'" As if to underscore its own ambivalence about the ostensibly patriotic and merit-earning half-brothers, the UP reporter followed up this quote thus: "A part of the indignation over Till's death stemmed from the fact that an impediment made his speech difficult to understand." In other words, black disability still trumped white female Mississippi beauty and white masculine Mississippi patriotism in the imagination of the reading public. But despite "the outrage of the nation, the state and her own neighbors," Mrs. Eula Lee Bryant had made important inroads into changing how white Mississippians viewed her boys. Meanwhile, her daughter-in-law was still being sought by Sheriff Strider.[7]

That search ended the next day, or so it seemed, depending on which newspaper Mississippians were reading. Many newspapers were headlined by the sudden and dramatic end of the search for the "woman" in the kidnap-murder investigation. Nearly all papers chose to name that woman as "Mrs. Roy Bryant." Thus had Moses Wright's initial description—a voice "softer than a man's"—been transformed into an indictment. And yet the *Meridian Star* quoted Deputy A. W. Shanks, who claimed that a warrant had not only been issued for Mrs. Bryant's arrest but that "we know where she is and we feel sure we can pick her up when she's needed." Of course anyone, male or female, who had an outstanding warrant issued because of potential involvement in a murder would be considered "needed," but Mississippi justice had a decidedly gendered bias. As the weekend arrived, Leflore County District Attorney Stanny Sanders remarked simply that "there were 'no plans at present for picking up Mrs. Bryant.'"[8]

Meanwhile, Mamie Till was literally shown being held up. On its front page, above the fold, the *Clarion-Ledger* featured a picture of the grieving mother as she met the bier carrying her son's corpse back in Chicago. Captioned "HER SON COMES HOME," the article shows three clergymen supporting the overwrought mother. Subtly, though, and despite her palpable grief, she was rendered different from Carolyn Bryant: "Mrs.," a term of respect, was not and would not be accorded her.[9]

31
"Comely Carolyn" (September 2–September 6)

And yet despite this sympathetic depiction, many papers, including the *Clarion-Ledger*, were still in a fighting mood from Wilkins's comments initially reported on September 1. And, instead of attacking only Wilkins for his intemperate words, the editors went after the group he represented: "It is by reason of incidents of this kind that such radical groups as the NAACP are able to raise large sums of money for expansion of its strife-breeding business." These indictments of the NAACP for opportunism would be extended in coverage of that day's singularly macabre and shocking event.[10]

A generation or two of black Americans know the name "Emmett Till" not from Mississippi newspaper coverage nor even from the tragic kidnap-murder. Rather, Emmett Till became something of a household name, a cautionary trope, because of what his mother decided to do upon viewing her son's horribly disfigured body. In moving detail, Mamie Till recounted in her memoir how she insisted that the pine-box casket be opened; she needed to see her son to know that it was in fact his body. Despite the objections of A. A. Rayner, the lye-packed box containing Emmett Till's body was opened; his mother recalls smelling an awful stench blocks away from the mortuary. Working from his toes to the top of his head, she looked diligently for identifying marks of her son's once-living body. "I decided that I would examine him from his feet to his head. I knew I could do it that way. I needed to do it that way. I just could not bear to examine his face. Not yet. I would have to get my courage back, let it build up again slowly as I moved back up his body to his head," she remembers. She found her son, but slowly. She paused at his midsection to see if he had been "unmanned" in that signature southern lynching gesture. He had not: "Everything was still there." After completing this heartbreaking task, in a mixture of grief and anger, she turned to Rayner and said she wanted an open-casket funeral. He asked if he should "retouch" Emmett. "No," she answered, "let the world see what I've seen." And with that decision made, the "world" would indeed see what a wolf-whistle might get a black kid in Mississippi.[11]

White America would generally not see Emmett Till's postmortem—not yet. While his mother allowed thousands of Chicagoans over the course of four days to view her son's remains, more importantly, she allowed photographers to take pictures of her son's badly mutilated face; thus was the "seeing" panoptic, not local. The photographs were published shortly thereafter in *Jet*, *The Crisis*, the *Chicago Defender*, the *Pittsburgh Courier*, and the *New York Amsterdam News*, among other publications. They would not appear in a single predominantly white newspaper. Black America now had a face to go with a name, and Mississippi was thrust on the defensive even more. Given the condition of the body, it is little wonder that Sheriff Strider wanted Till buried

"Comely Carolyn" (September 2–September 6)

immediately in the small Church of God in Christ cemetery in Money. That body would change its audience in a way that perhaps no other corpse could. Was it any coincidence that the esteemed arbiter of national news, the *New York Times*, ran its first story on the case that weekend?

News of the pornographic postmortem quickly spread back in Mississippi. The *Jackson Daily News* led its page-one story by dramatically stating, "Thousands of Negroes crowded into a church today to gaze on the battered face of a 14-year-old boy who was killed in Mississippi because he allegedly whistled at a white woman." Details followed: "The boy's face showed evidence of a brutal beating before his murder. Almost all of his teeth were knocked out and the right side of his face was almost unrecognizeable [*sic*]." The *Clarksdale Press Register* provided one key detail that the *News* had missed: "Young Till's disfigured face was left uncovered at the insistence of his mother." And, in the *Biloxi Daily Herald*, "the mother's" motives were laid bare: "Let the people see what they did to my boy." The *Tupelo Daily Journal* rendered her motives slightly differently: "Leave it like that, let the people come to see what they did to my boy." The latter quote suggested a physical visitation to Till's corpse (now a somewhat distanced "it") rather than a "viewing" that would occur in newspapers later in the week. In any case, what perhaps mattered most was the key term "they": Just who was the grieving mother referring to in expressing why she was allowing "the people" see the decayed corpse of her only child? Surely, many Mississippians would have argued, "they" were only J. W. Milam and Roy Bryant.[12]

Even as Mississippi newspapers reported the Chicago viewing, they also editorialized about it. While the *Press Register* noted simply that the large crowd walking through the funeral home had caused a "front window" to be broken, readers of the *News* might have thought that a full-scale riot (against Mississippi?) had broken out at A. A. Rayner's: "The press was so great that practically every window was shattered and the chapel was left 'a shambles.'" Similarly, the *Meridian Star* noted that "every window in the Reynar [*sic*] & Sons funeral home was shattered and the chapel itself was left 'a shambles' a funeral home spokesman said." But even more insidious than the near riot conditions prevailing inside the funeral home was what might have been causing that reaction: "There were reports that left-wing organizations passed out pamphlets outside the funeral home." For an increasingly defensive white Mississippi reader, the pieces might have been put together thus: an angry Negro mother, manipulated by Communist and northern agitators, was roiling the racial waters with cheap and opportunistic exhibitionism, and the violence would not likely be limited to windows in the near fu-

"Comely Carolyn" (September 2–September 6)

ture. In fact, the possible "violence" would migrate south before Emmett Till was even in the ground.[13]

The ambivalence in the Mississippi press manifested itself in connection with details other than the Chicago funeral home. While many papers mentioned Bryant and Milam's patriotic credentials—increasingly their service was merged so that both men became "World War II veterans"—and the glowing racial accounts of their mother, others hinted at their guilt. The *Greenwood Morning Star*, for example, wrote that Milam and Bryant were being held in separate cells and were being denied all visitors and that "the prisoners told officers they let the boy go. But they fell silent after the body was found." The mere conjunction "but" strongly suggested that the body was not only Emmett Till's but that the weighted cotton gin fan had incriminated the two would-be patriotic sons of the South. Silence might indeed be an index of guilt. But the *Star* went further, quoting an eager "Sheriff Stirder [*sic*]": "We haven't been able to find a weapon or anything, but we are not leaving a stone unturned." "[O]utrage from over the nation" had prompted the extensive house-to-house search for evidence bearing on the case.[14]

In addition to the shocking news of Till's public viewing in Chicago, the odd and unexplained "acquittal" of Carolyn Bryant and reports of the intensive investigation in and around Leflore and Tallahatchie Counties September 3 brought one other twist to the case: for the first time Mississippi papers reported on each other. In both the *Laurel Leader-Call* and the *Biloxi Daily Herald*, the AP summarized editorials from newspapers in major cities. From Greenwood, Laurel, Vicksburg, and Greenville to Jackson, Hattiesburg, and Clarksdale, editorializing was put into digest form; the lead indicated the state's continued ambivalence: "Mississippi newspapers condemned the kidnap-murder of a 14-year-old Negro boy who whistled at a white woman as 'a ghastly and wholly unprovoked murder,' and blistered the National Association for the Advancement of Colored People just as strongly." On one side stood the polio-induced stuttering, feeble-minded boy from Chicago; on the other was the "trashy talking" Roy Wilkins and the opportunistic northern organization he represented. By Sunday morning, though, that ambivalence would shift—and profoundly.[15]

Mississippians were greeted with a shocking revelation on the September 4: above the fold on page 1, Sheriff Strider publicly expressed his doubts that the body found in the muddy Tallahatchie on August 31 was Emmett Till's. "The whole thing looks like a deal made up by the National Assn. for the Advancement of Colored People," noted the heretofore justice-seeking sheriff. Strider continued, "He didn't look like the picture that was run in

34
"Comely Carolyn" (September 2–September 6)

a Jackson, Miss., newspaper of Till." Strider elaborated that the body had "a pug nose whereas the published photograph of Till showed a narrow, long head." Beyond the absurdity of forensic phrenology done with a grainy newspaper, the *Jackson Daily News* also reported that Strider claimed that "the body also appeared to be that of a grown man instead of a boy." Was this the sheriff's rhetorical code for the mythological black penis? Or did it reflect a body engorged by the murky waters of the Tallahatchie?[16]

And yet, somehow, the editorial writers of the *News* had not yet caught up with their UP-wire stringer. Or had they? Still smarting three days after Wilkins's rebuke of all white Mississippians, the editors again rebutted the charges—and only after reprinting the quote in full: Governor Hugh White had done "all that any Governor is permitted or allowed to do"; the district attorneys "pledged to work to the utmost of their abilities to obtain convictions"; Sheriff Smith had made two arrests, "all he is permitted to do under the law"; no Mississippi newspaper "read by this writer" had expressed anything "other than shock at the crime"; and surely no "sincere Christian" would approve of "this frightful murder." Conspicuously missing from the editorial was Sheriff Strider. Was the *News* editorializing by omission? Did they doubt the veracity of Strider's doubts? Or, had Strider's bombshell revelation—made nearly four full days after Emmett Till's corpse had left the state—completely reconfigured the case in the *News*'s editorial mind?[17]

If they had access to Sunday's newspapers in the county jail, no doubt J. W. Milam and Roy Bryant breathed perhaps their first sigh of relief: slowly but surely Mississippians were rallying to their cause; they now had the top lawman on their side. But the *Delta Democrat-Times* was not ready to turn the men loose quite yet, and, unlike the *Clarion-Ledger* and *Jackson Daily News*, it also questioned the timing of the sheriff's publicly expressed doubts: "Strider did not explain why the identification of the body as Till's was originally reported without qualification or why he waited until today to voice his doubts." The *Democrat-Times* also reported a rebuttal by Leflore County deputy, John Ed Cothran; he "completely disagreed" with Strider. Furthermore, Cothran had been with Moses Wright when he identified the body as that of his great-nephew. "There wasn't any doubt in Moses' mind, and there's none in ours that the body was that of Emmett," Cothran stated, as reported in the *Greenwood Morning Star*. Wright had indeed initially been unsure that the body belonged to Till, but an item taken from the corpse clarified the identification: a silver signet ring, engraved with "May 25 1943" and the initials "L.T." confirmed for Wright that Emmett's corpse had been found. This was Emmett's father Louis Till's ring, which had been shipped back from Italy after his death during World War II and which his son had worn with great pride to

"Comely Carolyn" (September 2–September 6)

Mississippi. Emmett's erstwhile father and his ring would remain in the news for months.[18]

For all intents and purposes, the official murder investigation ended that day in Tallahatchie County. While Cothran (and presumably his boss, George Smith) believed "there was another man and we will get him before we are through," the lawman charged with aiding the prosecution's case would now be the defense's best witness. One is left to wonder what might have happened in the courtroom had Till's corpse been found on the Leflore County side of the Tallahatchie River. But we might also wonder why Strider so suddenly changed his mind. Mamie Till would soon receive a death certificate, dated September 1, 1955 and signed by Sheriff Strider, that the body returned to her was her son's. Recall, too, that Strider had initially claimed that the body had been in the river but two days. That number would grow to twenty-five by the trial. With Cothran, a second person also publicly registered his surprise: the Hernando County district attorney who would prosecute the case, Gerald Chatham, told the *Columbus Commercial Dispatch* that it was "news to me"; he had been assured that "there is no question of corpus delicti." The fallout from Strider's public doubts registered immediately; the *Greenwood Morning Star* noted that the "Sheriff has changed his line of talk in view of the investigation thus far. 'It just seems that evidence is getting slimmer and slimmer,' he said today." With his dramatic change of heart, the sheriff commenced a very public campaign of "reasonable doubt."[19]

Roy Bryant might also have been smiling for another reason: his now "pretty" wife was completely off the hook—and in both counties. Even as the *Jackson Daily News* continued to report that she was in the car to identify Till as the offending whistler, Sheriff Smith stated, "We aren't going to bother the woman. She's got two small boys to take care of." And so what had been a page-one "manhunt" just a few days earlier had fizzled to an inconvenient daycare situation by Sunday.[20]

The specter of violence also returned the day after it supposedly erupted in a south-side Chicago funeral home. The *Meridian Star* reported that "the crowds were orderly but an undercurrent of tension could be felt in the heart of Chicago's vast Negro section." That tension was fueled by the "mourners [who] caught sight of the boy's face." Those same mourners expressed outrage over the "southern atrocity." That "outrage" went by a different name in the *Clarion-Ledger's* page-one headline: "Chicago Hysteria Called Hinderance [sic] in Delta Slaying." That so-called hysteria, generated by the horror over Till's corpse, might have a palpable expression: black Chicagoans would soon "invade" Mississippi; talk was rife that they were coming "to tear up Greenwood," where Milam and Bryant were still being held. Stoking fears

"Comely Carolyn" (September 2–September 6)

of an imminent northern invasion, the *Greenwood Morning Star* reported that the state patrol had arrested and charged thirteen black people traveling in Illinois-licensed automobiles near Clarksdale and that "patrolmen said they found a 12 gauge shotgun in one of the cars." Jay Milner, in a front-page *Clarion-Ledger* article, reported on the locals' fears: rumors of a northern "invasion" had "spread over the state Saturday like a forest fire." Other than the Clarksdale incident, newsmen from around the region had tired by midnight "from chasing rumors about the reported 'invasion' from Illinois"; "nervous residents and officials hoped it remained just a rumor." Those hopes would be translated into material precautions by the next day.[21]

Several newspapers, including the *Jackson Daily News*, also ruminated explicitly for the first time on the likelihood that justice might be impeded by northern outrage. In a page-one UP story, the logic was laid bare: "Authorities investigating the kidnap-slaying of a Negro boy said today a mass demonstration of Negroes in Chicago might hamper the prosecution of two white suspects." That the "mass demonstration" was a postmortem viewing and not an organized political rally did not matter: "Any outside demonstration would tend to 'build up resentment.'" One "authority" weighed in on the legal ramifications: "'This is not helping the prosecution's cause at all,' said Leflore County Attorney John Fraiser, Jr. He said local people resented 'outside agitation' in the case." Thus had Mississippi newspapers also entered the case as an important "witness" for the defense: the press was loudly featuring stories of the "Negro" northern "agitation"; presumably any "mass" gathering of black people signaled an organized resistance not only to Till's kidnap-murder but to the South's way of life more generally. Even though white Mississippi "resentment" was building, officers in Leflore County "said they had a 'air-tight' kidnapping case." But in the *Clarion-Ledger*, Sheriff Smith could clearly see the scales of justice moving in an unfavorable direction; he noted that "'sympathies are still with the boy' despite angry reactions from the north." The qualifier "still" must have registered ominously among some readers.[22]

By Monday, September 5, the rumors had clearly overwhelmed Sheriff Smith: readers awoke to see his deputy, John Ed Cothran, and Captain Joe Heard of the 114th Field Artillery of the local National Guard with guns at the ready. Based on threatening letters and phone calls from nearby Jackson, Smith had requested "battle equipped troops" from Governor White. The governor acquiesced to Smith's worries: thirty men from the local battalion of the National Guard were positioned around the perimeter of the Leflore County jail. Threats of mob violence and lynching precipitated his prompt decision. No doubt Smith's concerns were being fueled by his counterpart

"Comely Carolyn" (September 2–September 6)

to the north: Strider reported that "members of the Bryant family and other persons had their cars forced off the road over the weekend by automobiles bearing Illinois license plates." He had also received a death threat against J. W. Milam's brother James. As if to keep local Greenwood black people away from the jail or to prevent any plotting, Edward Cochran, president of the Greenwood NAACP, claimed that the case "could have happened anywhere. The case is primarily our concern. I believe sincerely that justice will be done [and] satisfy the common decency of people everywhere." Was Cochran appeasing a white reporter, or did his optimism reflect a genuine belief that (white) local justice would prevail?[23]

Other Mississippi blacks were less convinced that white Mississippi justice—blacks rarely sat on juries—could or would prevail. NAACP leader and head of the RCNL, T. R. M. Howard, from the all-black town of Mound Bayou, predicted a second "civil war" if the "slaughtering of Negroes" continued. Furthermore, Howard derided two prominent Mississippi blacks, including *Jackson Advocate* publisher Percy Greene, as "the biggest 'uncle Toms' in the United States because of their support of the continuance of Negro public schools." Howard's remarks, carried in Greene's newspaper, were met with a stern rebuke: the physician was nothing but a race-baiting Pied Piper who was largely "responsible for keeping racial tension at fever heat in the state." Emmett Till's murder and aftermath provided a new proxy for an ongoing and heated debate among Mississippi black leaders: Should blacks continue to press for school integration, or should they press the fight for equality from segregated quarters? Howard and Greene would continue their increasingly hostile fight in the pages of the *Jackson Advocate*—a fight in which the publisher held a definite advantage.[24]

Meanwhile, Strider's conspiratorial pronouncements were also persuasive in at least one other prominent venue: the Mississippi press employed a new phrase in referring to Emmett Till. Instead of "the murdered body of Emmett Till" or the "badly beaten body of Emmett Till," the identity of the body was now rendered as "a body, believed that of Till" or "a body identified as that of Till." Of course, the "believing" and "identifying" had been done only by those closest to the young boy. And what normally would have been the most persuasive evidence of the body's identity had become something far more sinister as the grand jury convened to hear evidence. Strider reported his new lead in the case: "I'm chasing down some evidence now that looks like the killing might have been planned and plotted by the NAACP." Moses Wright and Mamie Till had already identified the body as Emmett's, but this was all part of the alleged conspiracy being carefully orchestrated by the NAACP and Roy Wilkins. If the NAACP could make the

"Comely Carolyn" (September 2–September 6)

case symptomatic of race relations more generally in the South, so could the southern Sheriff make the case symptomatic of a Negro organization bent on dismantling Jim Crow. To many white southerners, sheriff Strider stood heroically between the South's way of life and "a deal made up by the NAACP."[25]

And what of the evidence? Rather than just the picture in the *Jackson Daily News* and his memory of seeing the bloated and disfigured face as it came out of the Tallahatchie River on August 31, Strider had explosive new evidence: "'Two burly Negroes' whom he said accompanied Till from Chicago on his visit with relatives here 'seem[ed] to be connected' in the case." Who or where these "burly Negroes" were remained elusive, but the sheriff was clearly on the case. Perhaps more important were the implications for the grand jury hearing that day in Tallahatchie County—at which Strider would testify. The *Tupelo Daily Journal* quoted Strider as saying that "he didn't 'see how' storekeepers Roy Bryant and J. W. Milam can be indicted for the boy's slaying on the 'slim evidence' now available."[26]

The *Daily Journal* sensed a burgeoning story; its front-page headline began, "Officers Offer Different Opinion in Race Slaying." The UP story led thus, "Mississippi officers today appeared at loggerheads over the investigation of a race slaying of 14-year-old Emmett Till of Chicago." While the bulk of the story reported Strider's explosive allegations, "other authorities" —and presumably Sheriff Smith was one of them—"were confident they had a strong case against the two white men being held in the case." Gerald Chatham, however, was hedging his bets: "In light of Strider's statements," the district attorney would convene a meeting of "all the authorities involved" before the grand jury met to see if there was "sufficient evidence for a murder indictment." Recall that the grand jury would hear evidence bearing primarily on the murder of Emmett Till; Leflore County, meanwhile, would convene a grand jury to hear the kidnap charges in October or November. Such legal details went to the heart of the alleged NAACP conspiracy. Milam and Bryant, after all, had already confessed to Sheriff Smith of taking Till out of Moses and Elizabeth Wright's house. Based on this abduction (and Till's purported release), the theory went, the NAACP had had enough time to find a corpse and plant it in the Tallahatchie River, thus framing Milam and Bryant for a race murder that might go a long way toward dismantling segregation.[27]

But the conspiracy, however far-fetched, did not explain one important detail—one that the *Delta Democrat-Times* reported on its front page: "Strider had said last Wednesday [August 31] when the body was fished from the Tal-

"Comely Carolyn" (September 2–September 6)

lahatchie River, 'we've got a good case against the men.' But yesterday he said, 'I'm chasing down some evidence now that looks like the killing might have been planned and plotted by the NAACP.'" The *Democrat-Times* was one of the few, perhaps only, Mississippi papers to draw attention to the sheriff's sudden and decisive change of heart.[28]

While the Greenville-based newspaper, published by the progressive Hodding Carter, was the only newspaper we noted calling attention to Strider's contradictory claims, many others insinuated that the Tallahatchie County sheriff might at least be wrong about whose corpse actually came out of the river on August 31. Newspapers around the state announced in page-one headlines that on Tuesday morning, September 6, an eighteen-member, all-male, all-white grand jury meeting in the tiny town of Sumner had indicted Milam and Bryant on kidnapping and murder charges. The murder indictment, as reported widely in an AP wire story, "apparently cleared up any doubt as to the identity of the body." In other words, an all-white Mississippi grand jury surely would not have indicted the two white men for murder if the corpse's identity was still in question. Strider's "slim evidence" had become a decisive indictment in less than twenty-four hours—despite the fact that Strider, a mortician named Nelson, and Dr. L. B. Otken had testified before the grand jury that the body likely was not Till's; the body, they argued, looked too old and it had deteriorated too much to have been in the river only three days.[29]

Several newspapers, however, did not make mention of the apparent confirmation of the corpse. In fact, the *Jackson Daily News* gave a lengthy account of testimony questioning its identity; furthermore, the article written by Chester Marshall and James McBroom stated, "It was also learned that George Wright [sic], uncle [sic] of the Chicago Negro youth, with whom the boy was visiting near Money, did not definitely identify the body as that of Till. He told Sheriff Strider and other officers that he thought it was Till's body, but that he could not be sure." This was true—but very partially so. After Moses Wright learned of the signet ring Till had been wearing, the identification had been made without qualification. The *News* also fanned the racial flames by reprinting parts of several letters sent to Strider. One letter sent from Chicago and addressed to Roy Bryant was quoted: "We are going to kill the first Hill Billy that say he is kin to you up there. We are beading and killing Southern Hill Billy and will kill youal." By giving voice to Strider, Otken, Nelson, and the anonymous Chicago letter writer, the *News*'s hard reporting on the case was clearly being influenced by the Tallahatchie sheriff.[30]

40
"Comely Carolyn" (September 2–September 6)

In which direction hard reporting was being influenced was clearly spelled out in that morning's *Clarion-Ledger*, whose page-one hopeful headline read, "Doctor's Testimony May Alter Inquiry." Jay Milner, whose fondness for the adjectival was becoming a hallmark of his reporting on the case, led with this: "Testimony of a Greenwood pathologist [Otken] may cause a dramatic turn in the grand jury investigation of the explosive kidnap-slaying of a 14-year-old Chicago Negro." White Mississippians, Milner reminded his readers, who were "already nervously facing a loaded and cocked pistol of racial strife, were stunned and deplored the incident for its tragic aspects and gross untimeliness."[31]

And then there was Carolyn—finally. Four days after she had been deemed "comely," the first photograph of Carolyn Bryant was featured prominently in Tuesday's *Clarion-Ledger*. Appearing above the fold on page 1, the large portfolio picture featured a younger Carolyn, her head tilted demurely and with her gaze mesmerically meeting the camera. The flattering photograph seemed to demand corresponding textual embellishment and the *Clarion-Ledger* did not disappoint: the "mother of two," "Mrs. Roy Bryant" was the "alleged victim of a wolf-whistle." No longer was she the woman on the lam from the constabulary or the angry pistol-seeking storekeeper; instead, she was a "victim," someone who clearly needed protection, if not retribution. The photograph, and several others clearly shot at the same time, would circulate around the state—on front pages, in the sports pages, even in the classifieds. It was yet another white Mississippi beauty photograph, and such photos knew no generic proprieties; they were fit to print wherever space allowed. From September 6 until well after the trial, Mrs. Carolyn Bryant would always have a "pretty," "attractive," or "comely" attached to her name; in fact, it would become something of a title. Retrospectively and prospectively, the photograph also changed the "looks" of Roy Bryant and J. W. Milam, even as the *Biloxi Daily Herald* ran the increasingly ubiquitous side-by-side patriotic photographs of the smiling half-brothers on the same day.[32]

Even as the tides of public opinion and "official" evidence swung in the suspects' favor, editorialists from around the state clung to a desire to see justice done. Henry Harris of the *West Point Daily Times Leader* opined, "The whole South looks upon the recent Delta murder tragedy as a personal problem," even as other states "do not hold Mississippi to blame for the incident. Rather, they stand ready to join with us in telling the world that we want to see right prevail. The guilty persons should receive the full impact of an unbiased jury decision." But that decision was increasingly imperiled by reports of what had recently transpired in Chicago: "The NAACP is hurting rather than helping the cause of justice in creating a demonstration such as the

41
"Comely Carolyn" (September 2–September 6)

one linked with young Till's Chicago funeral. Making a public display of [a] water-rotten unembalmed body was almost as dastardly a crime as the initial murder itself." That the NAACP had nothing to do with Mamie Till's decision was beside the point for Harris; increasingly, Roy Wilkins's comments were being uncritically coupled with the grieving mother's postmortem activism. That a child's murder might be "almost" as morally freighted as a public viewing spoke decisively about how many white Mississippians interpreted the "hysteria" and the "screaming crowd of Negroes" inside the A. A. Rayner funeral home.[33]

Many, but not all white Mississippians came to this conclusion. Editorialists at the *Delta Democrat-Times* lamented that "the friends of two white men" were seeking their acquittal. Among those friends "apparently can be counted Sheriff H. C. Strider.... Whoever heard of a sheriff offering on the flimsiest construction of fact, the perfect piece of evidence for the defense? Without a corpus delicti, there can be no murder conviction—of anyone." While the paper said "that the information that the body found was that of Emmett Till was accurate enough" and that it had been "identified by relatives" and the "boy's mother," still the Strider conspiracy theory persisted. And then the writer delivered perhaps the most devastating and complete debunking of the conspiracy ever written: "Had such a murder been planned to replace another body for Till's, the ring, engraved 1943 LT (for the boy's father, Louis Till) someone would have had to have been killed before the boy was abducted, the ring stolen from young Till, and placed on the dead person's finger." And then came the most improbable implication: "Without the prior knowledge that Roy Bryant and his half-brother would kidnap young Till, as they admittedly did, such a conspiracy defies even the most fantastic reality." Strider's tortured logic revealed but one possible conclusion: Milam and Bryant would have to have been in cahoots with the NAACP. One plausible ending was already in sight: "They are calling this a lynching in some places outside of Mississippi. Well, it wasn't. But it may well become a lynching post-facto, if the courts in Mississippi are unable to accomplish justice in this matter. And if this happens, we will deserve the criticism we get." The *Delta Democrat-Times* imagined a more plausible conspiracy being choreographed by the NAACP: "All the macabre exhibitionism, the wild statements and hysterical overtones at the Chicago funeral of the Till child seemed too well staged not to have been premeditated with the express purpose of (1) inflaming hatreds and (2) trying to set off a reaction in reverse in Mississippi, where there had previously been honest indignation." Things may not have been quite what they seemed—either in the Delta or in Chicago; it was all getting rather confused and confusing. What

"Comely Carolyn" (September 2–September 6)

had been a "tragic and brutal murder" had become a two-fold local and national conspiracy. Somehow, Emmett Till had become a racial Rorschach test in less than a week. The *Greenville Morning Star* could only conclude grimly in its editorial that the "dangerous situation . . . might erupt into a holocost [sic]."[34]

While the NAACP had clearly become the target of much of the press' editorial anger, it was not the only national civil-rights-oriented organization making public comment on the case. In a little-reported story of September 6, the *Meridian Star* featured on its front page the National Urban League's formal statement on the case; it was the only Mississippi newspaper to do so. Like the NAACP, the League called Till's murder "a lynching," and it fingered "a tragically irresponsible attitude of substantial elements of the state and its leaders." The League, though, chose not to name names nor yet groups of people in the way that Wilkins had less than a week earlier. Moreover, the rhetorically nuanced statement sought to transcend the specifics of North-South racial unrest: "This atrocity transcends racial considerations. It brings into focus a deterioration in civil liberties and an alarming growth of hate and of contempt for human dignity, which we have come to associate not with America but with certain other parts of the world." According to the League, the Till case was less about white Mississippians than American foreign policy: "It is an open invitation to exploitation by groups and ideologists hostile to American democracy." What had initially been a small-town murder had quickly become a potentially contested symbol in America's increasingly hot cold war. Readers of the *Star* might have read the League's statement with no small satisfaction: surely the NAACP was one of the "groups and ideologists hostile to American democracy."[35]

In McComb, Dr. Brumfield's front-page letter had been met with a stern rebuke from Robert B. Patterson, executive secretary of the Association of Citizens' Councils of Mississippi. That the Winona-based Patterson would even respond suggests that Brumfield's "white trash" letter had traveled quite far from home. "Such a letter would be expected from the NAACP," wrote Patterson, "but for a reportedly responsible citizen of Mississippi to hew so closely to the NAACP line is rather surprising." Nothing written or spoken in the name of the Citizens' Councils is "calculated to generate race hatred," he asserted. More local citizens were closing ranks quickly. J. Morris Jones of nearby Smithdale laid bare the white supremacist logic of "our way of life": "What is taking place in the larger cities in the South is just call for alarm. Negro Boys in groups whistling and eyeing our young girls on the streets. The risk a [white] woman takes to go out alone at night. . . . The Ne-

43
"Comely Carolyn" (September 2–September 6)

gro people are not ready for such a step [integration]. Socially, morally, educationally and physically, they aren't capable of taking such a step."[36]

Momentum was clearly growing among the Mississippi press toward the view that their state and its way of life had been unfairly maligned, and what had started as isolated editorials had become far "harder" news as the week wore on. That is, increasingly both AP and UP stories carried quotes from local citizens and attorneys speculating on the possible outcome of a trial. Part of that speculation was a function of a trial date having been announced by Judge Curtis M. Swango—September 19—but news reports of the preceding several days had clearly catalyzed Mississippi public opinion; thus had the press' extensive coverage become something of a self-stoking opinion shaper. Reporting of public opinion began in earnest on Wednesday. The *Greenwood Commonwealth*, for example, stated that "the attitude of Sumner [site of the pending trial] citizens seemed to be that the indictments were expected, but citizens also resented charges and influence of outside organizations, especially the National Association for the Advancement of Colored People." It reported further that C. Sidney Carlton, one of Milam and Bryant's five attorneys—the only five defense attorneys in Sumner—believed that "the people here are not convinced that the boys (Milam and Bryant) killed the Negro boy." The increasingly defensive *Jackson Daily News* quoted from Vernon Brett, a local Sumner grocer: "People in general have changed their minds as to what should be done in the case." W. V. Clutts, an automobile mechanic, added, "'If the evidence warranted, the two men should have been indicted,' but he and Brett 'doubt that there is enough evidence to convict the pair of murder.'" That the two Sumnerians had yet to see or hear any "legal" evidence strongly suggests that the white press had successfully turned the case into one of northern aggression. Their remarks, along with Carlton's, were carried in newspapers around the state.[37]

Less well publicized was the fact that Emmett Till had been finally buried on Tuesday in the Burr Oak Cemetery in Alsip, Illinois. His dead body had taken on a life of its own. A life that had been likely to have been lived anonymously, if happily, in Chicago near his doting mother had rapidly become a contested symbol in an increasingly national story. The singular tragedy of his death had been quickly eclipsed by the tectonic forces of race, class, politics, gender, geography, and culture. The local "fame" he had sought for talking "mighty big" outside the Bryant Grocery and Meat Market on a hot August night had become a national infamy. And many rural white Mississippians were just getting wind of that infamy.

Three

"Resentful of the Slant"
(September 7–September 9)

News of Carolyn Bryant's beauty migrated rather quickly following the *Clarion-Ledger's* September 6 publication. Downstate in Hattiesburg, the *American's* readers were greeted on September 7 to the same picture on its front page. More flattering photographs would appear immediately before and during the trial. In contrast, only a cropped and somewhat menacing picture of Emmett Till would appear during the same period. Gone from white Mississippi consciousness were the happy Tills circa Christmas 1954. The *Clarion-Ledger* also published the first post-war photographs of the indicted Milam and Bryant on its front page on Wednesday, September 7. The two men are shown conferring with "one of their attorneys" just "before pleading innocent" for kidnapping and killing Till, who "wolf-whistled at Bryant's pretty wife." The caption's terms subtly suggest that the men commanded resources (more than one attorney; they would in fact employ five); that they were using these substantial resources to prove their innocence; and, that Carolyn Bryant's racial privilege and honor were at stake, as were the privilege and honor of other attractive, white Mississippi women.[1]

Perhaps more interesting is the juxtaposition of the photograph of Milam and Bryant (and attorney J. W. Kellum) with another photograph, one that appears immediately under it. Taken from a distance, this AP wirephoto depicts hundreds of nameless and faceless black men and women watching Till's coffin being carried from a church towards a waiting hearse. Read in the context of the threatening letters and possible lynching of Milam and Bryant reported just two days earlier, the crowd of "about 2,000" retroactively redeems Governor White's decision to employ the National Guard. In fact, black Chicagoans seemed so threatening that the *Greenwood Morning Star* reported that very day that Milam and Bryant had been moved from Greenwood south to Greenville—and that authorities had purposefully lied to reporters that the two had been moved to Vicksburg as a decoy in order to prevent the lynching scenario. In these photos, rational and deliberative consultation with an attorney by the two white men stood in stark contrast to a teeming black mass assembled on Chicago's south side. This juxtaposition

"Resentful of the Slant" (September 7–September 9)

may have led some white Mississippians to wonder whether that mass might become "hysterical" in much the same way that Mamie Till did upon seeing her son's casket lowered into the ground. In its placement and framing of the two photographs, the *Clarion-Ledger* underscored the increasingly agonistic relationship between white Mississippians and black northerners.[2]

As Emmett Till's body was buried in Burr Oak Cemetery, and as newspapers editorialized via the visual, the press increasingly became the story. In an editorial in the *Greenwood Morning Star*, for example, the writer groused about the lack of balance in reporting the Till case versus the Dianne Kearney story: "The killing story has attracted nationwide publicity," while the "other side of the picture, which is much more typical of the actual pleasant relations between the races, was when the daughter of Mr. and Mrs. John Kearney of Money risked her life and the other Kearney children cooperated to save the life of their negro nurse who fell into the Tallahatchie river." The "bad publicity" from the Till case had done "untold harm to Greenwood," as northerners might conclude that "Leflore County people condone and encourage the wanton killing of negroes." Meanwhile, the Kearney story had "received very meager notice in the newspapers outside of Greenwood"; the only significant copy had appeared in the area's *Kiwanis Bulletin*. The writer concluded by appealing "to the management of the press services and other news sources covering for outside publications to give Greenwood a fair break. Why not reveal the true side of the story, that the accused men were promptly rounded up and dealt with in quick order in the courts of justice?" Good and bad publicity about Leflore County "should receive the same play." Notice that the editorialist localizes the Till and Kearney stories to Greenwood and Leflore Counties; this is not a Mississippi race relations story, nor yet a Deep South one. In one of the few, perhaps only, Delta towns with two newspapers (along with the *Greenwood Commonwealth*), the *Star* still interpreted the Till press coverage within a very local frame. Of course, larger dailies such as the *Delta Democrat-Times* and the *Jackson Daily News*, among others, clearly viewed press coverage within a broader Mississippi context—and what that negative publicity might mean in a national theater where segregation laws and Mississippi's "way of life" were perceived to be at stake.[3]

While the *Star* was calling for "balance" in reporting "the good" and "the bad," the *Daily News* continued its onslaught on the northern press generally and the Chicago press specifically. In its lead editorial of September 7, the paper attacked the *Chicago Tribune* for its "rather gleeful and gloating first-page play-up to the killing of that 14-year-old Chicago boy at Greenwood," whereas the paper "could find only a single column head for the

"Resentful of the Slant" (September 7–September 9)

brutal murder of Joanne Pushis, a 17-year old high school senior at Calumet Park in that city." Pushis, the *News* reported, had been beaten, raped, and strangled by Henry Matthews, "an 18-year old Negro private in the 743th aircraft battery." Such abstemious coverage, the paper opined, was "after all" "the way for a newspaper to handle the story. Rape and murder are common crimes in Chicago. Classed as news they are merely routine events." Whereas Pushis got named by the *News*, Emmett Till was rendered with anonymous adjectives. Furthermore, to many white readers of the *News*, Pushis's race could not have been in doubt, even though it is not identified as such in the editorial. Interracial rape and murder were not big news in Chicago, the logic went, not by virtue of a biased press but because of its "routine" nature. As such, perhaps the anonymous "14-year-old Chicago boy" was only being true to the racial atavism of the Windy City.[4]

Ambivalence remained palpable among many Mississippi newspapers, including the *News*. The same day that it excoriated the city of Chicago, an article by Phil Stroupe appeared in the back pages; its headline read, "Delta Residents Expected Indictments and Want Justice Done in Till Case but Outside Interference Resented." Increasingly, though, "justice" was not linked to the indictments or possible convictions of Milam and Bryant; rather, as one of their attorneys, C. Sidney Carlton noted, "the people here are not convinced that the boys (Milam and Bryant) killed the Negro boy." Justice, in other words, was increasingly linked to an acquittal rather than a conviction, especially on the charge of murder.[5]

As for the issue of "outside interference," the irony was telling: that very interference was being overblown by Mississippi newspapers, not generated "by Northern radical groups." Save for Wilkins's initial statement and several calls for possible federal involvement, the NAACP and its affiliates were keeping a very low profile. What many white Mississippians seemed to be reacting to was the clearly hyperbolic reporting of outside interference. Black people had not arrived en masse from Illinois to "tear up" Greenwood nor was the NAACP aiding the prosecution—not yet anyway. Rather, perhaps largely because of the widespread publicity given to Sheriff Strider's NAACP conspiracy claim, the threatening letters, as well as the seemingly constant rerunning of Wilkins's initial inflammatory comments, "outside interference" gained a reality that belied any sense of the real.

While the *News* quoted several Delta residents regarding the ever-diminishing likelihood of a conviction, Henry Harris of the *West Point Daily Leader Times* was more sanguine: "The two white men charged with murdering a 14-year-old Chicago Negro boy will apparently go on trial this month. Northern rabble-rousers," editorialized Harris, "who have accused Mississippians of

47
"Resentful of the Slant" (September 7–September 9)

condoning murder may be in for a surprise." Clearly directed at Wilkins and the NAACP, Harris was one of the very few Mississippians at this point who publicly held out hope for a murder conviction. That a conviction of Milam and Bryant would come as a "surprise" spoke volumes for just how quickly public opinion could change in the Magnolia State.[6]

Elizabeth Wright, Moses Wright's wife, was also surprised. Speaking publicly for the first time about what had transpired in their house in the early morning hours of August 28, Emmett Till's great-aunt insisted that another man was still at large: "Three white men came to the door with flashlights. Only two have been arrested, I know, but there were three." Having fled to Chicago and leaving her sons and husband back in Money, Wright claimed that she knew what was coming but acted too late: "She had hoped to sneak him out to hide in the cotton fields that surround her farm home." Whether it was fear for her personal safety or something else, Elizabeth Wright would not appear at her great-nephew's murder trial. Nor had she testified at the grand jury hearing. Her husband would later claim that the mysterious "third man" was likely black. Meanwhile, as Mamie Till buried her only child and as a trial loomed, she continued to try to curry favor with white—and perhaps black—Mississippians: "I told him several times before he left for Mississippi that he should kneel in the street and beg forgiveness if he insulted a white man"—presumably a white woman, too. By articulating again the unwritten rules governing Mississippi race relations, Emmett Till's mother not only attempted to vindicate her increasingly pilloried status as mother, but she also suggested that her son knew those rules. Perhaps those so-called "ugly remarks" were Carolyn Bryant's invention, or that "wolf-whistle" was directed at an efficacious checkers move.[7]

For rural Mississippians, particularly those outside of the Delta region, Emmett Till and the specifics of the dizzyingly growing story might have still been obscure, now twelve days in. In fact, many small Mississippi weeklies, even some in the Delta, never made mention of the case, either in editorials or wire stories. As one of the defining stories of the twentieth century was breaking in their collective backyard, "news," instead, was often limited to a local agricultural report, an account of social goings-on about the town, perhaps a story about a local car crash, classifieds, scattered obituaries, a piece looking ahead to the fall football season—and always a story, often accompanied by photographs, of the latest beauty. Only one or two weeklies carried news about local black people, under a small "Negro News" section. Perhaps most striking in this "white out" of local newspaper coverage is the extent to which important stories involving local black people would not receive mention at all. For example, on May 7, 1955, Belzoni voting-rights activist

48
"Resentful of the Slant" (September 7–September 9)

and NAACP and RCNL member Reverend George W. Lee was murdered as he drove his car down a dark city street. While the murder made news in Jackson (initially it had been reported as an accident), the story never made Lee's hometown paper, the *Belzoni Banner*. One of the small Delta town's most prominent citizens murdered, and not one word could we find about it in the *Banner*. Perhaps not surprisingly, then, the Till story often was not a story in small-town Mississippi.

But even though most local newspapers did not publish hard news on it, the Till story did often merit editorial comment; that comment came in a first, sizeable wave on Thursday, September 8. In the south Delta, the *Yazoo City Herald* was quick to link the story to the historic May 17, 1954, Supreme Court decision: "Some of the young negro's blood is on their . . . hands also" because the court had put into jeopardy "the peace of the Southland" by forcing school integration. But the *Herald* was also quick to counter national culpability with local accountability: "Whoever is proven guilty we hope are shown to the . . . gas chamber." That the *Herald* so easily assumed a guilty verdict suggests that they had not been following the stories coming out of Greenwood and Jackson.[8]

NAACP leader Roy Wilkins's September 1 comments had also spread to Kosciusko, birthplace of James Meredith, who would integrate Ole Miss seven years hence. In a lengthy rebuke and rebuttal to Wilkins's remarks, the *Kosciusko Star-Herald* attempted to prove that equitable race relations governed the state and region by drawing on a recent case in Attala County where "three white men apparently on a drunken spree shot up a Negro family." The three whites were quickly "apprehended, promptly indicted and brought to trial. They were convicted by an all-white jury and are now serving long terms in the state penitentiary. One of them was given a life sentence." Wilkins simply did not know what he was talking about. And, as for the NAACP classifying the Till murder as a "lynching," the *Star-Herald* borrowed directly from the *Jackson Daily News*'s editorial in which four white youths accosted and murdered "a Negro man, sleeping on a park bench in New York City." That crime had not been labeled a lynching, so why would Till's murder be treated as such, the *Star-Herald* wondered? The NAACP was not just guilty of rhetorical malfeasance, its editors hypothesized, it might also have been complicit in Till's actions at the Bryant Grocery and Meat Market: "It is entirely possible that this Negro boy from Chicago was inspired by NAACP statements to 'show off' while he was in Mississippi." This conspiracy theory was not of Striderian proportions, but the *Star-Herald* thought it "possible" that Emmett Till's big talking was part of a larger plan. After all, "the NAACP was quick to seize the incident as an opportunity to issue lying

"Resentful of the Slant" (September 7–September 9)

and libelous statements concerning Mississippi," the paper noted, implying that the NAACP was willing, or even hoping, to endanger Till's life by colluding with him to throw a spotlight on Mississippi's racially retrograde ways. Absence of corpus delicti was not the far-fetched and fallacious argument in Kosciusko; *post hoc, ergo propter hoc* was.[9]

Nearby, to the south and west of Attala County, the *Madison County Herald* published one of the more insightful and measured commentaries on public opinion and the Till case. In a column called "Mullen Musings," the editor summarized what had transpired: "At first almost everybody condemned the murder of the Negro youth in the Delta and [the] cry for speedy justice was almost universal. Now we are hearing less about justice and more sympathy for the two young men who are believed to have perpetuated the crime"; that change in sentiment "comes mainly from some Negro section in Chicago and the visit to the Delta by some colored men whose intentions, if any other than merely to visit, have not been disclosed." In other words, the swift change in public opinion, according to Mullen, was a direct function of the Mississippi press' willingness to draw attention to how northern black people had reacted to seeing Till's disfigured body. Even talk "that the body found was not that of the missing boy"—part of Strider's conspiracy theory—was a function of how the press had inflamed passions with its reporting. Mississippians, Mullen advised, should well remember that "the charge against the two men is still murder and they should be held accountable for taking a life. . . . Let's let justice have its own way if that be possible in these days of prejudice." Mullen must have known that such a noble and impersonal plea was increasingly impossible in a region and state on the racial defensive.[10]

Further south, in Lincoln County, home to the town of Brookhaven, where black activist Lamar Smith had been gunned down on the courthouse steps less than a month earlier, Dave Langford also took a measured approach to the Till case, even as he broadened the immediate context of it. Langford was also one of the first white writers to give his blessing to a much-discussed term. He began, "1955 may well be remembered as Mississippi's 'black year.'" Labeling the murders of Lee, Smith, and Till as "lynchings," Langford fingered "the attitude of the better white citizens" as "frightening." Much like McComb's Dr. Brumfield and without naming them as such, Langford leveled the blame at Mississippi's "uptown Klan," the white Citizens' Councils, who had turned their backs "and let the lawlessness continue." Further, while Langford knew he would be "challenged" for using the inflammatory lynching label, it was "beyond questioning." Much like Mullen, Langford emphasized that Mississippi's redemption rested with solving its "problem through legal channels." And, as if to exhale, he closed, "Thank

"Resentful of the Slant" (September 7–September 9)

God that the grand jury has two men for the murder." If white Mississippians would only obey the "laws of God and man," the state's "black year" might prove to be anomalous.[11]

But in Houston, Mississippi, in Chickasaw County, not far from Mississippi State University, the *Times-Post* editor and publisher, Sid R. Harris, strenuously disagreed with Langford's designation. He began, "The brutal murder (not lynching) of 14-year-old Emmett Louis Till, mentally deficient Chicago Negro, . . . is regretted by the people of Mississippi, both white and colored." As if to prove his point, Harris also borrowed from the increasingly well-circulated *Jackson Daily News* editorial, apparently authored by its editor Major Fred Sullens, in which he mentions the torture and murder of a black New Yorker by several white youths. If this was not a lynching, Sullens and his followers argue, then neither was Till's. Harris's editorial also reveals something of white Mississippi masculinity: "Unconfirmed reports describe the language by Till as crude, vulgar and the type that could not go unanswered." Ostensible threats to white male privilege and territory needed "answering"; not to answer was to be neither fully white, nor fully male, nor yet fully heterosexual. The "attractive young mother" needed defending, so this masculine code dictated, even against (or perhaps precisely because of) pubescent black boys. Harris was confident that Mississippians would "see that justice is done," even as the case was "being used as a political football, designed to inflame race trouble, and picture the Magnolia State as a land of hoodlums and illiterates." One also wonders if Harris had been reading the public opinion reports on the impending trial.[12]

James Skewes of the *Meridian Star* was also hopeful that justice might prevail: "If justice is done, then it will serve as a lesson to others to let the law take its course—and to let no man, or men, take the law in his or their own hands." Clearly directed at Milam, Bryant, and their defenders, Skewes attacked the very mentality of retribution articulated by Harris: "answering" even vulgar interracial encounters by taking the law into their own hands, "the slayers have committed a second crime—and this crime is against the fair name of our state." Skewes's logic was the logic of Roy Wilkins; and, even though he did not go nearly as far, such an "entirely needless" murder had cast its dark shadow over all white Mississippians. Law and its "orderly process" would and should redeem the state, not the avenging and lawless ways of imperiled white masculinity.[13]

The editor at the *Scott County Times* also called on the law to take its course, though in far more specific ways, saying that the only solution is "proper punishment for the ruthless men who snatched the negro from his bed and took him away." Such a solution would put an end to "hot-headed action,"

"Resentful of the Slant" (September 7–September 9)

this editor thought, which promised to end more lives if justice was not done. Unlike some other editors, though, this one had a keen understanding of Mississippi journalists and their role in the case: "Bitter language of protest and condemnation has been written about the delta incident," and "the biggest tragedy of all" coming from such journalism was that it stirred "racial hatreds" across the state. And while the "death of the negro boy has stirred race feelings as no other incident in the history of Mississippi," the editor added, rabid (presumably white) rhetoric was only going to lead to more killing.[14]

Some of that very rhetoric was on open display in the *Brandon News*. While Thomas M. Alewine deemed Emmett Till's murder a "dastardly deed," it was also "made to order" for the NAACP. With its fundraising apparatus in high gear from the murder, Alewine mused over where that money might go: "One guess is as good as another . . . and our's [*sic*] is that the money the NAACP raises will be used for zoot suits and the financing of further agitation against white people in general and the south in particular." While Alewine openly mocked the seriousness of the NAACP via its presumed members' sartorial choices, he also could not resist a jab at Till's mother, who got "out of a wheelchair at the Chicago railway station and [ran] across three sets of railroad tracks to greet the baggage car bearing what was said to be her son's body." This alleged performance of overwrought grief was also in keeping with the NAACP's supposed fixation on maintaining a stylish appearance. For Alewine, and presumably many of his readers, people in reality have strictly pecuniary motives. But the editor also had his eye on the courtroom. In another editorial that same day, Alewine used the press' rumors of the Greenwood invasion by Illinois blacks as a future pretext for acquittal: "Such tactics if continued by outsiders of any race, will only bring a 'not guilty' verdict out of the jury room in Tallahatchie County." Langford and Skewes's ideal of blind justice made for quaint copy, but such a call missed the racial point for many white Mississippians: black people who got out of their place—even (or perhaps especially) northern ones—needed "answering" after all. Jim Crow justice demanded as much.[15]

Distance from the Delta also did not correlate with pro-Till sympathies. In fact, sometimes the most virulent editorials were published in far-away places, such as Picayune near the Gulf Coast. In the *Item*, C. H. Cole opened his editorial with a blistering assault: "A prejudiced communistic inspired NAACP organization will make little headway in their efforts to blacken the name of the great soverign [*sic*] state of Mississippi, regardless of their claims of Negro Haters, lynching or whatever." Sexual racial innuendo also mixed with the facts of what prompted Till's murder: "It is very likely that

"Resentful of the Slant" (September 7–September 9)

'wolf-whistle' was not all but certainly nothing justifies murder, and no Mississippian believes that it does." Such whistling and the great likelihood of other untoward sexually provocative acts toward "a white lady" still needed "answering" in Cole's world, however, perhaps not with murder but certainly with some sort of physical response. Like other editors, he also used Mississippi press reports to justify an aggressive response to outside interference: "It has been reported that hundreds of cars loaded with Negroes with Illinois licenses have swarmed onto Mississippi highways." To our knowledge, no Mississippi newspaper reported more than a few cars with Illinois plates having been seen on the highways of the state over the Labor Day holiday, but talk of loaded cars, swarming Negroes invading Mississippi, some with concealed shotguns—it was enough to stiffen a white spine like Cole's: "Mississippians, even Mississippi Negroes don't want this outside interference, and it shall not be tolerated. . . . We hope no innocent Negro has to suffer for these radical acts." But, it would seem in Cole's mind that if an innocent black person must suffer, that punishment would be warranted for the aggressive actions of radical Illinois black people egged on by "their NAACP organization," or perhaps for any perceived aggressive act.[16]

Cole's warning of impending violence helps explain much of the in-house nonviolence training which groups such as the Southern Christian Leadership Conference (SCLC), the Congress of Racial Equality (CORE), and the early Student Nonviolent Coordinating Committee (SNCC) would later emphasize: to be seen as even slightly provocative in a racially tense situation could engender a violent beating, if not death. The rhetorical genius of nonviolent protest was that it typically involved public space and bodies rather than words, and the violence that often accompanied it was sometimes caught on tape and replayed to large audiences. Beatings would hurt—but they would also eventually outrage the nation's moral conscience.

As rural Mississippians read their weeklies and began to form opinions on the happenings in Leflore and Tallahatchie Counties, at least one larger city daily was reporting on one of the hinterland's own. On the front page of the *Greenwood Commonwealth*, the paper reported that the *Collins News-Commercial's* editor, Jimmy Arrington, was asking Mississippi senator James O. Eastland to sponsor a federal bill which would ban the exhibition of bodies for the purpose of fundraising: "Human decency demands such a law and civilized people are entitled to one." This was a clear rejoinder to the Till showing in Chicago. What made the *Commonwealth's* reporting unique was its timing: Arrington's editorial appeal did not appear in the *Commercial* until the following day, Friday, September 9. The archsegregationist and

"Resentful of the Slant" (September 7–September 9)

powerful senator who chaired the Senate Judiciary Committee chose not to respond, at least not publicly.[17]

On its editorial page that same day, the *Commonwealth* published a curious letter. Authored by local resident A. B. Ainsworth and addressed "To all White Mississippians," the Greenwood shopkeeper called on his readers to donate money for a Milam and Bryant defense fund: "We should not sit idly down and see these two men railroaded and made the object of the combined forces now working against them in the North." To counter fundraising by the NAACP, the Urban League, "and various other groups in the North," Ainsworth asked anyone wanting to donate to drop by the store or mail a check made out to the "Bryant and Milam Defense Fund." News of the letter spread around the state; rumors later estimated the Bryant and Milam Defense Fund at ten thousand dollars. "Justice" in Mississippi was rapidly becoming rather parochial, and a generous contribution to this fund helped pay the premium on a policy designed to prevent the destruction of the South's way of life. It also helped Milam and Bryant, whose legal bills "could break them," according to Ainsworth.[18]

Further south in Jackson, the *Daily News* again sparred openly and bitterly with the NAACP; again the subject was motives, and Major Sullens clearly sensed what the grand jury's murder indictment really meant: the "NAACP has taken a stunning blow from this action [indictment] in Mississippi by Mississippians. . . . [The] NAACP obviously didn't want the reaction which made that organization and its leaders liars. They said the South condoned such actions. It was plain that it does not." In other words, instead of yet another notch in its propaganda belt, the NAACP would have to admit that Mississippi had acted swiftly and decisively in indicting Milam and Bryant. In the *News*'s increasingly puerile tit-for-tat refutation of Wilkins's September 1 statement, Strider's conspiracy theory was, on one level, refuted: the grand jury clearly did not believe the sheriff's testimony. Yet at another level, the *News* confirmed the NAACP's conspiratorial motives: the organization was only interested in the propaganda value of the case in helping to overthrow Jim Crow. Perhaps some Mississippians might have raised the obvious question: How might the increasingly Byzantine motivation game get interpreted in light of an acquittal? Would this prove the veracity of Wilkins's claim, or would it simply mean, to them, that justice had prevailed?[19]

Wilkins was also increasingly aggressive. The *News* may have delighted in the latest blast from the executive secretary: "In the name of humanity, in the name of all that is decent in American life . . . the NAACP calls upon the federal government to act decisively to prevent further bloodshed in

54
"Resentful of the Slant" (September 7–September 9)

Mississippi." This statement came on the heels of a meeting between NAACP officials and Assistant Attorney General Warren Olney III, and it connected the Till murder with those of Lee and Smith. This connection suggested that the "atmosphere of violence and intolerance"—what the group called a "jungle fury"—was a direct consequence of black Mississippians trying to gain political power. Wilkins might also have been reading some of the state's newspapers: the federal government "must take steps," he warned, "to prevent a whitewash of them (two men indicted for the alleged crime) in some farcical trial." It was already evident to Wilkins "that an attempt [would] be made to exculpate them of the brutal murder of the lad." Yet even if the federal government found compelling grounds to enter the case, a fundamental problem remained: an all-white, male, Mississippi jury would still hear the evidence.[20]

The following day, September 9, Tom Ethridge of the *News* apparently took exception to Wilkins's "jungle fury" comment. The executive secretary and his NAACP colleagues "have reverted to ancient tribal instincts. They have unsuccessfully tried to replace American concepts of justice with those of the African Congo in centuries past," he shot back. Note that the replacement concepts of justice were based on racial "instinct" rather than a less biologically determined "custom," implying that a genetic African tribalism was anathema to Anglo-Saxon American justice. The only possible point of agreement between Wilkins and Ethridge was metaphorical: each accused the other of a jungle primitivism in which only raw power and ferocity were the governing principles.[21]

Meanwhile, Mamie Till, who was widely rumored to be on the prosecution's witness list, tried once again to soothe the racial antagonism. Widely reported around the state was her statement that she was not "bitter against the white people because you can't judge a whole race by one or two persons." She added, "the color of a person's skin has never made any difference to me, and it never will. Some of my best friends are among the white race." Whether it was meant to counter Wilkins's hyperbole and pretrial pronouncements or serve as a corrective to her own "den of snakes" comment, the grieving mother carefully maintained a measured rhetorical presence in her home state. If she was indeed coming to Sumner to testify at her son's murder trial, she would need whatever sympathy an increasingly hostile state might grant her.[22]

In the same issue of the *Greenwood Morning Star* that carried Mamie Till's comments, the Kearney story moved from the editorial section to a prominent place on the front page. The nine-year-old girl from Money would be receiving the Red Cross' highest award for saving "the life of her negro

"Resentful of the Slant" (September 7–September 9)

nurse," who had fallen into the Tallahatchie River after becoming ill. While the brief article made no mention of the Till case, this was clearly the subtext for the publicity given the young girl's heroism. The *Star* would remain adamant that the Kearney story provided the true picture of race relations in Greenwood: white people, even children, would come to the rescue of imperiled, if dependent, local blacks. Of course, it helped that the unnamed black nurse had fainted from illness rather than transgressed racial protocol. The *Star's* local counterpart also gave prominence to the Kearney story: on its front page that same day, the *Commonwealth* published a large picture of Dianne Kearney receiving the Certificate of Merit Award. An accompanying article also revealed one important new detail: she had saved her black nurse, Jimmie Abrams—Dianne was not yet old enough for the "Miss" designation always attached to white women—on May 26. "Little" Dianne probably did not understand why the award had been conferred three and a half months after her heroic actions. Even more obscure was just how Roy Wilkins had made her award a page-one photo op.[23]

As the *Star* in effect editorialized on local race relations on its front page, its editors also continued to fixate on press coverage of the case: "We have heard a lot of comment about outside newspapers overplaying the Till murder case. Quite a lot of people are resentful of the slant which newspapers and radio and TV commentators have given this very unfortunate case." Without naming any newspapers, north or south, locals clearly resented the implication "that mistreatment and murder of negroes is a common custom in Miss." But with many Mississippi newspapers printing three or four ostensibly hard news stories per day, to go along with editorials and letters to the editor, it is clear that if anyone was guilty of "overplaying" the Till case it was the Mississippi press. As for the slant and sensationalism of much of the news outside of the state, the *Star* interpreted it as "a challenge to people in Miss. to improve race relations to the point that this cannot occur again." Despite its plea for fewer stories on the Till case, the *Star* ran a second editorial that same day; it apparently could not resist leveling a shot at the NAACP for accusing "the Citizens Councils of responsibility for the murder." Unlike some Mississippians who had spoken out against them, the *Star* maintained that the "Citizens Councils were set up to prevent such things as the Till murder."[24]

Just east of Greenwood in Grenada, the *Daily Sentinel-Star* featured a slightly different response to Roy Wilkins and the NAACP. Since the executive secretary had also fingered Mississippi clergy in his September 1 condemnation, Dr. John W. Landrum of Grenada's First Baptist Church claimed his "conscience demands it be refuted." Dr. Landrum condemned Wilkins's

"Resentful of the Slant" (September 7–September 9)

"vicious" overstatements, which "show to what ends the warped malignancy of hatred will lead a person who generalizes on one tragic situation and saddles venomous vituperation on more than 2,000,000 people." Reverend Landrum urged Wilkins to consult Revelation 21:8 to discover just who else would join the murderers in the sulphurous flames of the lake of fire: "liars of every kind." Without telling Wilkins directly that he was on his way to hell, the implication of his remarks needed no scriptural hermeneut to translate.[25]

A fellow Baptist a bit farther north begged to differ with Dr. Landrum. Reverend J. A. Parsons of Tupelo argued that Emmett Till's murder had fundamentally changed things for black Mississippians: "We are not afraid anymore," the minister said while speaking to the seventy-fifth annual meeting of the National Baptist Convention of America in Chicago. He added, "We are going to fight for what is right—as human beings—and we are going to be against this wrong." Given the often exceedingly high price to a Negro for speaking out in so public a venue—and having it carried by the UP wire and reported on the front page of the *Delta Democrat-Times*—one wonders what became of Parsons and his Tupelo congregation.[26]

While Mississippi clergy editorialized for the first time on the case, Carolyn Bryant had something of a coming out ceremony in three dailies: featured on page 1 in the *McComb Enterprise-Journal*, the *Clarksdale Press Register*, and the *Grenada Daily Sentinel-Star*, the beauty photograph of the "comely," "attractive," or "pretty" twenty-one-year-old mother of two boys no doubt had white Mississippi men talking. Since she was no longer wanted for questioning in the case, by this time her flattering photographs functioned less as prolegomena to a trial or arrest and more as the eye candy so prevalent in the Mississippi press. Meanwhile, images of Emmett Till and his mother remained in the visual void; white Mississippians were clearly not eager to see the once smiling, well-dressed family.[27]

Nor were they eager to hear from people offering their opinion on the case from out of state. One of the very few letters from out of state was printed in the *Delta Democrat-Times* on September 9. Perhaps a reader of the *Call and Post*, Cleveland's Marvin J. Barloon offered a lengthy and measured "American point of view" on the case. But before offering that view, Barloon was compelled to steer clear of Roy Wilkins: "It would be grossly unfair to suggest that the people of Mississippi are any less horrified by this crime than the people of any other state or to imply that crimes of this character are encouraged or condoned by the average Mississippian." It would be just as unfair to "cast aspersions upon the judicial system of Mississippi." Having cleared the rhetorical ground, Barloon argued that the "real problem"

"Resentful of the Slant" (September 7–September 9)

posed by the Till case was indicated before the murder even happened; that is, based on Moses Wright's account, it was clear that "a negro in Mississippi cannot defend his own household with his own hands from invasion." That Milam and Bryant could barge into the house and kidnap Till in the middle of the night, without threat of retaliation, suggested that the notion of place and space was governed completely by white privilege. An empowered landowner—white or black—should have forced the two men from his property, even at gunpoint, Barloon argued, thus saving the life of Emmett Till. Wright's obsequiousness in the face of a domestic invasion revealed less about the sharecropper's character and much more about Mississippi race relations. Whether Barloon sent his diplomatic and measured missive to other newspapers is unknown; suffice it to say that only the relatively progressive *Democrat-Times* published it.[28]

A far less measured, though vastly more influential, voice weighed in on the case the next day. From Rome came a scathing and apocalyptic rebuke from Mississippi's own William Faulkner. Perhaps surprisingly, it first appeared on the front page of the *Jackson Daily News*. And the Nobel laureate was not picking nits about race and place in his home state; rather, Faulkner situated "the sorry and tragic error" of the Till murder in its most global context. In an increasingly hostile world in which three-fourths of the earth's inhabitants were not "white in pigment," how could America hope to survive its own hypocrisies, he asked, adding, How could America survive if "when we talk of freedom and libertty [sic], we not only mean neither, we don't even mean security and justice and even the preservation of life for people whose pigmentation is not the same as ours[?]" America's survival was contingent on one condition, according to Faulkner: the nation must "present to the world one homogeneous and unbroken front, whether of white Americans or black ones or purple or blue or green." For Faulkner, the logical conclusion to such a crime against "an afflicted Negro child" was self-destruction: "If we in America have reached that point in our desperate culture when we must murder children, no matter for what reason or what color, we don't deserve to survive, and probaly [sic] won't."

In less than two weeks, the kidnap and murder of Emmett Till had been transformed from a three-paragraph local story to an apocalyptic tale symptomatic of America's probable decline in a nonwhite world. That it was one of the world's most famous writers narrating said demise reflected the extent to which the Till case had become emblematic of race in America. Perhaps even more telling, Faulkner did not even have to mention Till's name in the article; already, the supposedly "afflicted Negro child" needed no name—even for a world audience.[29]

Four

"The World Is Watching"
(September 10–September 18)

Perhaps because it was a UP wire story and many Mississippi newspapers subscribed to the AP wire service, Faulkner's blistering editorial did not receive a broad airing around the state. More likely, Mississippi editors simply wanted no part of yet another "outsider's" denunciation of their state. Even so, Faulkner was not keeping Emmett Till's name alive in the state's newspapers; the massive coverage already given to the case ensured that. Even though Milam and Bryant's trial was ten days away, the story would remain in the public eye. After all, white Mississippians had too much at stake in the case for it to simply fall off the front page or the back page for more than a week. In newspaper parlance, the story had considerable legs, and with each passing day leading up to the much-anticipated trial, the defense jockeyed for rhetorical angles that might ensure a victory. Perhaps not surprisingly, the formidable defense team of Sidney Carlton, J. W. Kellum, J. J. "Si" Breland, John W. Whitten, and Harvey Henderson—the only five defense lawyers in Sumner—tried repeatedly to further stoke an already antagonized and defensive Tallahatchie venire. Given the sentiments already articulated by several Sumner men—by law women could not sit on Mississippi juries—the fires did not need much stoking; the Mississippi press had already seen to that.

The prosecution's resources, though already very lean on account of having to gather and sift evidence and prepare a case in a mere thirteen days, got a boost on September 10 when Governor Hugh White, perhaps with the consent of Attorney General and Governor-elect J. P. Coleman, appointed former FBI agent Robert B. Smith III of Ripley as a special assistant attorney general. Featured in newspapers across the state, Smith joined James Hamilton Caldwell, Jr., who was recovering from a recent heart attack, and district attorney Gerald Chatham. Whether their case was compromised from the outset, as Caldwell believed, the prosecution would later get significant help in rounding up possible witnesses from Mound Bayou physician T. R. M. Howard and several members of the black press who were covering the trial. For now, Governor White's benefactions to the prosecution were registered

"The World Is Watching" (September 10–September 18)

in self-satisfactory terms: "The people of Mississippi are anxious to see justice done in this case according to the law and the evidence, and as governor I am glad to provide special counsel as evidence of our good faith in this prosecution." The question of why it took the governor almost four full precious days to name Smith was never raised.[1]

While White was attempting to assist the prosecution, the black *Jackson Advocate* and its fiery conservative editor Percy Greene continued to use the Till case to press its case against Howard, against school integration, and against the NAACP. In its first editorial on the murder, Greene quickly recontextualized the meaning of the event: "The incident touches at the very heart of the question whether Negroes can continue to make progress in the state in a parallel march beside its white people while avoiding those points of contact out of which friction is inevitable." This was code for continued separate-but-equal racial relations. For Greene, murders ("friction") were simply the natural result of too much interracial contact pressed by the "reckless ambition" of Howard, Wilkins, and an integration-seeking NAACP, and only the "friendship and goodwill of the white people of the state" would ensure future racial comity. Greene's logic was that of the Citizen's Councils: Mississippi blacks' attempts to translate the *Brown* decision into interracial fact were the chief cause of the problem.[2]

Despite the good news of Smith's appointment, prosecutor Chatham's anger with his key witness, Mamie Till, boiled over in the press. Because of her request for police protection while in Mississippi—she stated "[t]here's no sense in being foolhardy"—Chatham was said to be "plainly irritated." The district attorney's irritation, however, had less to do with issues of personal safety and more with interpretation: "If there [*sic*] trying to make a farce out of this trial that's a good way to go about it." While Mamie Till claimed to have taught her son the unspoken rules governing Mississippi race relations, she was either flaunting or ignoring others; for a black northern woman to ask for white southern (or, black or white northern) police protection simply antagonized prospective white male jurors even more. In a state where even getting "Mrs." placed before her name was rhetorically provocative, asking for police protection would border on the absurd to local eyes. Clearly getting Chatham's message, she eventually arrived with her father, John Carthan, and her minister, Louis Henry Ford, who had also preached the eulogy at her son's funeral.[3]

If Chatham was reading the papers on September 10, he might also have been angry with his star witness for talking too "loosely" about her future. Though he promised her "every reasonable" protection, Mamie Till was not reticent about her activism: "I was never much active in working for racial

"The World Is Watching" (September 10–September 18)

equality. Now I'm going to devote all the time I can. This has made me more aware of the problem." Most white Mississippians did not want to hear how their state had transformed an anonymous Chicago working mother into a civil-rights heroine—all because two undistinguished locals had taken exception to her vacationing son's interracial flirtation. Nor could they have been pleased to read that the budding activist had already received more than four thousand dollars from sympathizers around the nation.[4]

As the case entered this new phase of legal details, customs, and intrigue, Mississippi newspapers reran the basic "facts" of the case in almost every article touching on it. Those facts were quite slim: Emmett Till had "gotten fresh" or made "ugly remarks" and "wolf-whistled" at Carolyn Bryant on Wednesday evening; J. W. Milam and Roy Bryant had taken young Till from Moses and Elizabeth Wright's house early Sunday morning; the two men claimed to have released him once Carolyn said he was the wrong boy; a body "believed to be Till's" was discovered early on August 31 in the Tallahatchie River. But within this small group of facts germane to the upcoming murder trial, Mississippi papers often editorialized. For example, Carolyn Bryant's looks remained an ever-present detail clearly bearing on the outcome of the case: she was "Bryant's pretty young wife," "pretty Mrs. Bryant," "pretty Mrs. Bryant, 21," "Bryant's pretty 27-year-old [sic] wife," and "Bryant's attractive wife." In a profession dominated by white men, beauty journalism maintained its allure: the portfolio photographs continued to run in newspapers throughout the state. The full rhetorical import of her beauty would not be made manifest until her rather dramatic appearance at the trial. Silence and erasure also editorialize—and Emmett and Mamie were neither mentioned nor depicted in this coverage. The Christmas 1954 photograph, which revealed the youth and class of the murdered boy, had vanished. Eventually the Mississippi press would substitute a far more menacing and age-ambiguous picture of Emmett Till, one that was also tightly cropped, which functioned rhetorically to reframe its context.[5]

While Sidney Carlton had initially been the defense's point man with the press, by September 12 J. J. Breland—whom Mamie Till would later call an "attack dog" and a "ringleader"—had taken center stage. The elderly Breland—a sixty-seven-year-old Princeton graduate who had practiced law in Sumner since 1915—masterfully plied the press with a subtle blend of insinuation and expectation in a lengthy AP story run in papers stretching from the northern tip of the state in Corinth all the way south to Biloxi. That story contained but one brief quotation from the prosecution—"They got the whole Sumner bar," lamented Chatham—despite Breland's frequent references to what the other side would have to prove. In other words, it was a wholly lopsided, prodefense story.[6]

"The World Is Watching" (September 10–September 18)

The article began by noting that Circuit Judge Curtis Swango would draw a special venire composed of 120 Tallahatchie County white men—"both sides said no Negroes will be impaneled"—and not the more typical venire from just the judicial district in which a trial would be held. In other words, instead of drawing white men only from the western part of the county, Swango chose to include white men from in and around the Charleston area as well. According to Hugh Stephen Whitaker, this more demographically expansive venire worked in the defense's favor as white farmers in the hill country of eastern Tallahatchie County were often in direct competition with black farmers and sharecroppers; they did not share the sense of noblesse oblige not uncommon among plantation-owning whites in the Delta region.[7]

After introducing such factual details in the article, Breland held court. He began by expressing his certainty that "the state would ask for the maximum sentence," in this case, the death penalty. Breland would know this because the prosecution's evidence was largely circumstantial; they would likely not seek the maximum penalty. When that decision was announced, the prosecution's case would appear noticeably weaker; the defense might then feign their collective surprise at such an admission of weakness. Breland, however, was not done talking about the prosecution's case: "The way I see it, the state has got to prove three things: 1. That the boy was murdered. 2. That it happened in the second judicial district of Tallahatchie County. 3. That Bryant and Milam did it." If priority here was an index of strategy, then the defense was clearly holding fast to the grand jury testimony of Strider and Otken in which the corpse's identity was in doubt. Probably having sensed the corpus delicti strategy from the beginning, Chatham's subpoena of Mamie Till was strictly confined to her ability to identify the body as her son's. Breland of course knew that if number one could be proven, numbers two and three were beside the point; the likelihood of a racially motivated kidnapping— Milam and Bryant had already confessed to as much—leading to a killing surely did not stretch Mississippi credulity. Jurisdiction is a red herring in a murder case; plus, the defense could not have hoped for the murder taking place in a different county if for no other reason than Sheriff Strider would then be off the case. But Breland's point was not so much about strategy here as it was about public opinion and expectations; he stated as much: "It's all circumstantial, which is o.k. when you're returning an indictment but quite different when you've got to prove it beyond a reasonable doubt." The seeds of that doubt, if Mississippians were reading carefully, were already being sown in increasingly fecund soil.[8]

Breland did not forget his clients—the same clients who had been loudly denounced across Mississippi in the days immediately following the discovery of the corpse. He noted their "good mental attitude" and the possibility that he would call character witnesses. In fact, the defense would call six of them—a seventh if Breland was included: "I've known those two boys for years. They're men of good reputation, respected businessmen in the community, what I'd call real patriots . . . 100 per cent Americans." Beyond the equivocation between "men" and "boys," Breland articulated exactly what the initial newspaper visuals had suggested: here were two happy, fun-loving American patriots eager to defend their country and state. But their supposed pure Americanism might have registered as curious, if not contradictory, for some readers: Had William Faulkner not derided the two defendants and the state that nourished them as precisely anti-American? Breland was claiming a profound and perfect authenticity for the two men's image; Faulkner a perversion that augured physical ruin based on moral rot. For a man who rented out cotton-picking equipment and another who sold fatback and farming supplies to local blacks to have become palimpsests of American identity, even as they sat in the Charleston jail, J. W. Milam and Roy Bryant had never been farther or closer to home.

While Breland was editorializing about the forthcoming trial, local papers continued their defense of the state's race relations. Recall that the *Greenwood Morning Star* had called twice for fairer coverage of black-white issues in Greenwood and Leflore County. On September 13, the *Greenwood Commonwealth* also entered the media criticism fray—but with very odd examples of Mississippi justice. "For the past several weeks," the editorial opened, "the great northern press has roared its contempt and scorn for the reported killing of a 14-year-old Chicago negro somewhere in the vicinity of Leflore County, Mississippi." Their "screaming headlines," it went on, suggested that such crimes were "unknown to their section of the country," when in fact evidence of "vile and filthy crimes" proliferated in national periodicals. Furthermore, the *Commonwealth* opined, the northern press had "given the impression that the accused will be set free by a prejudiced Mississippi jury. What do they know about Mississippi justice?" The *Commonwealth* set about answering that question in a curious way: the "integrity, honor and mercy" of whites in the state was revealed by several cases in which local blacks had been spared the death penalty. Stated differently, Mississippi justice was demonstrated by convicting blacks of crimes against whites—but sparing them death. Perhaps "our jurors have been too lenient," the editorial suggested. Taken to its logical conclusion, it implied that justice was not about evidence, eligibility for jury pools, or legal representation but in showing blacks mercy with a life sentence—a most odd manifestation of noblesse oblige. "And now Mr. Northern Agitator," the argument concluded, "you have a few of the

"The World Is Watching" (September 10–September 18)

facts about Mississippi justice. We know why you jumped on the Emmet [sic] Till case. You just wanted to sell a few extra papers." While the *Commonwealth* apparently ruled out an NAACP conspiracy, or a conspiracy against Leflore County and Mississippi, this ostensible refutation of the northern press conveniently begged some questions: What if the north's "impression" proved true? What if Bryant and Milam were in fact "set free"? What then of Mississippi justice?[9]

Mrs. Charles Stewart of Vaiden, Mississippi, had her letter to the editor published in the *Commonwealth* on the same day; it bore notable similarities to the editor's position regarding the northern press. Stewart's sister, Mrs. Mozell Nelms, had been "murdered by a negro from St. Louis" one year earlier. The case "caused only a little stir in Mississippi and none whatever outside of the South. The reason of course, was that the victim was a white mother whose life no longer seemed to be of value compared to those of negroes." Clearly, Stewart had not been reading the *Belzoni Banner*, nor many Mississippi newspapers for that matter. But white resentment, as channeled through Stewart, was perhaps less about sectional biases in the press per se and more about the Till case: "I read that the NAACP displayed the negro's body in Chicago for three days to collect money and to incite hatred against the people of Mississippi. I certainly hope that the people of this nation catch on to the schemes of the NAACP before it is too late." That the NAACP had nothing to do with Mamie Till's decision made little difference; increasingly, the white Mississippi imagination conflated very disparate events to form a simple and compelling conclusion: the Till case was merely pretext and proxy for an attack on the South's way of life.[10]

Barry Rutherford said as much that same day in his editorial in the *Tupelo Daily Journal*. While he called on the "hot-headed leaders" of both sides to "avoid the excesses of emotionalism," he quickly parlayed publicity surrounding the Till case into an anti-integration argument. Reverend J. A. Parsons of Tupelo did not remain anonymous for long. As the black minister's statements from Chicago about Mississippi blacks being suddenly emboldened by the Till case were published in newspapers around the state, Rutherford interpreted Parsons's vague comments to mean that "local Negroes [were] behind demands for ending segregation." That Parsons said nothing about segregation mattered little. "Before any of the colored residents of our community or area are misguided by such leadership, however, we feel that it should be impressed upon them that segregation is going to continue in Mississippi.... There is not the slightest possibility that segregation is going to be ended in Mississippi in the foreseeable future," Rutherford warned. And while he decried organizations such as the Citizens' Councils,

"The World Is Watching" (September 10–September 18)

the Ku Klux Klan, and the NAACP for their extralegal emotionalism, he believed that segregation in Mississippi should and would continue "for a long, long time."[11]

While the Greenwood newspapers continued to castigate the northern press, at least one Mississippi editorial praised a northern peer for its stand on the case. The *Jackson State Times* noted with satisfaction that the *New York Times* had refused to "join in hasty, unjust accusations against Mississippi and its people." The southern *Times* said it was "gratifying" to see the northern *Times* praise the grand jury for indicting Milam and Bryant. That the nation's most influential newspaper—in Roy Wilkins's and the NAACP's backyard, no less—had praise for Mississippians and that the *State Times* reported on this with satisfaction clearly reflected on two aspects of the Mississippi press: it was reading (and voraciously) northern press accounts of the case and northern opinion still mattered to its own self image. Interestingly, though, and despite its geography, the editor of the *State Times* referred to the *New York Times* as an "eastern paper." Perhaps allies, even liberal northern ones, could not register rhetorically as "northerners."[12]

White Mississippi journalists were not the only ones eagerly and anxiously scanning northern newspapers for what they were saying about the Till case. In Washington, D.C., the virulently racist cold warrior J. Edgar Hoover had taken a keen interest in the goings-on in Mississippi—and also in Chicago and New York. In a three-page single-spaced letter sent by courier to Dillon Anderson, "Special Assistant to the President," and marked top and bottom with "CONFIDENTIAL," the director of the FBI suggested that President Eisenhower might be "interested" in the "agitational activity" of the "Communist Party, USA," "in connection with the murder in Mississippi of Emmett Louis Till, fourteen-year-old Negro Chicago boy." While many in the Mississippi press had labeled the NAACP a Communist or Communistic organization, Hoover was more concerned with explicitly communist organizations such as the Communist Party USA and its press organ, the *Daily Worker*. The director provided summaries of three recent *Daily Worker* articles, each of which advocated for federal intervention in the Till murder. Hoover called particular attention to Rayfield Mooty, a distant relative of Mamie Till's and "president of a Chicago steel union local." Mooty and others signed a petition urging the president to "call a special session of Congress in order to recommend passage of additional anti-lynch and anti[-]poll tax laws. Only in this way can we be assured that other Negro Americans will not meet a similar death."[13]

While Hoover's top-secret missive to the president did not recommend a course of action, the press coverage and Communist support clearly con-

"The World Is Watching" (September 10–September 18)

cerned him. That the Communists were in cahoots with civil-rights activists, along with labor leaders, suggested an unholy trinity to the director: it was a sinister alliance that would keep Hoover and his famed G-men busy for the next two decades. History has not recorded just how Eisenhower reacted to this confidential warning. But we do know that Mamie Till's personal appeal for federal involvement was met with a stern and telling silence from the White House.

Back in Mississippi and with no new "hard" news to report on September 14, several papers continued their defense of the state by attacking slanted media coverage around the nation. The *Daily Corinthian*, for example, perhaps taking its cue from the Greenwood papers, lionized Dianne Kearney and lamented the fact that her heroism "did not get national headlines." Those headlines were "reserved only for acts of violence when a Negro is concerned," and the NAACP would do everything in its power "to inflame minds" and utter "malicious" contempt for white Mississippians, according to the *Daily Corinthian*. The newsworthiness of saving a black life was equivalent to taking one in their view: "Let the heroism of this little girl in saving a Negro receive equal publicity and consideration as the murder of a Negro boy." Such press coverage would supposedly reflect the true state of race relations in Mississippi where there were "legions of Diannes . . . who live in harmony and respect with our colored population."[14]

Citizens' Council secretary Robert B. Patterson expressed a nearly identical sentiment in a letter to the editor sent to the *Kansas City Times* and reprinted in the *Clarksdale Press Register*. Regarding three black-on-white crimes committed in Tallahatchie County, Patterson remarked, "I am sure you had not heard of these crimes as the Northern press is only interested in crimes against Negroes." Patterson tartly closed his letter by asking the paper to send word of the next murder in Kansas City "and we will have some of our newspapers comment editorially on it." In Patterson's view, Kansas City did not "get" race precisely because they had not yet experienced Negro migration; just as soon as they did, though, their "paper [would be] better qualified to write about the race problem." Criminality inhered in black people, Patterson believed; the Deep South felt this in ways that many in the Midwest simply could not.[15]

But not far from Patterson's home in Winona, it was not just the northern press that was featuring stories of white-on-black crime. On the front page of the *Greenwood Morning Star*, a headline blared, "Kidnapping Near Columbus Brings FBI Probe; Stirs More NAACP Criticism." The UP story reported that the state of Alabama had filed kidnapping charges against three white men who had abducted and beaten a twenty-one-year-old black man, Matt

"The World Is Watching" (September 10–September 18)

Jones. NAACP regional secretary Ruby Hurley made the explicit link between Jones's abduction and the Till murder: "This thing is just frightening. With the Till case in Mississippi, and now this, it looks like anything can happen in that part of the country."[16]

A fellow member of Patterson's Citizens' Council, M. C. Durr, also editorialized on the Till case that same day in the *Brookhaven Leader-Times*. Recall that voting-rights activist Lamar Smith had been murdered on the courthouse steps in Brookhaven just a month earlier. "[S]ome good may come from the death of Emmet [*sic*] Till," Durr began. Specifically, Till's murder would encourage both white and black men to better respect women and stop their whistling ways. Stating that "members of the White Citizens' Councils deplore the act of any white citizen who without a right and just cause will take the life of another be it white or black," Durr begged the question of whether an insolent whistle and flirtation constitute a "right and just cause." For many white Mississippians, Till's offense was, as Sid R. Harris had made explicit, the sort of thing "that could not go unanswered."[17]

Meanwhile in the state capital, the *Daily News* continued its rhetorical campaign against all things Chicago. Instead of going after the *Chicago Tribune* and its coverage of the case, the *News*, thanks to an "offset publication called the 'South Deering Bulletin,'" attempted to recontextualize much of the anti-Mississippi sentiment; it was all about "the Negro vote in Chicago." The reason that "one Negro murder in Mississippi looms larger in Chicago than the hundreds which take place there each year" was because of a simple political calculus: "Negro crime in Chicago [is] a forgivable matter while any such crime in Mississippi becomes a national incident" because Chicago black people might vote for any politician willing to see the Till case not as a murder but as a civil-rights-related lynching.[18]

Privately, Mississippi's highest-ranking politician was not lobbying for votes but expressing his convictions about the impending trial. To District Attorney Armis E. Hawkins of Houston, Mississippi, Governor Hugh White wrote, "I am afraid that the public has become so aroused over the NAACP agitation that it will be impossible to convict these men." The outgoing governor had it slightly wrong: the arousal stemmed from Mississippi newspapers' incessant reporting and editorializing on the NAACP. But the governor had it right when it came to reading the juridical tea leaves: based on what locals had been telling journalists about the case in Tallahatchie County, convictions against Milam and Bryant grew slimmer with each news cycle. That White was "afraid" of such an outcome, combined with the appointment of special prosecutor Robert B. Smith III and his prompt reassurances to Wilkins and the NAACP, suggest that White understood something

"The World Is Watching" (September 10–September 18)

of the long-term consequences of a not-guilty verdict for his state. Mississippi newspapers would try to squelch those dire consequences via a most curious rhetorical method in the trial's aftermath.[19]

The arrival of Thursday, September 15, meant that rural Mississippians would get their weekly dose of the case, mostly in the form of editorials; but the great majority of Mississippi weeklies, perhaps because of few new developments, chose to remain silent on the impending trial. In prosecutor Smith's hometown of Ripley, however, W. H. Anderson of the *Southern Sentinel* editorialized for the first time on the case; he might have taken his position right out of the *Greenwood Commonwealth*, the *Daily Corinthian*, or the *Jackson Daily News*: "The story of the Till killing has been spread over the front pages of South-hating newspapers in Chicago and elsewhere. We doubt if the story of the little girl saving the life of the negro woman was even printed in the Northern newspapers." Dianne Kearney remained the standard rhetorical counterpoint to supposedly imperiled Mississippi race relations. But what so many editors refused to understand at this point was that the white Red Cross award-winner did not save her nurse because of her skin color while Emmett Till's abduction and murder had been framed explicitly by race all along. Race was thus incidental to the former; fundamental to the latter. Anderson also repeated a mistake made by many of his colleagues: the "story of the Till killing" had been "spread over the front pages"—and many back ones—of most Mississippi dailies since August 28; if anyone was guilty of sensationalizing the case, it was Anderson's colleagues in Natchez, Vicksburg, Tupelo, Jackson, McComb, Greenwood, Laurel, Hattiesburg, Clarksdale, Greenville, and Biloxi.[20]

One of the details the major dailies eventually got right was that Emmett Till was not retarded, nor slow or dim-witted. The Wright family's widely reported initial descriptions of their Chicago relative reflected a cultural disposition rather than a genetic inheritance. Emmett *did* come from a different planet from the one his southern cousins did. But Sid R. Harris of the *Houston (MS) Times-Post* maintained the initial misunderstanding, referring to Till as a "14-year-old stuttering, feebile-minded [*sic*] Chicago negro who the defense charges insulted the attractive wife of Bryant." Whether such descriptions reflected pathos or provocation at this point mattered little; Harris had gotten the larger point wrong: the defense was charging no such thing. In fact, the defense was doing its best to avoid the name Emmett Till altogether—for reasons that would become apparent with the "attractive" victim's testimony the following week. As for the likely verdict, Harris pulled his punches even while laying the extrajudicial logic bare: "The verdict could be an answer to outside meddling and interference. On the other hand it

"The World Is Watching" (September 10–September 18)

could be a reply to those who mock Mississippi's system of jurisprudence. Time will tell." That a jury would seek to "answer" or "reply" to anything beyond the legal evidence reflected the extent to which the case was not at all about J. W. Milam and Roy Bryant's guilt or innocence.[21]

And yet an editorial appearing in the *Forest Scott County Times* and reprinted in the *Clarion-Ledger* on September 16 tried to steer the context of the case back to Mississippi and what had transpired on the night of August 28: "Mississippi's race relations, already nearing a precipice under pressure of the NAACP, are in far worse condition than before the [D]elta slaying." Rather than demonizing the NAACP and the northern press, the editorialist averred that the "only solution is proper punishment for the ruthless men who snatched the Negro from his bed and took him away." If the state did not punish Milam and Bryant, the writer added—note that only the kidnapping is invoked and not the murder—black people would gain added momentum in their "current drive for racial integration." In other words, justice was still a proxy for many white Mississippians; if a guilty verdict could mitigate pro-integration activism in the state, then "justice" might indeed prevail.[22]

That same day in Greenwood, the *Morning Star*, perhaps wary of continuing its call for more balanced coverage of the case, adopted a new strategy on its editorial page: it simply reprinted two pro-Mississippi pieces, one that editorialized on press coverage, the other on Mississippi racial justice. Both came from out of state. The first, a letter by J. Jackson of Washington, D.C., shifted the focus from Till to the press: "There is a 'national outrage' here all right, but it is not the recent occurrence in Mississippi. It is the cockeyed slanted view of the Washington press." Once again the evidence took the form of a recent interracial killing, in this case a black man shooting a white Korean War veteran. Additionally, "one of the world's greatest newspapers" had encouraging news on Mississippi race relations. Recall that the *Jackson State Times* had made mention of the *New York Times*'s editorial on September 13. But the *Star* went further and reprinted the entire September 7 editorial, which ended thus: "The prompt action of the grand jury in the Till case indicates that the people of contemporary Mississippi are against this form of murder as against other forms of murder." A direct refutation of Roy Wilkins's September 1 charges, the *Times* editorial looks quaintly dated only nine days after its initial publication. The case was not really about murder anymore but a set of consequences, now that the nation was watching, that would accrue to the state from a guilty or not-guilty verdict.[23]

As the last weekend before the much-talked-about trial approached, the only germane news seemed to be Mamie Till's travel plans. On the front pages of the *Jackson Daily News* and *Clarion-Ledger*, fear of reprisals against the mother whose child had made race a national issue demanded secrecy:

69
"The World Is Watching" (September 10–September 18)

"I would just as soon not have too many people meeting me. There's no way to tell whether they are friends or foes." Not so secret were her plans to attend an NAACP-sponsored speaking event in Cleveland, Ohio. One group of people anxious to "meet" the aggrieved mother was the out-of-town press, which had begun to arrive in Clarksdale. In one of the only articles authored by a woman bearing on the case, Lois J. Schultz in her "Strolling—Around Clarksdale" society column—and this was the only type of newspaper column that white Mississippi women wrote in 1955 (with one notable exception)—reminded her readers that "citizens of Clarksdale and the entire Mississippi Delta will be on the witness stand, so to speak." While differences with the northern press would no doubt persist over the race question—she discreetly referred to it as "our own local programs"—Schultz added, "We welcome the opportunity of showing them that Clarksdale likes company. . . . In other words we knew they were coming and put out the welcome mat." In other words, Mamie Till need not fear for her safety, nor any blacks covering the case for that matter. For as long as the trial lasted, Schultz wanted to assure everyone, blacks would be treated well by a region "famed for her hospitality." That Mamie Till might indeed stay in Clarksdale during the trial was suggested by the *Jackson State Times*, which reported that Fulton Ford, the brother of her pastor, Louis Ford, was a Clarksdale businessman.[24]

Residents of Sumner, however, were publicly expressing less than hospitable sentiments to the assembling press. In a UP story that ran throughout the state, Sumnerians "expressed surprise that the world is watching the small courthouse here." Residents of the tiny community of 550 "said they couldn't understand what all the fuss was about." One man reportedly shouted to arriving newsmen, "You're making a mountain out of a mole-hill. The NAACP is really making you work." The heckling did not augur well for a prosecution hoping to find local residents who might adjudicate evidence in a fair and evenhanded manner. Nor did it bode well for the attempt to localize the case as a relatively straightforward revenge-motivated kidnap and murder.[25]

On the same Saturday that Schultz's column ran in Clarksdale, readers of the *Laurel Leader-Call* in the southeastern part of the state were treated to more gender-specific commentary on the case. Just when and where the photograph had been taken was not disclosed, but for the first time readers had a second view of the alleged victim. Pictured prominently on page 1, above the fold, in a dark, high-collared dress was an older and less finely coiffed "Mrs. Roy Bryant." With her hands folded and wearing a slight frown, a puffy-eyed Carolyn Bryant posed with her twenty-seven-year-old sister-in-law, Mrs. J. W. Milam. Juanita Milam, sporting an open-colored, large-buttoned white blouse, looked to be consoling her younger relative. The photograph can be read as both defiant and pathos-inducing; after all, white Mississippi women were not typically featured in photographs beyond a context that commented directly on their beauty. Glum, if not grim, Carolyn and Juanita also tried hard to feign a class mobility belied by their unadorned appearance, dour expressions, closely cropped hair, and weathered working hands. Perhaps the five lawyers defending their husbands coached them on the pose of insulted white womanhood. Perhaps they only reluctantly agreed to be the public faces of their incarcerated, class-bound husbands. Perhaps it was just a lousy picture.

But it was a picture that was not featured the following day in the *Clarion-Ledger*. Instead, editors finally put together—literally—the two principals in the case, in side-by-side photographs. On the left was one of the now-familiar beauty shots of a younger Carolyn Bryant. On her right was a picture of Till new to readers, at least in the Jackson area. Rather than a cropped 1954 Christmas picture, the *Clarion-Ledger* ran a cropped close-up of Emmett looking over his left shoulder. In the somewhat age-ambiguous photograph (in fact he appears to have a moustache), Till looks to be staring rather fixedly at a nearby object, perhaps at something or someone who had suddenly gotten his attention. In the context of what supposedly transpired on August 24 at the Bryant Grocery and Meat Market, this was an interesting editorial choice. But the editors still could not get the details of the case right: the caption under Till's picture reads "Emmett Till, teenaged Negro boy who was slain and his body dumped in a river because two men say he whistled at one's wife." Roy Bryant and J. W. Milam had said nothing of the sort; in fact, they explicitly denied killing Till since Carolyn Bryant claimed that he was the "wrong one."[26]

In Sam Johnson's lengthy AP story that featured the side-by-side photographs, key details bearing on the case were reviewed, including the claim that the two men had released Till unharmed. Johnson also noted in passing that the 125-man special venire drawn up for the trial contained the names of no black men nor any women, adding, "That's customary in Tallahatchie County" and "Women do not serve on Mississippi juries." In a mere twelve words, race and gender were dismissed as irrelevant to the outcome. Johnson also quoted from an anonymous defense source that the trial would likely last only two or three days and that the state "seems to have little evidence." That same source also foreshadowed the defense's theory that the body was not Till's; this was a theory already being espoused by many: "Local citizens are still asking the question: Was it Till's body that was pulled from the muddy river?" Moses Wright's positive identification of the body

"The World Is Watching" (September 10–September 18)

was not invoked by Johnson—at least not in the version of his story that ran in Jackson. Further south and west in Natchez, the *Democrat* ran a more expansive version of Johnson's AP article that same day in which both Mamie Till and Moses Wright offered rebuttal evidence. Such partial renderings of AP and UP stories was a not uncommon editorial tactic employed by newspapers around the state.[27]

Back in the Delta, the *Greenwood Morning Star* was less subtle in making known its pretrial biases: large page-one headlines blared, "Defense Predicts State Cannot Prove Murder; Till Trial Opens Monday." Only one short paragraph was devoted to the defense's predictions—"'We don't believe the state has a case,' C. Carlton Sidney [*sic*] reportedly stated"—but that sufficed as headline fodder for the editors. The UP article also repeated the now-standard description of Carolyn Bryant as "the pretty young wife."[28]

Certainly not all Mississippi newspapers displayed a prodefense bias on the trial's eve. Most notably, in Tom Ethridge's *Jackson Daily News* column, many pro-Till letters were featured in a digest of local and regional opinion. "A Christian" wrote that "our whole state will be judged by Mississippi's bar." Mrs. M. Patton of Dallas, Texas, in a letter clearly recalling Roy Wilkins, issued an "indictment" of Mississippi's press, schools, and clergy for what the murder said about them "singly and collectively." An attorney from Jackson, perhaps having read the September 6 *Delta Democrat-Times* editorial, thought the idea that the NAACP had foreknowledge of the crimes "absurd" when in fact it was "a clear-cut case of kidnapping and murder!"[29]

Sunday, September 18, marked just the three-week anniversary of the Till case. And yet given its vast coverage in both urban and rural areas, many Mississippians had a fairly settled opinion about the guilt or innocence of Roy Bryant and J. W. Milam. Based on Tallahatchie County resident Hugh Stephen Whitaker's interviews with jurors, lawyers, and townsfolk, white Mississippians did not doubt their guilt. In a state that took its Jim Crow ways with a lethal earnestness, incredulity did not extend to a man many locals did not like and another who was just plain feared. Despite this fairly settled belief, white Mississippians had rallied to the half-brothers' side: Ainsworth's appeal helped raise more than ten thousand dollars for their defense, which was initially rejected by all five defense attorneys in Sumner, but the same five quickly got back on board. Fueling such loyal support was a Mississippi press that had clearly taken things quite personally. Bryant and Milam, regardless of class, were still "their" boys. And Carolyn and Juanita were "their" women. And Jim Crow represented "their" way of life.[30]

Indeed, the Till case was very personal.

Five

"Every Last Anglo-Saxon One of You"
(September 19–September 23)

The most sensational trial in Mississippi's history officially began on September 19. The Mississippi press, along with Mamie Till and the NAACP, ensured a national and even worldwide audience for the week-long proceedings. Reporters from as far away as England descended on the sultry and roiling Delta town of Sumner—the western county seat of Tallahatchie—to document how southern racial justice would play out. And it did not take long for the reporters to note a morbidly ironic advertisement for the town: on a roadside billboard, Sumner touted itself as a "good place to raise a boy." Perhaps Jim Crow had become so naturalized, so much a part of the physical and lexical terrain, that a Delta chamber of commerce had clearly missed the irony. As for womanhood, white or black, the categories were so promotionally inconsequential as to be invisible.

While some out-of-town reporters stayed in Sumner, the small contingent of black reporters found accommodations in the all-black community of Mound Bayou, home to the prominent surgeon and activist T. R. M. Howard. At least one of them was immediately struck by an initial impression of white and black Sumnerians: "Either this thing is being over-played or these people aren't reading the script. Everybody acts like nothing out of the ordinary is taking place." Similarly, two reporters for the *Jackson State Times* noted that "[i]f there was any 'racial tension' in Sumner on the eve of the Emmett Till murder trial, it wasn't apparent on the town square Sunday." Had these reporters been reading the previous weeks' papers, they would have known that some serious dissembling was afoot. Long a skill critical to blacks' survival, white townsfolk could dissemble, too. Perhaps to get worked up around northern "nigger newsmen" would have belied a hostility anathema to the much-vaunted southern hospitality. Readers of the *Clarion-Ledger* were treated to more overt forms of apparent Sumner interracial harmony: its front page described the cordial gathering of whites and blacks at the funeral services for Kid Townsend, a local black who had died of a heart attack. Local whites generously contributed money and food to

73
"Every Last Anglo-Saxon One of You" (Sept. 19–Sept. 23)

Townsend's widow. They also sat in a "special section of the church reserved for them" so as not to transgress racial sensibilities.[1]

Sunday, September 18, was the last day the tiny county seat would remain unknown to Mississippians and the nation. Much like the hamlet of Money, the Till murder trial would give it a special infamy in civil-rights history. That trial would last all of five days—and jury selection would account for two of them. The prosecution's first witness, Moses Wright, would not take the stand until Wednesday morning at 9:15. Milam and Bryant's defense would take but part of Thursday afternoon and most of Friday morning. A verdict would be reached by 3:43 on Friday afternoon. By contemporary standards such a radically truncated trial seems criminally short. In fact, defense attorneys publicly argued that the trial would last only until Tuesday afternoon or Wednesday morning at the latest. We should also remember that Friday's verdict would have been reached much sooner had not Howard and members of the assembled black press located and persuaded several local witnesses to testify. Presumably the verdict would have also come sooner if the jury had not been urged to "make it look good" and if they had not fouled up the paperwork.[2]

Spectators entered the courtroom in single-file; deputies searched each person for possible weapons as a precaution in the wake of more than 150 threats. Three hundred eager men and women strained the room's 180-seat capacity. As Circuit Judge Curtis M. Swango banged his gavel promptly on Monday at 9:15 A.M., Mississippi newspapers finally had something to report on other than the press, Mamie Till's travel itinerary, and Dianne Kearney's heroics. Sheriff Strider made sure that the packed courtroom remained strictly segregated: "The colored people will be in one section and the white in another," the "270 pounder" bellowed, adding, "We've kept the races separated for a long time and we don't intend to change now." Swango's courtroom rules were few: no photographing or sketching while court was in session, no loud talking, and no exiting or entering the courthouse except through the front door. Smoking was permitted, and, given the stifling heat, men were encouraged to take off their jackets. The small cadre of black reporters—there were only six present on Monday morning, and the *Jackson Advocate's* Percy Greene was not one of them—were herded into a corner and given only a small card table. Strider had in fact argued with Swango over whether black reporters should be allowed in the courtroom at all. The white press had front-row seats proximate to the jury, Swango, and the witness chair, as well as two large tables. Jury selection officially began at 9:25.[3]

The headline item of the day for most newspapers was one of omission:

74
"Every Last Anglo-Saxon One of You" (Sept. 19–Sept. 23)

District Attorney Gerald Chatham had not asked prospective jurors for their views on the death penalty. As such, the state was tipping its hand: its evidence would be largely circumstantial. Chatham, however, broached the issue of racial prejudice with each juror, asking "if they had 'any prejudices because the defendants are white and the deceased was colored.'" Chatham (and Smith and Caldwell) knew their audience: prejudice was not interrogated in a general sense, but only as it related to the present case. To have asked each juror for his racial views more globally would have completely flummoxed a system built and sustained on a presumption of white (male) supremacy. That justice could be expected in a context in which no blacks (or women) were eligible to vote was simply beyond debate. Chatham did, however, make special mention of the press: "Because of the wide publicity in this case, the prosecution will take special pains to see that fair and impartial men are selected to try the case on law and evidence and on nothing else." Chatham had clearly been reading about the case and the verdict already rendered by many Delta residents and by many perhaps unwitting journalists.[4]

The language of the Mississippi press continued to foreground Milam and Bryant's assumed innocence—they were "confident," in "good spirits," and expressed a "jovial attitude"—and Emmett Till's supposed "guilt." This language became even more revealing as the trial commenced. Almost universally, the Mississippi press had a new designation for the murdered youth: Emmett Till was now a "husky negro lad who stuttered," "a husky negro lad," and "a stuttering husky Negro lad." Only the *Delta Democrat-Times* referred to the victim as "young Emmett Till." Markers of youth had been replaced by those of size and perhaps mental acuity. While Till was deemed "normally intelligent" by his great-uncle in an extended interview with the *Clarion-Ledger*, a "husky lad" was certainly not a "14-year-old Chicago boy." Till's now conspicuously missing hometown also made his alleged "wolf-whistle" that much more incriminating: a crime had been committed against white southern womanhood rather than a teenaged prank by a northern black boy meant to impress his southern cousins. But perhaps above all else, size mattered to aggrieved white southern men—and Till had clearly grown in stature in three short weeks.[5]

Meanwhile, and perhaps predictably, Till's more imposing physical stature was concomitant with Carolyn Bryant's increasingly universal beauty. While the "victim" remained "attractive" and "pretty," the *Jackson Daily News* emphasized that she was "highly attractive." The *Clarion-Ledger* went further: she was "a 27-year-old [*sic*] Mississippi-born girl with dark good looks inherited from Italian-born ancestors." By the close of the trial, Carolyn's good

"Every Last Anglo-Saxon One of You" (Sept. 19–Sept. 23)

looks would migrate to her entire family. Class also subtly insinuated itself into the journalist's reporting. Juxtaposed to the "humble" "six-room shack" inhabited by the Wright family was the attire of Carolyn and her sister-in-law, who were "clad in summer print dresses and high-heeled shoes." No longer a "shopkeeper" catering to local black sharecroppers and left unprotected by a truck-driving husband, the Bryants and Milams were certainly more upwardly mobile than initial reports had suggested. Whereas the Wright "shack" was decorated with a "cardboard framed picture of Esther Williams," the seasonal dresses and stylish shoes worn by Carolyn and Juanita, to say nothing of the employment of five attorneys, suggested social and economic mobility. The *Clarion-Ledger* did report that Moses Wright was seen by local whites as a "cut above" most blacks of his age and station because of "his volubility and his ability to express himself vividly." Such abilities were not reflective of a formal education; rather, as trial testimony would reveal, Wright was an occasional preacher at the nearby Church of God in Christ.[6]

Nearly forty-eight hours before Wright would lead off the prosecution's case, Sam Johnson of the AP reported that eleven of the thirteen jurors had been selected by noon on Monday, September 19. Far more notable was the fact that Carolyn Bryant and Juanita Milam were each permitted to sit next to their nonuniformed and unshackled husbands—along with each of the defendants' two sons. Rather than keeping their young sons at home—the four boys were all under four years old—the defense team clearly encouraged their clients to make a show of their families. The *Natchez Democrat* was one of the only newspapers to comment directly on the strategy: "Mississippians said it is not unusual for a defendant to bring in a small child." But they quickly added, "In many parts of the country it is unprecedented." It would prove to be a stroke of rhetorical brilliance as members of the press fixated on the families, particularly the cute children. Moreover, how could twelve fellow white male Deltans convict such affectionate and playful fathers and husbands? While Milam and Bryant would not take the stand in their own defense, their supposed innocence was underscored by courtroom protocols that recontextualized them, not as cold-blooded child murderers but as family men. Such reassuring visuals would be prominently pictured in local newspapers that week. Mississippians could thereby see for themselves, if they were so inclined, that loving family men were incapable of such a barbarous act.[7]

Readers of the *Vicksburg Evening Post* also got some important visuals as the trial opened. In a front-page matrix, key principals were paired: Emmett with Carolyn, Bryant with Milam, and Moses with Mamie. The *Post* used the more menacing picture of an older-looking Till alongside the younger

"Every Last Anglo-Saxon One of You" (Sept. 19–Sept. 23)

beauty picture of Carolyn; it was the same side-by-side strategy used by the *Jackson Daily News* just one day earlier. The *Post* also used a less-than-flattering photograph of Mamie Till. Unlike Carolyn's closely cropped photograph that concealed any cleavage, Mamie's open, dark, wide-lapelled blouse revealed a suggestive décolletage. Many readers would likely ask, Was this the appropriate outfit for a grieving mother? Did her sartorial choices bespeak an opportunistic promiscuity? As they followed her upward gaze toward the picture of her dead son, the context of the photograph was redrawn—away from a sympathetic display of white feminine beauty so familiar to southern newspaper readers to a crass and entirely inappropriate sexuality.[8]

While the *Post* subtly editorialized on mother and son, they got information about Moses Wright wrong. Instead of Emmett Till's great-uncle, they reported that he was the "boy's grandfather." But the *Post* was not alone in making basic factual errors, despite the daily publicity surrounding principals, dates, and key events connected with the case. Many reporters still could not get the ages of Milam, Roy Bryant, Carolyn Bryant, or Mamie Till correct; others still insisted that Till had made his infamous "wolf-whistle" on August 27. James Featherston of the *Jackson Daily News* also claimed that an autopsy had been performed on the murdered youth. The first and only autopsy on the corpse would take place more than fifty years later. One important detail the press did have correct was Mamie Till's speaking schedule on her way south. Before an NAACP audience in Cleveland, Ohio, she told two thousand listeners that "my son is a martyr, and I want to work and help so that his death will not have been meaningless." That the much-reviled NAACP now had its hooks into Emmett Till's mother was further proof that the "communistic" civil-rights organization was using the case as a proxy for an assault on desegregation more generally. Mamie Till's radicalization did not bode well for her reception in the Delta, nor in the courtroom. But reports of her speaking engagement in Cleveland also suggested a misleading chronology; that is, by September 17, Mamie Till was already safely ensconced at T. R. M. Howard's compound in Mound Bayou. The story in the *Hattiesburg American* and other newspapers, in light of her absence during Monday's court session, implied that the crusading mother was too busy stumping for the NAACP instead of preparing for her critical testimony. The slant would prompt many to ask, What kind of mother could be so opportunistic in the face of her son's alleged murder? What kind of mother would be speaking rather than mourning? In hindsight, it is clear that Mamie Till had purposefully misled reporters as to her whereabouts. Even as the trial opened, District Attorney Gerald Chatham thought she was still in Chicago. A small article in the *Jackson State Times* quoted Till's attorney, William

"Every Last Anglo-Saxon One of You" (Sept. 19–Sept. 23)

Huff, to the effect that she would not leave Chicago until she was called as a witness.[9]

The *Daily News* didn't miss the opportunity to comment on the NAACP, which was using the case to push its "completely unrealistic goals"; in so doing it was sacrificing the "harmony between the white and Negro races in areas where the Negro population is heaviest." Part of that harmony was vouchsafed by white paternalism that sympathized with black inferiority and that would now be jeopardized by calls for equality: "Mississippians have long understood the inability of the Negro to live with comprehension in a white man's complicated society without minor rebellions and backsliding into his ungoverned heritage. That understanding has made for a double standard of social mores throughout the South." The logic recalled the recent editorial in the *Greenwood Commonwealth* which argued that blacks had actually been treated deferentially by the state's justice system. Furthermore, the *Daily News* claimed, "[i]t has been a kindly double standard and one calculated to let the Negro live with as few overlapping regulations from a society he is ill-equipped to meet as a social equal as possible." Whether blacks' "inability" to live in such a complicated society was genetic or cultural mattered little. But if the NAACP really wanted equality, the rules would have to change since "[n]egro justice is substantially softer than white law." In this rather remarkable assertion and defense of white supremacy and paternalism, the logical implications were unavoidable: the justice system would have to be far more punitive towards blacks. Or, to equalize things in the opposite direction, perhaps white juries would have to treat white defendants with more leniency. Perhaps it was a bit of both; it all depended on just how much "substantially softer" the double standard was. In any case, the legal calculus did not bode well for the prosecution—nor for black Mississippians more generally.[10]

Before one word of testimony was even recorded, for example, Virgil Adams, who published the *Greenwood Morning Star*, interviewed two dozen locals, and "not one expressed the opinion that the men would be found guilty." Note that those surveyed did not express the opinion that Milam and Bryant were innocent of the crime. As Hugh Stephen Whitaker has shown, based on his interviews with locals, most whites in Tallahatchie County believed that the men had in fact committed the crime. Adams's rather crude "survey" merely suggested a hoped-for outcome rather than an opinion based on legal evidence.[11]

By Tuesday, September 20, the twelve members and one alternate of the all-white, all-male jury had finally been seated, and testimony was set to begin the following day. The lengthy jury selection process was exacerbated by

"Every Last Anglo-Saxon One of You" (Sept. 19–Sept. 23)

"widely-circulated 'money jars'" to which many in the 120-man venire had contributed. But according to James Featherston, the "highlight" of day two was Mamie Till's highly anticipated appearance in the Sumner courtroom. Accompanied by her father, John Carthan, and her pastor, Louis Henry Ford, Mamie Till's appearance in the packed, steaming room had clearly not taken Sheriff Strider by surprise. With dispatch, the plantation-owning sheriff marched up to her, issued her a subpoena, and loudly announced, "You are now in the state of Mississippi. You will come under all rules of the state of Mississippi." A surprise visitor was Michigan congressman Charles C. Diggs, Jr., whom Featherston labeled as "a bitter critic of the South and segregation." Local whites were incredulous that a black man could possibly be a congressman. Reporter James Hicks heard one deputy say to another, "This nigger [Hicks] says that other nigger is a congressman." "A nigger congressman? It ain't possible. It ain't even legal," came the reply.[12]

Predictably, Mamie Till's much-anticipated appearance in the courtroom set off a "photographic circus"; it was also met with talk of her physical appearance. The *Jackson Daily News*'s Featherston offered readers the most detail: "Dressed in a black shantung dress, a black velvet hat studded with rhinestones and a considerable amount of costume jewelry, the 33-year-old Mamie Bradley [was] small, plump, and appear[ed] very neat." Just how Featherston concluded that the "plump" mother's jewelry was not the real thing remained a mystery. Far less mysterious was a subtle yet profoundly important omission: Mamie Till would never be addressed by the white Mississippi press with the title of "Mrs." or "Miss"; that appellation was reserved exclusively for white women. Featherston might well have been sharing his observations on Mamie Till with Sam Johnson, who described her for the wire service as "[a] small, neat woman, somewhat on the plump side." "Neat," which perhaps registered as good hygiene, was as close as the white Mississippi press would get to saying something salutary about Mamie Till's looks. To have explicitly stated that Emmett Till's mother was attractive or even pretty would have transgressed racial decorum; it would have also put her on equal physical terms with Carolyn Bryant. The most positive description of Mamie Till was rendered by the *Jackson State Times*: "Dressed stylishly in a grey dress with white collar and a small black hat, the youthful woman was given a seat at the Negro press table." Most notably, the weight of the "youthful" and "stylish" mother was not commented upon. The same writer also commented favorably on her ability to handle the throng of "jammed-up reporters": "She appeared to be completely at ease and smiled frequently." In a preview of her testimony as well as a harbinger of the defense's strategy, the aggrieved

"Every Last Anglo-Saxon One of You" (Sept. 19–Sept. 23)

mother also talked frankly about identifying her son's mutilated corpse: "I looked at his teeth and looked for the other things I knew about him. There is no doubt in my mind but that the body was that of my boy. If I thought it wasn't my boy I would be down here looking for him now."[13]

Mamie Till was not the only person receiving careful physical scrutiny. As we noted earlier, Carolyn Bryant's "attractive" looks rapidly migrated to her immediate family as the jury selection ended and testimony was about to begin. On a page-six special of the *Daily News*, hyperbolic headlines read, "Cast in Impelling Court Drama Matches Movies." Roy Bryant was cast, with no small flattery, first: he "looks like a college athlete and is handsome enough to be a movie star." Three reporters, the article continued, "couldn't make up their minds whom he resembled. One said he looked somewhat like Mississippi-born Dana Andrews. Another said he was more like Jeff Chandler. Still a third said Bryant was handsome in a similar fashion as Bill Holden. Bryant is tall and athletically-built." In a different article on the same page, Bryant was described as "ruggedly handsome," and his "wife and children also are unusually attractive."[14]

Milam did not possess the supposed rugged movie-star looks of his half-brother—unless one was reading Ralph Hutto of the *State Times*. In another drama-inflected trial preview, Hutto described both defendants as "handsome men. Bryant, 24, is slim and curly-haired. Milam is 36, his half-brother, is balding and portly but handsome nevertheless." Hutto did not leave it there: "Both defendants have beautiful wives. . . . Carolyn Bryant, 22 [*sic*], subject of the 'wolf whistle,' is a brunett [*sic*] with dark eyes. Juanita Milam, 27, is better looking of the two, with a fair complexion, blue eyes and light brown hair." In a culture consumed with white female beauty and where cultural capital flowed to those associated with such beauty, Roy Bryant and J. W. Milam already had one foot out of the Charleston jail.[15]

But in addition to the powerful allure of beauty, the *Daily News* and the *Clarion-Ledger*, in particular, feted the half-brothers for their racial bona fides. The "logic" of good looks suggested that such men could not have perpetrated such vile, racially motivated revenge—even if to defend southern white womanhood. In this effort to redeem the half-brothers, family members, friends, attorneys, and neighbors came to their rescue. Mrs. Louie Campbell, Milam's sister, claimed that her brother "once saved the life of a little Negro polio victim by rushing him to the hospital in Memphis in the nick of time." Emmett Till had also been a polio victim. That the "much-decorated veteran of World War II" would drive two hours to save a dying black boy countermanded images of a brutal racist operating under the

"Every Last Anglo-Saxon One of You" (Sept. 19–Sept. 23)

cover of darkness. World War II heroism also underscored compelling sacrifices in the name of freedom and equality. And Milam's color-blind heroism was not an anomaly: according to his attorney Sidney Carlton, he had "dived into the Tallahatchie River and saved a little Negro girl from drowning." Surely, readers would respond, this could not have been the same man accused of drowning a black boy in the same muddy river. To punctuate these textual appeals, the *Daily News* ran a large picture of a playful and laughing Milam holding his two young sons, Bill and Harvey, in the "oven-hot" courtroom. Perhaps surprisingly, the black *Jackson Advocate* ran a nearly identical article featuring Milam's interracial heroism.[16]

In a page-one story in the *Clarion-Ledger*, Jay Milner focused similarly on Roy Bryant's racial sensibilities. Unlike those of his heroic half-brother, Bryant's allegedly progressive attitudes on race were underscored by his service in the Korean War. According to neighbor and "long time friend" Johnny Tupman, Bryant "didn't seem to mind" that he served under a Negro noncommissioned officer: "He told us the Negro was a good soldier and that they understood each other." Clearly, readers would likely conclude, the young man who was "handsome in the William Holden manner" and married to the "uncommonly attractive" victim could not have possessed the ugly racial prejudices needed to carry out a race killing, and if Roy Bryant would willingly risk his life taking orders from a black man in the service of his country, then surely race played no role in whatever might have happened on August 28, or at least race did not exacerbate it. Or, was race so interlarded with events at the Bryant Grocery and Meat Market that, good military behavior notwithstanding, Roy Bryant had to act? Perhaps defending one's country against Communism trumped racial mores of place and authority, but not so when defending one's woman in the Jim Crow South.[17]

Of course, Milam and Bryant's racial sympathies were emphasized precisely because they were under assault by the prosecution, as well as by the national media. But the articles in the *Daily News*, *Jackson Advocate*, and *Clarion-Ledger* can also be understood as rhetorical scaffolding for a larger defense strategy. That is, newspapers around the state reported on September 20 that the defense would not feature the corpus delicti arguments promulgated by Sheriff Strider at the grand jury hearing; perhaps the defense was leery that Mamie Till's positive identification might hold sway with jurors. Instead, newspapers reported that the defense expects "to establish that Mrs. Bryant was assaulted by the victim, Emmett Louis Till, while he was alone with her Aug. 24. The word was used in the legal sense which implies any untoward incident and did not imply actual physical attack or rape."

"Every Last Anglo-Saxon One of You" (Sept. 19–Sept. 23)

Only in hindsight does the defense's strategic disclosure register as something of a bombshell.[18]

It is clear that the defense was not engaged in a strategic bluff; its star witness would be Carolyn Bryant, as was revealed on Thursday, September 22. By foreshadowing its strategy, the defense was rather baldly announcing that Roy Bryant and J. W. Milam had in fact murdered Emmett Till—but on justifiable grounds. Having "assaulted" the former beauty queen—and her testimony would claim an assault of a sexual nature—it was open season on the "stuttering" and "husky Negro lad." Remarkably, it appears that the defense was betting that a jury would acquit the half-brothers on the grounds of justifiable homicide; and, based on this revelation of strategy to the local press, they were also hoping for an acquittal in Mississippi public opinion as well. Coupled with the stories about Milam and Bryant's supposed race-neutral proclivities, the defense hoped to show—using the graphic testimony of the aggrieved and "unusually attractive" Mrs. Bryant—that the early-morning kidnapping and murder were entirely justified. In other words, the case was about race and place, not merely race hatred; as such, it was a case of simply enforcing a code of conduct. Thus did M. C. Durr of the *Brookhaven Leader-Times* get an answer to his September 14 editorial: the alleged interracial sexual assault of a white woman in Tallahatchie County did constitute a "right and just cause" for taking a life.

The defense's strategy, however, ran afoul of at least two evidentiary matters—to say nothing of sane human interaction. First, recall that both Milam and Bryant had confessed to Leflore County Sheriff George Smith and his deputy John Ed Cothran that they had taken Till from the Wright house but had released him once Carolyn could not identify him as the alleged assailant. If Carolyn testified that Till was in fact the assailant, she would be making a liar out of her husband and half-brother since she allegedly told them he was not the offender in question. On the other hand, if Milam and Bryant released the boy, an assault by Emmett Till had not taken place, thus making a liar out of Carolyn Bryant. Clearly, the defense would need to keep Smith and Cothran's potentially damning revelations away from the jurors. As it turns out, the defense had already anticipated the lawmen's possible testimony.

The other problem with the assault and justifiable homicide defense involved witnesses: if Carolyn Bryant was permitted to testify to a physical assault, presumably the prosecution could call upwards of eight witnesses who had watched as Till acted out the high-stakes dare. Certainly white male jurors would be inclined to believe one of their "own," but the sheer number

"Every Last Anglo-Saxon One of You" (Sept. 19–Sept. 23)

of potential rebuttal witnesses could prove problematic. Moreover, perhaps a black child could be even more compelling a witness than an adult since motivations pertaining to race might yet elude them. Furthermore, prosecutors might ask, if Emmett Till had assaulted Carolyn Bryant, wouldn't his family have put him on the next northbound Illinois Central train?

Regarding more overtly rhetorical matters, we are still left with the question of why the defense would reveal its hand to the prosecution on the eve of the trial. Assuming the story was not a leak, prosecutors would wonder why the defense would possibly strengthen their admittedly circumstantial case. If the defense team would indeed mount a defense—and there was some hint that they might rest without one—why not argue the absence of corpus delicti, as claimed by Sheriff Strider and the pathologist Dr. Otken? Did the grand jury indictment suggest that such a far-fetched defense might not work with this jury, either? Had the *Delta Democrat-Times* exploded it back in early September? Or, was the issue less about legal evidence, speculation, and testimony and more about a southern way of life that needed no public apology? The *Greenwood Commonwealth* seemed to answer the question: "In talking with some of the people around the crowded building, the *Commonwealth* reporter found that there is strong desire to see Milam and Bryant, the defendants, acquitted."[19]

Before Tuesday's early recess because of courtroom overcrowding and the prosecution's claim that it had to interview potential new witnesses, several reporters took the defense's alluring bait: the four Milam and Bryant sons had become "the darlings of the newsfolk." Arthur Everett described the "boys' thin wails" and "childish laughter" as they wandered around the courtroom. Jay Milner described both the "well groomed and uncommonly attractive" wives and their rambunctious brood whose "bright-eyed young faces shone from scrubbing." Hygiene was also on John Herbers's mind as he described the four boys being "scrubbed and decked out in Sunday best." By the afternoon, though, all four boys roamed the courtroom bare chested. "More than once their fathers or mothers had to leave their seats to retrieve one of the lads," Herbers added. The *Clarion-Ledger* also carried a large photograph of the two men on their way from their attorney's office across the street to the courthouse. Carefully choreographed, each man held one child while leading the other by the hand. If a reader did not know better, the context might have been a church service rather than a murder trial.[20]

More overt forms of editorializing were sparse as the testimony phase of the trial neared. The *Greenwood Morning Star* continued to fan the flames of northern racial hostilities, specifically those in Chicago. Editors quoted liberally from the *South Deering Bulletin*: "It is the common and accepted thing for

"Every Last Anglo-Saxon One of You" (Sept. 19–Sept. 23)

black bucks to toss rude, insulting and suggestive remarks to white women. The white women consider themselves lucky if that is all the negroes do to them. . . . The south learned long ago that to keep negro attacks on white women down to a minimum, strong and direct action had to be taken." By publicizing this south-side Chicago editorial, the *Morning Star* hoped to show that race relations in Emmett Till's hometown were "much more bitter" than anything seen in a Mississippi newspaper. Perhaps too, the Deering editorial functioned rhetorically to give proxy vent to "amalgamation" fears, suspicions, and punishments that migrated easily across the Mason-Dixon line.[21]

While the Jackson and Greenwood papers argued explicitly and implicitly for acquittal, at least one Mississippi newsman predicted a win for the prosecution. In his "Pencil Shavings" column, Henry Harris, owner and publisher of the *West Point Daily Times Leader*, conceded that, even though the prosecution was not seeking the death penalty, "there are few Mississippians who would like to trade places with either of the accused men. A verdict of 'guilty' is very probable." Harris clearly had not been reading his colleagues' reporting from in and around the Delta. Regrettably, Harris did not allow his one and only reporter, a twenty-one-year-old Harvard graduate hired in August, to cover the case for the Clay County daily. David Halberstam would not, however, miss a fascinating follow-up story involving J. W. Milam's close friend Elmer Kimball.[22]

The trial got underway in earnest on Wednesday, September 21, and testimony from Moses Wright proved explosive; it was not the only revelation, though, that took many Mississippians by surprise. Most newspapers carried detailed accounts of Wright's testimony, including his dramatic rendering of the early morning abduction: Milam barked orders while carrying a flashlight and a .45-caliber pistol, his wife frantically attempted to bribe the two intruders, a third man came to the door with Milam and Bryant and "acted like a Negro," and a fourth person in the car with a voice "a little lighter than a man's" identified Emmett as the offender in question. Newspapers also detailed Wright's positive identification of the body, as well as the defense's attempts to question Wright's ability to identify Milam, Bryant, and the corpse removed from the muddy Tallahatchie River. Perhaps the detail that received the most prominent play involved Wright's willingness to stand and point to Milam and Bryant as the men who had abducted his great-nephew. With a forceful "thar he," Wright did what Mississippi blacks were not supposed to do: confront a white man, under oath, with an alleged crime, before a room full of hostile witnesses no less. It was a gesture immortalized in an "illegal" photograph taken by the *Chicago Defender's* Ernest Withers. Wright also detailed identifying the silver signet ring on the body pulled to

"Every Last Anglo-Saxon One of You" (Sept. 19–Sept. 23)

shore; his family reminded him that Emmett had worn his father's ring on his journey south. He was certain that the body discovered on August 31 belonged to his great-nephew.[23]

While newspapers recorded many of the same details of Wright's testimony, the *Jackson Daily News* not-so-subtly attempted to discount the sharecropper's testimony with the large page-one headline, "Dim Light Casts Some Doubt on Identity of Till's Abductors." With only Milam's flashlight as a source of light, defense attorneys attempted to discredit Moses Wright's identification of the defendants. Clearly the defense was betting on Judge Swango not allowing either Smith or Cothran to testify since, on their account, the identity of the kidnappers was not in question.[24]

The *Clarion-Ledger*, having gone to press before Wright's testimony, was even more inflammatory in commenting on the case. Jay Milner, for example, wrote that the "pretty 21-year-old wife of one of the defendants, will tell the jury that Emmett Till, not only directed a wolf whistle at her, but exposed himself indecently in her presence." Coupled with the previous day's allegations of assault, it was increasingly clear that Emmett Till was not being tried for merely flirting with Carolyn Bryant; rather, his alleged offense was attempted rape. Milner also attempted to recontextualize Mamie Till's dramatic courtroom appearance: "The state's case may have been hampered psychologically by the furror [sic] surrounding Mamie Bradley's courtroom entrance. Tallahatchie Countians, jurymen included, stared in wonderment, as reporters and photographers swarmed around the small Negro woman hanging on each word of her few words." In other words, Milner gave voice to white Tallahatchians' resentment that an uppity northern negro—and a woman at that—would command attention (and perhaps respect) from white and black media members. On the topic of the media, Milner quoted locals asking, in effect, "How come those blankety-blank newspapers are making all this fuss?" Milner, too, described the "hard crust of prejudice against the South that encloses the minds of some northern newsmen here." To punctuate the prodefense, anti-North position, the *Clarion-Ledger* ran an exclusive photograph of the Bryant family, taken in a law office, with a radiant and neatly coiffed Carolyn Bryant, her two children, and a smiling husband. The sizeable photograph might well have been an advertisement for *Ladies Home Journal*.[25]

After Wright's dramatic testimony, the prosecution wasted no time in calling its next witness, Leflore County Sheriff George Smith. Attorneys Chatham, Smith, and Caldwell clearly wanted a white police officer on record—as he had been during the grand jury hearing—stating that Emmett Till

"Every Last Anglo-Saxon One of You" (Sept. 19–Sept. 23)

had in fact been kidnapped by J. W. Milam and Roy Bryant. Not surprisingly, the defense objected strenuously; Smith's testimony would likely destroy their sexual-assault/justifiable-homicide argument. Swango compromised: he excused the jury but agreed to let Sheriff Smith testify. Reporters noted that the sheriff found Roy Bryant at his store around 2 P.M. on Sunday, August 28: "Bryant told him he 'went and got Till from the house of Mose Wright but then he found he was not the one and let him loose.'" Swango ruled that he would not allow Smith's testimony "until testimony had been presented on the actual facts of the slaying." "All we have is proof that Till is dead," stated the judge. "We don't have proof he died in an unlawful manner." That proof was forthcoming with the next several witnesses. Given Swango's ruling and given a list of witnesses that would include undertakers as well as Mamie Till, the defense perhaps realized that a corpus delicti case was increasingly likely.[26]

Mississippians also learned on Wednesday that the list of the prosecution's witnesses had grown. Recall that a day earlier, Judge Swango had recessed court early to allow prosecutors to interview potential new witnesses. Readers of the *Delta Democrat-Times* learned that T. R. M. Howard claimed to be able to produce "at least four or five witnesses" to the Till killing. Howard also claimed that the murder likely took place on the Sheridan plantation in Sunflower County, which was managed by J. W. Milam's brother Leslie Milam. District Attorney Stanny Sanders called it a "startling development," one that might force the case to move into his jurisdiction. And while several lawmen had not found blood at the plantation barn where a beating had supposedly taken place, they "noted that the gin fan was missing. A gin fan was found tied to Till's floating body in the Tallahatchie river." The brief front-page article closed with another loaded revelation: Howard claimed "that two Negroes who worked on the plantation 'have not been seen or heard from since.'"[27]

The *Greenwood Commonwealth* picked up the story where the *Democrat-Times* had left off: the two missing plantation workers were identified by Howard as Leroy "Too Tight" Collins and Henry Lee Loggins. In reporting this story, though, the *Commonwealth* was reporting on what another paper had already printed; by prior arrangement, *Memphis Press-Scimitar* reporter Clark Porteous broke the Collins/Loggins story, which was immediately picked up by papers around Mississippi. Left unstated at this point in the reporting was the fact that Collins and Loggins possibly had a direct hand in the beating and/or murder at the Sheridan plantation. Also left unstated was just how a white Memphis reporter had discovered such potentially stunning details. It

"Every Last Anglo-Saxon One of You" (Sept. 19–Sept. 23)

would be several more weeks before the full story of the Porteous reporting broke. For now, Mississippians were led to believe that Howard had somehow simply coaxed several black sharecroppers to come forward.[28]

While new witnesses and important new information was on the horizon for the prosecution, the *Jackson State Times* filled in key details of Wednesday's juridical strategies, though perhaps without intending to do so. Once Swango ruled that the prosecution would need to establish that Till had been killed unlawfully in order for Sheriff Smith's testimony to be heard by jurors, thus establishing motive, prosecutors quickly put Chester A. Miller on the stand. Note that Swango did not ask the prosecution to prove that the corpse was Emmett Till's; in the judge's mind, apparently, that was an unproblematic fact. A Negro undertaker from Greenwood, Miller had been called to the scene once the corpse had been discovered on Wednesday morning. In questioning conducted by special prosecutor Robert B. Smith III, Miller testified, based on "certain parts of the body, that he was a youth and not an adult person." Miller also said under oath that the victim was around 5′4″ and weighed approximately 160 pounds—precisely Till's height and weight. Furthermore, Miller testified that "Till died from a crushed head and a wound in the side of his head above his right ear." In other words, Miller confirmed that this was Emmett Till and he had died from what appeared to be a fatal beating.[29]

During cross-examination, the defense still clearly had Sheriff Smith and his deputy John Ed Cothran on its mind. According to the *State Times*, "J. J. Breland asked him [Miller] if the wound could have been inflicted after the death, possibly by accident. Miller said he could not tell whether this was true or not." Breland's question, at first blush, may appear rather odd: What difference did it make, if in fact the corpse belonged to Till? The question, though, speaks directly to Judge Swango's objection to Smith's initial testimony: in order for jurors to hear the sheriff's testimony, the prosecution needed to show that Emmett Till had met with an "unlawful" death. If he had drowned accidentally, for example, Bryant and Milam's kidnapping confession was moot. Moreover, if Smith testified to the half-brothers' confessions, the sexual-assault/justifiable-homicide defense would become impossible, since both men claimed to have released the boy. But readers of the *State Times* and other papers reporting on the Smith and Miller testimony would not be able to suture together the logic of the defense until Thursday or Friday, depending on when Carolyn Bryant's testimony was reported. Given that the defense chose not to seriously question Wright or Miller as to the identity of the body—and Miller testified that he and his helpers were the ones who removed the signet ring from Emmett's finger and gave it to

"Every Last Anglo-Saxon One of You" (Sept. 19–Sept. 23)

Wright—it was clear that Milam and Bryant's attorneys still hoped to keep the Leflore County lawmen out of the Sumner courtroom.[30]

So eager to argue the sexual-assault/justifiable-homicide angle was the defense that attorney Sidney Carlton all but delivered Carolyn Bryant's testimony a day early. Virgil Adams of the *Greenwood Morning Star* quoted Carlton: "Mrs. Bryant said the Till boy came into the store and propositioned her. Further than that, she said he grabbed her and unsuccessfully tried to assault her. It got so bad that one of the other boys had to go in and get him out. We believe the other boys had egged him on, because of his big talk and told him there was a pretty woman in the store, to go in and see what he could do." Not coincidentally, Carolyn's claims about "the Till boy" would vanish by Thursday afternoon.[31]

Adams also joined Jay Milner of the *Clarion-Ledger* against the out-of-town press: many "objectionable characters" had "invaded" the state, including Rob Hall of the Communist newspaper the *Daily Worker*—who actually hailed from Pascagoula. The unwieldy press contingent also slowed the trial proceedings; Adams looked forward to the day when Mississippi could be "rid of these characters." The press was also at least partly to blame for a rape revenge crime that had recently taken place in nearby Memphis. The usually temperate editors at the *Delta Democrat-Times* thundered: "The thing that sets this beastly crime apart is that they [four young Negroes] attempted to justify themselves by referring to the Emmett Till 'wolf-whistle' murder case." In a curious leap of logic, the *Democrat-Times* fingered the NAACP: Since the group was so willing to blame all white Mississippians for the death of Emmett Till, is it now "ready to take the blame for inciting these four young Negroes to commit rape? It is certainly as logical." It was more logical that the editors look in the mirror in accessing culpability: not only had Mississippi newspapers deliberately fanned the flames of racial animus, but editors had frequently portrayed the southern black person as an uncivilized savage eager to act out his predatory ways against unsuspecting white womanhood. Oddly, given the explosive nature of such a crime and confession, no other Mississippi newspaper picked up the story.[32]

Some papers did, however, run a race story coming from downstate, out of Brookhaven in Lincoln County. Despite at least thirty or forty witnesses to a crime committed in broad daylight Saturday morning on the courthouse steps, not a single witness had come forward in the all-white grand jury hearings on the murder of voting-rights activist Lamar Smith. Said District Attorney E. C. Barlow, "I've had just about as much cooperation in the case as a Methodist preacher would get out of the devil at a protracted meeting." Despite Barlow's pledge to "continue the investigation," indictments would

"Every Last Anglo-Saxon One of You" (Sept. 19–Sept. 23)

never be returned in the murder that took place just days before Emmett Till's arrival in the Delta.[33]

Thursday, September 22, would prove to be the most consequential day of testimony in a trial that many newspapers were calling the most sensational in the state's history. "Never in the history of our state," the *Meridian Star* declared, "has so much out-of-state interest been taken in a case involving white and negro." So, too, in state. But sometime between Wednesday's recess and Thursday's opening, the Ku Klux Klan struck: a large wooden cross had been torched in front of Sumner's only hotel. Was this the Klan's way of expressing to the northern press, several of whom were rumored to be staying at the hotel, that it did not take kindly to their brand of "radical" journalism? Or was the cross burning merely the "[j]uvenile prank" that the *Greenwood Morning Star's* Virgil Adams claimed it to be? Only John Herbers wrote a brief story about the incident, which appeared in the back pages of the *Delta Democrat-Times*; he noted that it "went almost unnoticed" in town. Without irony, the *Jackson Daily News* ran a photograph of the burned cross with the caption "Cross Burning Is Ignored." Clearly, the Klan had not been reading Lois Schulz's hospitality advice from the previous week's *Clarksdale Press Register*.[34]

If the Klan was miffed about the presence and the prose of the assembled press, it was not alone. Adams editorialized, "Frankly we are anxious for the Till murder trial to come to a conclusion before there are any incidents which might further aggravate Miss. race problem [*sic*]." Adams himself had talked with several so-called radical newsmen the day prior, "all of whom," he imagined, were "probably spreading vicious propaganda about Miss. in New York and foreign newspapers." While lacking the overt paranoia of Adams, Velma Taylor of the *Holly Springs Southern Reporter* in her "Just Ramblin'" column apparently could not resist resuscitating the Dianne Kearney story: "No national recognition has been given so heroic a deed. Why? Because to recognize that act would be to recognize the fact of good race relations in Mississippi such as do not exist in the north." Sid R. Harris of the *Houston (MS) Times-Post* argued similarly: "Sound thinking Americans must admit that the raping of a white woman in Chicago or New York gets little play in the daily newspapers of those cities. On the other hand a case of similar nature is the lead story in those newspapers when it happens in Mississippi." Recall that Harris's editorial of September 8 defended Milam and Bryant to the extent that Till's actions in the store "could not go unanswered." Two weeks later the retaliation-minded newsman boasted that, if the NAACP decided to march in Mississippi, "whites will not tolerate" it. Such intolerance would not only prove prescient, but it would be catalyzed

"Every Last Anglo-Saxon One of You" (Sept. 19–Sept. 23)

to great rhetorical and political effect over the course of the next decade by many civil-rights groups. Harris was also prescient in pronouncing that the Till case "will echo for years to come." South of Jackson, in Simpson County, N. H. C. of the *Simpson County News* claimed that the presence of Rob Hall constituted "tacit admission that the Red propaganda machine is working overtime." And while white Mississippians might be able to ignore the likes of Congressman Charles Diggs and his ilk, "Hall stirs our ire," the Simpson County reporter asserted. Presumably, though, Hall and other northern newsmen were invited to "stick around our state long enough to see the true relationship between Negroes and the whites." The suprahyperbolic Jay Milner did not dwell on north versus south but rather the edgy journalistic atmosphere: "Close friends among the press corps now mistrust each other. A lone reporter leaves the hotel at night to buy a pack of cigaretts [*sic*] and immediately the hotel switchboard gets a frantic flurry of calls from other reporters trying to find out where the smoke-hungry reporter might be going." Such "explosive tension" reflected the fact that the press was increasingly becoming an important component of the unfolding drama.[35]

While the Mississippi press alternately brooded and welcomed the presence of their northern peers, eighteen-year-old Willie Reed, a black man, would capture most of Thursday's headlines, save for those of the *Clarion-Ledger*. Because most of the press had filed their stories before Wednesday afternoon's court appearances, the profoundly important testimony of Sheriff George Smith and Deputy John Ed Cothran did not get the headlines it deserved, except for in Jackson's morning daily. Beneath a flattering front-page picture of Moses Wright on the witness stand, the *Clarion-Ledger's* somewhat misleading headline read, "Defendants Admit Kidnaping Till Boy but Deny 'Murder.'" Milam and Bryant, of course, admitted nothing in court; the half-brothers would remain silent all week. And their attorneys had clearly hoped to keep the half-brothers' confessions out of the Sumner courtroom.[36]

Over "vigorous defense objections," Smith and Cothran both testified late Wednesday afternoon that Bryant had confessed to the sheriff that he had taken Till out of the Wright house, while Milam admitted the same thing to the deputy. Additionally, the half-brothers claimed to have "turned him loose," once Bryant's wife failed to identify him back at the store. While prosecutors apparently did not make the connection overt, such confessions ran afoul of Wright's testimony earlier in the day. In recounting the details of the abduction, Wright had clearly stated that the "one who did that talkin' at Money" was his great-nephew. In other words, based on Wright's admission, Milam and Bryant did not need Carolyn's identification to avenge the flirtation. But regardless of the contradicting testimony, the prosecution got

"Every Last Anglo-Saxon One of You" (Sept. 19–Sept. 23)

admitted into evidence the ostensibly damning admission that they had eagerly sought. Such eagerness was reflected in twinning Wright's testimony with Sheriff Smith's—before Swango had ruled it inadmissible (as of yet) earlier that morning.[37]

The *Clarion-Ledger* noted that before allowing Smith and/or Cothran to testify, Swango "spent some time listening to defense objections with the jury out of the room. Eventually, however, the judge permitted both men to testify before the jury about the purported admission of abduction." According to Arthur Everett, those objections involved the fact that neither lawman warned their admitted "friends," Milam nor Bryant, that what they said could be used against them in court. Pre-Miranda, Swango admitted the testimony. In their cross-examination, defense lawyers could only reiterate their earlier objections—but with a political twist. The following is an exchange, recorded by Ralph Hutto of the *Jackson State Times*, between J. J. Breland and Sheriff Smith:

Q. You and Bryant were good friends, weren't you?
A. Yes, sir.
Q. You trusted him and he trusted you.
A. Yes, sir.
Q. In this last election when you ran for representative, he supported you, didn't he?
A. Well, I hope he supported me.
Q. When you talked to him you requested he come to your car so you could confer privately.
A. Yes, sir.
Q. You asked Deputy Sheriff Cothran to leave the car while you talked with Bryant.
A. Yes, sir.
Q. You did so to talk confidentially.
A. I asked him about his troubles and he came out to talk.
Q. What you said was just between you two, wasn't it?
A. That's right.
Q. Did you tell him you came to arrest him?
A. Not at the time.
Q. You had no warrant.
A. No.
Q. You didn't tell him you were investigating for the sheriff's office. You went up as a friend, didn't you?
A. I went up as a friend.
Q. And of course you didn't tell him any statement he made might be used against him.

"Every Last Anglo-Saxon One of You" (Sept. 19–Sept. 23)

A. He didn't make any statement. We were just talking. No, I didn't tell him that.
Q. Did you arrest him that afternoon?
A. Yes.

Based on this testimony, Breland asked Judge Swango to strike Smith's testimony from the record on the grounds that it was not given freely and voluntarily, it was obtained under improper circumstances, and the defendant had not been advised of his legal rights. Breland also moved to have the testimony stricken because the state had not proved the corpus delicti. Judge Swango overruled both of these objections.[38]

Similarly, C. Sidney Carlton later asked Deputy Cothran "whether he warned Milam in advance of taking the oral statement from him that he was under arrest and anything he might say would be used against him. 'No, sir,' Cothran said." Flummoxed on this key legal point of admission, the defense went after Moses Wright's identification of the corpse. And while Cothran claimed that Wright initially said, "I could be mistaken, that might not be him," this doubt had been expressed "when the body was face down in the boat." Cothran also testified that the head "was torn up pretty bad," but he refused to say that the hole above the right ear had been caused by a bullet. The defense's cross-examination of Deputy Cothran subtly insinuated a possible corpus delicti argument, but much more pervasive were questions about the condition of the body. Implied in such questions, one of which involved the all-important condition of Till's genitals—Carlton inquired, "Had the boy's privates been mutilated?"—was the possibility that Till had not in fact been murdered. Given the half-brothers' admission that they had set the boy free at around 3 A.M. outside of the store, the defense was limning the possibility that Till had not died at the hands of the two men. Left unexplained was how Till's body had been recovered more than fifteen miles from the store with a blast wheel from a gin fan tightly barbwired to his neck.[39]

While most newspapers did give coverage to Smith and Cothran's important testimony, far more attention was paid in the press to the new witnesses promised a day earlier by T. R. M. Howard. The Mound Bayou surgeon had initially promised reporters that he would be able to provide five or six witnesses to the actual beating, and likely murder, of Emmett Till. By the morning of September 22, that number had shrunk to three: Willie Reed, Amanda Bradley, and Add Reed, Willie's grandfather. Walter Billingsley was not called to testify, while Frank Young mysteriously left the courthouse before he could be called as a witness. All five either lived or worked on the

"Every Last Anglo-Saxon One of You" (Sept. 19–Sept. 23)

Sheridan plantation in Drew, Mississippi; the Sunflower County plantation—there was some speculation that a new trial would have to be held—was managed by J. W. Milam's brother Leslie.

The testimony of eighteen-year-old Willie Reed would prove to be something of a Rorschach test among Mississippi journalists, for the young man would dramatically transform the evidentiary basis of the case from circumstantial to eyewitness. And in insinuating that J. W. Milam and at least three other white men—they were never identified—beat and likely killed Emmett Till in a storage shed, the state's case had taken on new life. Reed testified that in taking a shortcut across the Sheridan plantation on his way to a local store between 6 and 7 A.M. on Sunday morning to pick up some cigarettes, he saw a green and white 1955 Chevrolet truck—with four white men in the cab, and three black men in the bed, two of whom sat on the rails, while one sat on the bed facing the cab. Based on a picture he had seen in a local paper, Reed claimed that the seated person was Emmett Till. Later, on his way back home from the store, Reed testified to hearing "hollering" and "a whole lot of licks" coming from the storage shed; furthermore, he claimed to have seen J. W. Milam come out of the shed to get a drink from a well; he was wearing a pistol holstered to his waist. Upon cross-examination, J. J. Breland reminded Reed of what he had said in a Wednesday discovery meeting with defense lawyers: that Milam was four hundred yards away when he had seen him draw a drink from the well. If such a distance was to be believed, of course, J. W. Milam would have been completely indistinguishable, to say nothing of the supposed holstered pistol he was wearing. On redirect, prosecutor Smith tried to show that the measurement of four hundred yards had been misleadingly suggested by the defense and that Reed had merely agreed with their estimation. Left unstated was that a painfully anxious and frightened black youth would be highly agreeable before five white attorneys in such a volatile racial climate. "In other words," special prosecutor Smith concluded, "you don't know how to put yardage on it?" Reed agreed.[40]

Reporters telegraphed their feeling about the surprise witness—typically in their lead sentences. Sam Johnson of the AP, for example, began his lengthy article with "A teen-age Negro farmhand. . . ." By way of contrast, UP's John Herbers opened with "A witness testified today. . . ." Articles that featured the race-specific and demeaning Johnson nomenclature also usually drew attention to the fact that eighteen-year-old Willie Reed was only a ninth-grader at a local school and that he testified in an unlettered whisper. Even Mamie Till would state in a speech delivered in Baltimore five weeks after the trial that "Little Willie Reed" was "not a good witness." The grieving and crusading mother quickly turned Reed into a Deep South object lesson: "Willie Reed had a story, but he couldn't tell it. It was locked inside of

"Every Last Anglo-Saxon One of You" (Sept. 19–Sept. 23)

him. It would have taken education to put the key in the lock and turn it loose. Every word that was gotten from Willie had to be pulled out word by word." She continued, "That's because Willie is 18 years old and has probably been to school only 3 years. What he learned in school was not enough really to have gone to the trouble to go there every day." Form and content had become tragically imbricated: a story of torture had devolved into a tortured story.[41]

Of course, Mamie Till did not make such feelings known to Mississippi journalists, many of whom clearly did not agree with her assessment of Reed's testimony. Even the *Jackson Daily News*'s James Featherston reported that Reed's testimony "was the most damaging introduced thus far"; he had "electrified the court" as he "spoke in a low voice" before the "jammed" and "deathly quiet" courtroom. Similarly, Herbers described Reed's "sensational testimony" that sent a "murmur of excitement [that] swept throagh [sic] the crowded second-story courtroom." So compelling was Reed's account of that Sunday morning that the defense had to couch its objections in claims of irrelevance. Breland objected to Swango: "This testimony is not related in any way to the disappearance of Emmett Till or to the location of a body." The judge overruled the objection. The jury, though, would latch onto Breland's move to dismiss Willie Reed. As would *Greenwood Commonwealth* writer David Bready, who deemed Reed "a very poor witness." As if to further discredit Reed, Bready added that "[s]peculation as to the outcome of the trial is still much in favor of the two defendants." Tom Alewine of the *Brandon News* agreed with his Leflore County colleague: "We would not attempt to predict the weather but we'll predict that the jury will return a 'not guilty' verdict up at Sumner where two white men are charged with the kidnap-slaying [sic] of a Chicago negro boy."[42]

That the Sumner jurors were more predictable than the boiling, late-summer Mississippi sun spoke volumes about public opinion in the state. Alewine's prediction was premised on three grounds: circumstantial evidence (which Willie Reed's testimony quashed), doubts about the body (which Moses Wright's testimony refuted), and, most insidiously, the mere presence of "outsiders." According to Alewine, jurors were "bound to resent the appearance of the motley crowd of carpetbaggers in the courtroom where the trial is going on." Just as likely was the resentment of Mississippi journalists who increasingly rallied around the defendants by proclaiming their innocence. That a not-guilty verdict could be based on the mere presence of the northern press (and Congressman Diggs) gave telling testimony to just what the trial had come to mean for the Mississippi press. Other journalists tried to hedge their bets. In Coffeeville, just forty miles east of Sumner, the editor of the *Coffeeville Courier* aimed for equivocation but tellingly

"Every Last Anglo-Saxon One of You" (Sept. 19–Sept. 23)

missed: "The outcome is unpredictable, but an amazing lack of essential evidence seems likely to put a cog in the wheel." More "amazing" yet was that such a prediction had been offered before even Willie Reed or Mamie Till had testified.[43]

The principal reason that Mamie Till had been subpoenaed was her ability to identify her son's body; given Strider and Otken's grand jury testimony, the state clearly understood that a corpus delicti defense would be raised at some point during the trial. Before jurors heard Willie Reed's bombshell revelation of "hollering and licks," the "small, plump woman"—the more liberal *Jackson State Times* called her "the pudgy mother"—who had been roundly pilloried in her home state, took the stand on Thursday morning. At precisely 10:03 A.M. (CST) and with special prosecutor Smith careful to call her "Mamie" to not run afoul of Mississippi racial decorum, she testified that the silver signet ring with the initials L. T. had belonged to her first husband, who had died overseas while serving in World War II. Instead of the cufflinks she wanted to give her son on his trip south, Emmett selected the ring—which now properly fit his finger. Surely the ring would impress his southern cousins. She was also asked by Smith to identify the corpse, first the one she greeted back in Chicago and then the one that came out of the Tallahatchie. In so doing, the state was being careful to follow the corpse all the way from the muddy drift to the dirt of Burr Oak Cemetery. The waterlogged and bloated corpse was even more gruesome than the lye-packed corpse she had examined in Chicago; the picture had been taken immediately after the body had come out of the river on Wednesday morning. Reportedly, "she quietly took off her glasses, wiped her eyes and lowered her head in one hand. While the picture was shown to the jury, she shook her head slightly from side to side, an action she kept up for several moments." "I looked at it all over and very thoroughly. I knew beyond a shadow of a doubt it was my son," she testified. Invoking a mother's intimacy, a corporeal epistemology bound up with something quite sacred, she said this was her "Bo."[44]

In conducting a cross-examination while condescendingly seated, Breland did not attempt to question the veracity of "Mamie's" identification; he was saving other witnesses for that. Instead, he asked about the double-indemnity life insurance policy she had taken out on her only child; while yet to collect, she had indeed taken out a policy totaling four hundred dollars. She also testified to the racial etiquette she had taught her son before he headed south: he was always to use "yes, sir" and "no, sir" and to "humble himself if necessary by going on his knees whether he thought it was wrong or right." She had also instructed him "to be careful how he walked the streets."[45]

The resilient mother, though decidedly not as "pretty" or "attractive" as

"Every Last Anglo-Saxon One of You" (Sept. 19–Sept. 23)

Carolyn Bryant, nonetheless elicited a grudging admiration from the press. Even the dour David Bready had to admit that the "fashionably dressed 33-year-old negro woman had an air of confidence and determination as she swore that the body found in the river was that of Emmett Till, her 14-year-old son." Her answers were also given "using good English." Similarly, Herbers described her as "composed and speaking firmly." In other words, Mamie Till had exonerated herself and, by proxy, her son on the witness stand. She was not the hot-headed, NAACP caricature in cahoots with Roy Wilkins to finger all white Mississippians in the death of her child. Neither was she poor, hysterical, uneducated, or lacking in charisma or courage. Even the *Jackson Daily News* had to admit that she was "more intelligent that [sic] her many self-appointed spokesmen." In a word, Mamie Till was credible—even to inflamed white Mississippians.[46]

While the grieving mother had earned her credibility in the heat of 1955's final summer days, Carolyn Bryant's was vouchsafed by the double inheritance of good looks and the caste system of southern white female beauty. In a public culture dominated by white men, white women "spoke" as surrogates, their minds held hostage to a rigidly delineated body culture. Wandering off the society pages typically meant that a Mississippi "girl" was betrothed or beautiful, often both. A "nigger girl," by contrast, was prohibited from taking her place in such a public culture; her beauty and body were marked privately, if at all, both tempting and promiscuous; in the white male imaginary, it was also readily available. As if to temper the grudging enthusiasm for Mamie Till, the *Daily News* could not resist a puff piece on Carolyn Bryant's looks before she led off the defense's case on Thursday afternoon. The article by W. C. Shoemaker, headlined "Mrs. Bryant Won 2 Top Beauty Honors," contextualized Carolyn Bryant's importance to the case, less as a potential witness and more as a singularly beautiful white Mississippian. The fourth of seven children, she had been "named prettiest girl at both the Delta high schools she attended." At both Leland High School and a high school in Indianola, the former Carolyn Holloway "was chosen the prettiest." "So beautiful" was she that after only a few visits from the older and "handsome Roy Bryant," the two were married; she was sixteen, he was nineteen. Not surprisingly, supplying the beauty information to Shoemaker was none other than her "attractive greying mother," Mrs. Frances Holloway. The story punctuated a rather remarkable twenty-five-day transformation in the press: in that brief span, Carolyn Bryant had gone from a "white shopkeeper" elusive to police interrogation to a well-dressed, "unusually attractive mother" who had been assaulted, perhaps sexually, by a "stuttering and husky Negro lad."[47]

"Every Last Anglo-Saxon One of You" (Sept. 19–Sept. 23)

But was that "lad" Emmett Till? Or did Carolyn Bryant dare not name him?

If order indicates priority, Carolyn Bryant was to be the defense's star witness, in the same way that Moses Wright had led off for the prosecution. The state rested its case at 1:56 P.M. on Thursday with Mandy Bradley testifying that she had seen four white men walking between a green and white truck and the storage shed on the Sheridan plantation. She also saw the truck back into the shed. She could not identify any of the four white men. Following a brief recess, the defense called Carolyn Bryant as its first witness.

"[D]ressed demurely with a Peter Pan collar at her throat," Bryant lowered her head as she began to testify. But as she started to describe the events on the evening of August 24, the state objected: the story could not be used as evidence, Smith argued, because "[o]ur proof started Sunday at 2 A.M. when the boy was taken from Moses Wright's house. We have offered no proof of anything that happened prior to that time. Mrs. Bryant has not been brought up in any way. We have not mentioned her name." Carlton countered with the argument that when Wright testified that Milam said they "wanted to see the boy who done the talk at Money," the incident in question needed to be explained. In other words, just who the boy was and what talk had been "done" required a defense or at least an explanation. Judge Swango split the difference: he would allow the testimony but for now out of earshot of the jurors. Carolyn Bryant's testimony would only be admissible "if there was some question of who was the aggressor at the time of the crime, or overt acts of the deceased at the time of the crime." In brief, the jury would hear Carolyn Bryant's testimony if and only if she named names.[48]

Perhaps the more important question is Why did the prosecution object to Carolyn Bryant's testimony in the first place? If she was going to testify to a possible sexual assault, wouldn't this work to its advantage? Upon cross-examination, wouldn't the prosecution try to show that the offending person in question was in fact Emmett Till? If so, wouldn't such an admission make liars out of her husband and half-brother? At this point, wouldn't the prosecution's case be even stronger? Had the prosecution made a mistake in not beginning its case at the Bryant Grocery and Meat Market? If members of the Wright and Crawford families could describe what happened when Emmett entered the store, wouldn't such testimony force Carolyn to take the stand and admit that the offender was Emmett Till? In hindsight it seems that the prosecution was unusually careful in steering clear of what happened on August 24; it stands to reason that they actually feared a justifiable homicide defense—even if they had caught the perpetrators in a big lie.

C. Sidney Carlton was extremely careful in questioning Carolyn Bryant to steer her away from identifying the culprit—even as Swango stipulated that

"Every Last Anglo-Saxon One of You" (Sept. 19–Sept. 23)

she would have to in order for jurors to hear her testimony. But since her testimony would never be heard by the jurors, Carlton knew that Mississippians yearned to hear from the woman with whom many had cast their lot; bloodlust, as Whitaker's interviews starkly suggest, needed a quasi-official justification. The *Jackson State Times* was one of the only papers to reprint nearly all of Carolyn Bryant's rather sparse testimony in full:

Q. Who was in the store with you?
A. I was alone.
Q. Was there anyone in the living quarters of the store?
A. Mrs. J. W. Milam was there with her children and my children.
Q. Did any incident take place that made an impression on you?
A. About 8 o'clock a Negro man came in the store and went to the candy case. I walked up to the candy counter and asked what he wanted. I gave him the merchandise and held out my hand for the money.
Q. Did he give you the money?
A. No.
Q. What did he do?
A. He caught my hand in a strong grip and said, 'How about a date baby?'
Q. What did you do then?
A. I turned around and started to the back of the store, but he caught me at the cash register.
Q. How did he catch you?
A. He put both hands on my waist from the side.
Q. What did he say?
A. He said, 'What's the matter baby, can't you take it?'
Q. Did he say anything else?
A. He told me, 'You needn't be afraid.'
Q. Did he use words that you don't use?
A. Yes.
Q. It was unprintable wasn't it?
A. Yes. He said that and added, 'with white women before.'
Q. What happened then?
A. Another Negro came in and dragged him out of the store by his arm.
Q. Did he say anything further?
A. He said goodbye.
Q. What happened then?
A. I called Mrs. Milam, and then went out to the car and got a pistol from under the front seat. He was still standing on the porch, and he whistled.
Q. (Carolton [*sic*] whistled). Was it like that?
A. Yes.
Q. Have you ever seen that man before or since?
A. No.

"Every Last Anglo-Saxon One of You" (Sept. 19–Sept. 23)

Q. What size was he?
A. He was about 5 feet, six inches tall, and weighed about 150 pounds.
Q. Did he have a walking or speech defect, did you have trouble understanding him?
A. No.
Q. How did you feel when this happened?
A. I was just scared to death.
Q. Do you know most of the Negroes around Money?
A. Yes.
Q. Was this Negro man one of those?
A. No.
Q. Did he talk with a Southern or Northern brogue?
A. Northern.
Q. Did you have any white men around to protect you?
A. No. [She testified that Juanita Milam stayed with her while her husband hauled shrimp to Brownsville, Texas, so she "wouldn't be alone."]

And with that the "former high school beauty" was "dismissed with no testimony about the incident on the record." The *Jackson Daily News* was quick to underscore that such unseemly interracial disclosure "seemed to offend [the] delicacy" of the "shapely and slender 21-year-old." The *News* also reported that the very first question Carlton put to the witness was about her height and weight (5′2″ and 101 pounds).[49]

In the courtroom that afternoon, as she later reported in her memoir, Mamie Till understood quickly what Carolyn Bryant's salacious testimony was intended to do: "She had added so much to this brief encounter to try to justify what her husband and brother-in-law had done to my son. . . . But the damage was already done: You could be sure the jury would hear it." Mamie Till understood better than any journalist in the courtroom the rhetorical function of Carolyn Bryant's testimony: it was a juridical justification for the murder of her son; not mentioning his name was but a technical, irrelevant matter, one perhaps cleared up by details of the suggestive size, weight, and accent thrown in for good measure at the end. A black "man" had sexually harassed and talked inappropriately to a white woman—such news could travel fast between the courtroom and the sequestered jurors at the Delta Inn Hotel across the street.[50]

Predictably, on Friday, before the verdict was reported, Mississippi newspapers led with the "high drama" of Mrs. Bryant's testimony. "A young Mississippi white mother claimed today she was molested by a wolfwhistling Negro boy. Three days later," Arthur Everett continued, "a visiting Chicago Negro lad was abducted and slain, allegedly as the molester who tried ob-

"Every Last Anglo-Saxon One of You" (Sept. 19–Sept. 23)

scenely to date her." Only Everett's second paragraph actually revealed that the testimony was ruled inadmissible. Tellingly, Everett took the bait: hands on the waist had become a "molestation," even if erroneously perpetrated by a "boy." Herbers, too, reported that Bryant had been "molested," but he also added that she "did not identify" the black perpetrator. While other reporters noted that the "attractive, brunette Mrs. Bryant" did not identify the perpetrator as Emmett Till, no reporter attempted to put the suggestive evidentiary pieces of the puzzle together.[51]

Far more suggestive was the large front-page picture of Roy Bryant and his bride featured in the *Clarion-Ledger*: with eyes closed, the "delicate" and "becoming" Carolyn rested her head on her husband's shoulder; a fitting compliment to the family photograph featured just days earlier. The *Greenwood Morning Star* ran a similar picture on its front page with the caption "Accused Man Comforts Pretty Wife during Recess." The toll taken earlier in the day on the "plump" and "pudgy" Mamie Till was never visually recorded; instead, the *Jackson Daily News* ran a photograph of her conferring with the much-maligned black congressman from Michigan, Charles C. Diggs, Jr. Opposite the photograph, on the same page, Mrs. Eula Lee Bryant was shown lovingly wiping perspiration from her son J. W. Milam's face. Almost without exception, the Mississippi press pictured the Bryants and Milams in the context of family, whereas Mamie Till was shown either alone, consulting with supporters such as Diggs and Howard, or with other would-be witnesses. Only a careful reader would have known that her father, John Carthan, had even accompanied her to the Delta.[52]

Curiously, another spouse, the "unusually attractive" Juanita Milam, followed her sister-in-law to the witness stand. She briefly recounted for jurors the time of her marriage to her husband, details about their children, and her husband's much-noted war record. Mrs. Milam would be one of several character witnesses for her husband, who was being portrayed as a devoted family man and a patriot. That the defense felt compelled to have a spouse actually testify in court as to the character of J. W. Milam spoke volumes about the man who later bragged of knowing how to "work Negroes." Even Carolyn Bryant was not asked questions about the good name of her husband, though she was asked about his war record.[53]

With their sexual-assault defense ruled inadmissible, Bryant and Milam's attorneys quickly regrouped around the corpus delicti strategy—the same set of arguments introduced weeks earlier at the grand jury hearing. Tallahatchie County Sheriff H. C. Strider was the first of three witnesses called to induce doubt as to the identity of the corpse. Under questioning by John W. Whitten, Strider testified that he first looked at the body on the morning of

"Every Last Anglo-Saxon One of You" (Sept. 19–Sept. 23)

August 31 at 9:15 A.M. Even though the corpse was still in the boat, Strider noted that that body was in "mighty bad shape," and the skin was "slipping on the entire body." The head also revealed three large gashes and a hole above the right ear, which Strider probed with a small stick. The tongue was out of the mouth "about three inches" and the left eyeball was "out enough to call it out." The stench from the body was such that an undertaker had to douse the body with two "deodorant bombs" just to be able to get close to it. Whitten then moved to matters of identity: based on once having seen a corpse taken out of the water that had been immersed for three days, Strider estimated that this corpse had been in the Tallahatchie River for "at least 10 days, if not 15." Furthermore, the sheriff claimed that the body was so bloated that he could not even tell if it was a black or white man; the only discernable black characteristic was that it had "kinky hair," but Strider quickly added, "I've seen a lot of white men with kinky hair." Strider went even further for the credulous jury: "If one of my sons had been missing I couldn't have told it was him. All I could tell it was a human being." In other words, Mamie Till, in her role as mother, was telling lies. Whitten then showed Strider a photograph of the corpse taken in Chicago: the Sheriff noted that said corpse did not look like the one he had seen; the one he had seen had been much lighter. Left unstated was the conclusion that the body had either been tampered with in Chicago to make it resemble a Negro, or it was not the corpse actually removed from the river.[54]

On cross-examination, special prosecutor Smith could only feebly ask Strider about why he had signed a death certificate with the name Emmett Till on it. Yes, a death certificate had been issued, the "big gray-haired man" affirmed, but he had not identified the body as Emmett Till's. But had Smith (or Chatham or Caldwell) not been reading the newspapers back in early September? followers of the case might have asked. Had the *Delta Democrat-Times* not quoted the lawman to the effect that the corpse had only been in the river a mere two days? Had new forensic evidence emerged to change his mind? Furthermore, that Strider could testify without public ridicule about the science of forensic pathology, based apparently on only one corpse he had ever seen retrieved from the river, indicates just how flimsy the defense's case really was.[55]

Next to testify was L. B. Otken, a physician from Greenwood. He claimed that the body had been in the water from eight days to two weeks. Asked if "anyone" could have identified the body, the physician replied, "I don't think so." Pressed further about the possibility of a mother identifying it, Otken said, "I doubt it." Coupled with Strider's testimony, Otken's "doubts" were becoming far more certain. On cross-examination, though, the sixty-

"Every Last Anglo-Saxon One of You" (Sept. 19–Sept. 23)

six-year-old doctor did admit, with Strider, that a badly injured body would deteriorate more rapidly in warm water. He was also forced to admit that he had only viewed the body and had not been able to make a pathological examination because of the stench. The final person to cast doubt on the identity of the corpse, and the last person to testify on Thursday, was Cleveland, Mississippi, undertaker H. B. Malone. Like Strider and Otken, he claimed that the body delivered to him in Tutwiler for shipment to Chicago had been in the water a minimum of eight to ten days and a maximum of twenty to twenty-five. In addition, the embalmer estimated the corpse he examined to be 5'10", six inches taller than Emmett Till.[56]

Thus closed a dramatic and consequential day of testimony—and the defense team was most pleased with the outcome. The *Clarksdale Press Register* reported that the Sumner barristers, Carlton, Breland, Whitten, Kellum, and Henderson, were "confident" of an acquittal. That confidence was perhaps based less on the testimony of Strider, Otken, and Malone, as the *Register* reported, and far more on a leak, also reported by the *Register*, that "[s]tate attorneys privately voiced doubt they would get a guilty verdict." Similarly, reporters agreed among themselves that "the defendants will be set free." That said, some of the newsmen, who confessed as much to David Bready, also wondered just how testimony regarding the ring might be reconciled with corpus delicti arguments. As the *Delta Democrat-Times* had made manifest back in early September, if the ring had really been part of an NAACP conspiracy, Milam and Bryant would have had to have been in on it.[57]

One wonders if the *Commonwealth's* Bready consulted with fellow journalist Rob F. Hall, who had become something of an object of fascination throughout the week. In similar pieces for the *Jackson Daily News* and the *Delta Democrat-Times*, W. C. Shoemaker and Harry Marsh interviewed this "son of the south"—Hall hailed from Pascagoula and had close ties to Hattiesburg—to try to find out just why a white Mississippian had become a convert to the cause of socialism. Covering the trial for the *Daily Worker*, headquartered in New York City, Hall traced his genealogy as a devout leftist to the treatment of impoverished workers he had witnessed firsthand. But beyond biography, Shoemaker and Marsh emphasized that even Hall believed that the trial was "being conducted fairly" and that townsfolk had conducted themselves hospitably. Hall's summary judgment would be invoked frequently in the coming days and weeks as the jury hurtled towards its verdict. What was often overlooked is the fact that Hall's comments and many others' reflected on method, not substance. A "fair trial" did not mean that justice had been done.[58]

At least one member of the Mississippi press, though, was not racing

"Every Last Anglo-Saxon One of You" (Sept. 19–Sept. 23)

ahead to write self-satisfied post-mortems on the "just" outcome. B. J. Skelton of the *Clarksdale Press Register* posed several important and unanswered questions that were directly related to the case. First, just who was the "third man" identified by Moses Wright who "moved around like a Negro"? Second, who were the black men in the back of the truck identified by Willie Reed? Were they Leroy "Too Tight" Collins and Henry Lee Loggins? If so, where were they now? And what had happened to Frank Young, part of T. R. M. Howard's cohort of potential witnesses to the beating and possible murder on the Sheridan plantation? Skelton also raised important questions about the identity of the body: If it wasn't Till's then just whose was it? If it wasn't Till, then where was he? Was there another black man reported missing from the same area? Skelton also aimed critical comments at the defense, an unwieldy contingent who occasionally ran afoul of what each other was doing, such as by objecting to a question that one of its own members had raised. Unfortunately, Skelton chose not to critique the witnesses for the defense, nor the defense's initial strategy of arguing sexual assault rather than corpus delicti.[59]

It took the defense less than an hour to conclude its side of the case on Friday morning. Jurors heard briefly from seven character witnesses: Lee Russell Allison, L. W. Boyce, and Pete McGraa for Milam and Grover Duke, Harold Perry, James Sanders, and Franklin Smith for Bryant. The only snag in the proceedings occurred when the prosecution cross-examined Allison: the defense objected vigorously when the state leadingly asked if it was true that Milam had "been charged and pleaded guilty on quite a number of charges." Indeed, Milam was known in the area for bootlegging, among other things, but Judge Swango upheld the objection. By 10:22 A.M., the defense rested its case. After a brief recess, District Attorney Gerald Chatham would begin the final summation and closing arguments; Swango gave each side seventy minutes to finalize its case. By early afternoon, jurors would hear from nearly every attorney involved in the case; they would also hear a curious mix of trial facts, southern protocol, human motivation, and racial conspiracy. The defense in particular offered up a bilious bouillabaisse steeped deeply in Mississippi white supremacy and xenophobia.[60]

Chatham began dramatically: "The killing of Emmett Till . . . was a cowardly act." Riffing on the defendants' vaunted military service, Chatham said that Till got "a court martial with the death penalty imposed." Reportedly "sweating profusely," the district attorney exclaimed, "The first words that entered this case were literally dripping with the blood of Emmett Till." Chatham strategically tried to locate a motive, one that jurors could only infer from Moses Wright's opening testimony: the pivotal words in the slaying

"Every Last Anglo-Saxon One of You" (Sept. 19–Sept. 23)

were "I want the boy from Chicago who did the talking at Money." In other words, Chatham wanted jurors to know about the incident at the Bryant Grocery and Meat Market; without it, questions of motive might remain unresolved. While trying to navigate carefully around the shoals of interracial sexual assault, Chatham also addressed himself to southern masculinity and southern racial politics: "I was born and bred in the South. I'll live and die in the South. The very worst punishment that could have occurred or should have occurred if they had any idea in their minds that this boy had done anything was to take him over a barrel and give him a little beating." This was the masculine way—even when it involved a black "boy," and Chatham was very careful to draw attention to youth: "A man deals with a child accordingly as a child not as man to man." Chatham then artfully turned to the matter of race: "I . . . am not concerned with the pressure and agitation of organizations outside or inside the state of Mississippi. But I am concerned with what is morally right—to be concerned with anything else will be dangerous to the precepts and traditions of the South." At one level, Chatham's rhetoric aimed at transcendence: morality should always trump race, and yet at another level Chatham implied that an acquittal would do grave violence to the southern way—in a word, segregation. The tangled knot of southern morality could not be untangled quite so simply since that morality was premised in the very first instance on strict racial rules, or the more courtly "precepts."[61]

Special prosecutor Robert B. Smith III appealed to practicality in his closing remarks: "If J. W. Milam and Roy Bryant are turned loose it will serve the purpose of the very organizations that have come down here to stir up trouble." Emphasizing little of morality or justice, Smith, later described by the *Greenwood Morning Star* as "the swarthy heavy set prosecutor," calculated that the jury had other concerns: "If you convict them no one can use this to raise funds to fight us in our defense of southern traditions." The logic was sacrificial: convicting the hometown boys was far more efficacious than dealing interminably with the obstreperous Roy Wilkins and his NAACP mercenaries.

The NAACP and its affiliates also bulked large for the defense. Whitten moved to give motive to a conspiracy: "There are persons who are trying to widen the gap which has appeared between the white and colored people in the United States. Those people would welcome the opportunity to focus national attention on Sumner, Mississippi." The young Princeton graduate continued, "They would not be above putting a rotting, stinking body in the river in the hope it would be identified as Emmett Till. They are not all in Detroit and Chicago. They are in Jackson, Vicksburg and Mound Bayou,

"Every Last Anglo-Saxon One of You" (Sept. 19–Sept. 23)

too." In a somewhat remarkable concession that Mississippi blacks may be protesting their servile state, Whitten was clearly putting T. R. M. Howard and the new NAACP Mississippi field secretary Medgar Evers in his crosshairs. And while Howard would eventually flee the state—apocryphally, under the disguise of a coffin and northbound hearse—Evers would remain in the supremacist's crosshairs until his assassination shortly after midnight, on June 12, 1963. Planting a corpse was not so fantastic an idea, claimed Whitten: "Most of you can remember 35 years ago when the Ku Klux Klan tried to reorganize and three Negro bodies were taken from the Mississippi river. A great hue and cry went up about the land. But investigation later proved that those three bodies had been embalmed before they were tossed in the river." Whitten also gets credit for the line most often quoted from the closing: "Every last Anglo-Saxon one of you has the courage to free these men."

Harvey Henderson even got in on the defense's closing: he reminded the twelve "sun-tanned" men that they must be "convinced beyond a reasonable doubt and moral certainty" should they be inclined towards reaching a guilty verdict; furthermore, he added, the defense team was not required to prove anything since the burden of proof rested entirely with the state. But the defense, Sidney Carlton quickly reminded jurors, had in fact proved that the body was not Emmett Till's: "Sometimes mothers believe what they want to believe. I'm sure Mamie Bradley thinks that body was her son, but the scientific facts show otherwise." Beyond the planted corpse, he averred, the state had no case at all: "We think we could have rested our case when the State rested. The State didn't prove anything."

Perhaps most interesting of all the remarks made during the tense and emotional closing involved motive. Once Swango ruled Carolyn Bryant's testimony inadmissible because she never identified Till as the assailant in question, Carlton attempted to capitalize on the seeming lack of evidence: "Where's the motive? Where's the motive?" the lead attorney bellowed. "The state did not link up the dead boy with the defendants. The only testimony that Emmett Till did anything in connection with these defendants was Moses Wright's testimony that he heard the boy had done something wrong." Carlton continued to pursue this tortured line of logic: "If he [Wright] had known Emmett Till was involved in something down there, he would have gotten him out and whipped him himself." As for the problem of Wright having identified Milam and Bryant in his home, Carlton dismissed his testimony because of lighting problems and because there were many "Mr. Bryants" in the state of Mississippi. In Carlton's view, Wright's identification posed another sort of problem: "If that's identification, if that places these

"Every Last Anglo-Saxon One of You" (Sept. 19–Sept. 23)

men at that scene, then none of us are safe." As for the far greater catch of George Smith and John Ed Cothran's testimony placing Milam and Bryant squarely in Moses Wright's home on August 28, Carlton conveniently ignored it. The closing was pure sophistry: having claimed sexual assault in the court's official transcript and having done everything but name Till as the perpetrator—because Carlton did not ask—Carolyn Bryant had made the motive clear and compelling. One would think that anyone could have seen through Carlton's fog of deceit and non sequiturs.

J. W. Kellum's extrajuridical closing was nearly as remarkable as Whitten's: "I'll be waiting for you when you come out. If your verdict is guilty, I want you to come to me and tell me where is the land of the free and the home of the brave." The threat was made even more personal: "I say to you, gentlemen, your forefathers will absolutely turn over in their graves."

By 2:36 P.M. (CST), with final instructions from Judge Swango, the jurors went to work on a verdict. The *Jackson Daily News* was openly leery that the jury might have been swayed by the "Roman circus" of outside media: "If justice is done, it will have been done despite the steady flow of slanted and reckless copy which has come from the trial scene." The *News* hoped that the twelve men would not be swayed by the "intensely repulsive" acts of "Negro publications" and others such as the grandstanding Congressman Diggs. Mamie Till left the Sumner courthouse quickly with T. R. M. Howard, on their way back to Mound Bayou; she confessed that she did not want to be around for a not guilty verdict. She was not the only one apparently expecting an acquittal: many Mississippi newspapers quite literally "held the presses" with the expectation that a verdict might be rendered with dispatch. In fact the *Sumner Sentinel*, with a circulation of 686, released its weekly paper a day late in order to shoehorn in news of the verdict. As they awaited the outcome, and despite the heat, humidity, and occasional thunderstorms, the Milams and Bryants posed comfortably for pictures; some papers reprised shots taken earlier in the week of Milam playing with his "tots."[62]

At 3:43 P.M., jury foreman J. A. Shaw blurted out the verdict: "not guilty." A shout of approval followed the dramatic pronouncement, but the judge quickly intervened: the jury would need to deliver the verdict in proper legal form, he insisted, and the twelve men were led back out of the courtroom. Not long thereafter, the verdict was read correctly to the still-assembled throng: "We, the jury, find the defendants not guilty." So ended the murder trial of J. W. Milam and Roy Bryant. Crowds quickly formed around the men as many offered handshakes and back slaps. Both men lit up victory cigars. Observers quickly learned that the sixty-seven-minute verdict would have

"Every Last Anglo-Saxon One of You" (Sept. 19–Sept. 23)

been rendered sooner had not the jury been asked to pause for a pop to "make it look good." The black journalists "stood, after court was recessed, and stared at the crowd blankly."[63]

Reporters seemed overeager to finally unsublimate all the sexually suggestive material they had written about for nearly four weeks: "As photographers and cameramen surrounded the defendants and their attractive wives after the verdict, Milam gave 27-year-old Juanita Milam a long, forceful kiss. Bryant hesitated until photographers induced him to kiss his wife, too." The "petite and pretty Mrs. Roy Bryant," with a "radiant smile," said suggestively to the press, "Well this is one way to make up for lost time." Captured on film, the Bryants' passionate kiss seemed a fitting response to the oversexed press; such a public display of intraracial sexual desire finally redeemed the southern way from the northern threat.[64]

Six

"Forgotten as Quickly as Possible"?
(September 24–September 30)

The more liberal daily in the state capital duly recorded these osculations: above the fold on page 1 of the *Jackson State Times*, Roy Bryant is pictured "flush with joy" kissing his "pretty young brunette" wife while, opposite them, Juanita Milam is pictured enduring "a long, forceful" kiss from her acquitted husband. Ralph Hutto, whose byline was on many of the Till stories for the newspaper, snapped both pictures. Perhaps the multitalented Hutto had also drafted the paper's editorial that ran immediately next to the photos. Titled "The Truth Remains," the editorial was one of the most measured responses to the verdict in the Mississippi press. "The Emmett Till case," it began, "is not completed." Praising Swango for his fairness—a judgment repeated frequently in and out of state—and the prosecution for being vigorous, it predicted that the acquittal would ensure that the state and its residents would be "maligned" by "vicious distortions" in the days to come. More important than the inevitable finger-pointing was the matter of collective conscience: "The truth is enough for responsible citizens to face, and one inescapable truth is this: A particularly brutal slaying has occurred in the state, leaving a blot Mississippians feel can be erased only by finding and punishing the guilty person or persons. The task continues to weigh heavily upon the state's conscience." The *State Times* would be one of the very few Mississippi newspapers that chose to remind its readers that a particularly awful race-related murder had taken place and that the culprits were still at large; in this sense did it see justice at a micro-level. Others were quick to measure the case and its conduct in far more salutary, macro terms.[1]

The outspoken Virgil Adams at the *Greenwood Morning Star* editorialized, for example, that "[s]ometimes they [the NAACP and other radicals] wore your patience thin, but Miss. people rose to the occasion and proved to the world that this is a place where justice in the courts is given to all races, religions, and classes." As such, the state and its citizens, he believed, have "been raised in the opinion of many who are in position to be competent critics in this matter of justice." Adams's qualifier was telling: just two days prior he had roundly denounced the "vicious propaganda" coming from the pens of

"Forgotten as Quickly as Possible"? (September 24–September 30)

"radical newsmen." To be from New York City or Chicago, for example, signaled incompetence to him. He simply disqualified black journalists from the outset; justice or qualified judgment could not result from anything they wrote. Adams rested comfortably knowing that the "top newsmen" agreed that the trial was "fair and impartial."[2]

But in his zeal to promote Mississippi justice, Adams confused method for substance; legal protocol had become the measure of justice rather than outcome. As lawyers for the Justice Department would argue well into the next decade, playing by extant legal rules was beside the point in the Deep South; the problem was in the rules. An exclusively white and male venire, formed according to the most scrupulous attention to legal procedure, often rendered the most unjust verdicts—especially on the explosive issue of race. Adams and many of his colleagues would feign great confusion in the coming days as northern newsmen would talk openly about the farce they had witnessed in Sumner. That confusion was typically resolved at the level of contradiction by the Mississippi press: northern newsmen said one thing in the south, but, safely back home, they told another story to appease their antisouthern readers.

Congressman Charles C. Diggs, Jr., would come to embody the seeming contradiction most pointedly. The observing Democrat from Michigan was quoted by the *Jackson Daily News* following the verdict: "I think the judge was fair and I think the presentation by the prosecution was impressive," noted Diggs, "but apparently the deep-rooted prejudices of the jurors would not permit any kind of objective consideration of the case." Diggs well understood that form and substance could mean two very different things in a southern courtroom. The *News* saved its invective for the editorial page: Diggs was "an insolent, arrogant, South hater . . . a meddlesome Negro politician" seeking both votes and violence on his journey to the Delta. The thinly veiled hatred could hardly surprise: even the idea of a "nigger congressman" was thought to be illegal among Tallahatchie lawmen. That he came to Sumner, sat in the courtroom, and offered a public and contrary opinion was almost as inflammatory as whistling at a white woman.[3]

So incensed was the *News* that they again lambasted Diggs in an editorial the very next day, blaming him in no small measure for the not guilty verdict: "The case for the prosecution was not helped the least bit when an impudent, South-hating Negro Congressman from Detroit named Diggs journeyed all the way from his home city, accompanied by three lawyers, and squatted themselves in the court room at Sumner as spectators." That the judicious Judge Swango allowed Diggs to "squat" did not matter to the *News*

"Forgotten as Quickly as Possible"? (September 24–September 30)

editors; in their eyes, an uppity Negro with no sense of race and place had brought "the NAACP atmosphere" into the courtroom. They believed that such a blatant violation of racial decorum "surely must have had an adverse effect on the state's case. Mississippi's courts do not like covert attempts at intimidation." In other words, a northern black man with democratically elected powers merely sitting in on a trial was interpreted by them as a hostile act of intimidation.[4]

In a telling aside, the *News* disclosed something of its motives in going after the black congressman. Even though the prosecution had not proven its case and the defense had created reasonable doubt, it suggested, "many think it was a case of the old Scotch verdict, 'guilty but not proven.'" Rather than blaming white Mississippians Chatham, Smith, and Caldwell and their presentation of the evidence, the *News* fingered Diggs (and implicitly T. R. M. Howard and Mamie Till) for the acquittal. Had Tallahatchians been left to their own legal devices, they would have convicted the half-brothers, so went the logic. By "merely" violating the Deep South code of race and place, the *News* argued, Diggs had proven an able, if unwitting, facilitator of the very white supremacy he was sworn to oppose. According to this argument, Emmett Till's blood was now on the congressman's hands. Perhaps this was blood that the *News* shared, a possibility that the editors could not admit. It was now painfully clear that some evidence bearing on the case, whether circumstantial or not, implicated Milam and Bryant—but the *News* could bring itself to admit publicly that "the boys" had likely kidnapped and murdered Emmett Till only after the trial.[5]

Maybe the *News* was right about one thing. Maybe Milam and Bryant might have been convicted if the NAACP and the northern press had not pressed quite so hard. What if Roy Wilkins had not indicted all white Mississippians, the northern press had not thrown a spotlight on the state's Jim Crow ways, Mamie Till had suffered in silence, and Representative Diggs and his cadre of black lawyers had stayed home? The perversity of Jim Crow racism meant that blacks could only hope for the best in white people while simultaneously affirming the worst. Optimism about white paternalism was married to a self-loathing that many blacks, north and south, were beginning to tire of in 1955. Some could perhaps discern that their optimism was nothing if not the vestigial and corrosive effect of a system created in fear and imposed by terror. The *News* closed its editorial with an odd request: "It is best for all concerned that the Bryant-Milam case be forgotten as quickly as possible. It has received far more publicity than [it] should have been given." For the newspaper which covered the case in greatest detail and with the most polarized

"Forgotten as Quickly as Possible"? (September 24–September 30)

editorializing, a request for mnemonicide was indeed a curious rejoinder to the ostensibly just verdict. Its own staff vigorously ignored this request in the coming weeks and months.[6]

Editors to the south and west of Jackson in Natchez were similarly ambivalent about the verdict: "We do not say that the verdict was the correct one"; the paper even entertained the possibility that the acquittal had been "a mistake" and that the men "were guilty." But justice would not be denied since the "defendants are being judged at the bar of Heaven." While the *Natchez Democrat* emphasized a transcendent court, its editors believed that more egregious verdicts had been rendered in the earthly realm, specifically the Supreme Court's recent *Brown* verdict: "The Supreme Court's anti-segregation decision subverted the very foundations of our judicial decision. It strayed far from Constitutional law and sought to appease the rising tide of sociological and political opinion." A mistake in the Till decision "is infinitestimmal [sic]," as they saw it, "in comparison with what the Supreme Court did in the segregation cases." By invoking the striking contrast of a small-town murder with an extrajuridical national ruling that ended a way of life, the *Democrat* subsumed Emmett Till into the vortex of racial politics. One small injustice did not quite add up to the cataclysm of *Brown*. In the realm of argumentative topoi, the *Democrat's* framing of the verdict was pure red herring.[7]

Across the state, a straight shot east from Natchez, editors at the *Laurel Leader-Call* also invoked segregation, but not as a comparative judicial calculus: "We hear a lot of talk about preserving our 'way of life' in the south. By this most of us mean a segregated society, for the 'way of life' that has been the southern pattern is a thing of the past, but a segregated society can and should be preserved." Adopting the posture of white paternalism, the *Leader-Call* looked to the short-term future: "We think that, as time passes and the colored people become more aware of what integrity of race means and pride in their tradition and in their people, they'll want segregation, too." *Brown* would be rendered largely meaningless since both races would voluntarily choose to remain separate. But the *Brown* decision was not the impetus for the *Leader-Call's* editorial, nor was it brought into a faulty comparison, as it was in the *Natchez Democrat*; rather, both "the trial at Sumner" and the "incident" at Brookhaven suggested to the *Leader-Call's* editors that a peaceful future between the races required a respectful separation. That the incident in question—the murder of black activist Lamar Smith on the courthouse steps (not far from Laurel) and the ensuing refusal of witnesses to testify at the grand jury hearing—did not engender a critique of white supremacy and its enforcement was most revealing. For the *Leader-Call*, mur-

"Forgotten as Quickly as Possible"? (September 24–September 30)

dering black men and black boys for their intrusion into heretofore "white space" was simply part of that same nostalgic "way of life."[8]

Similar to the *Jackson Daily News*'s first editorial pointing to fair conduct of the trial, was the *Greenwood Commonwealth*'s praise for "one of Mississippi's finest jurists, Judge Curtis Swango." Since neither the defense nor prosecution heaped anathemas on the venerable Hernando judge, the *Commonwealth* concluded "that the trial was as fair as any ever held." The editors, though, were quick to parse opinions on the verdict: the "fine newspaper reporters" who represented "the accredited and recognized news agencies" all "to a man" had high praise for how Judge Swango had conducted the trial; however, the NAACP, radicals, and "other alien elements" who covered the trial "for left-wing newspapers, would condemn every part of the hearing." With one broad brushstroke, the *Commonwealth* editors dismissed a significant part of the press contingent, whose ideologically inspired journalism had "backfired" in their opinion. The editorial concluded with a final parsing: "Mississippi can handle its affairs without any outside meddling and its long history of proper court procedure can never be questioned by any group." Like its peer to the south, the paper equated a just outcome with just procedure and argued that emphasizing testimony, evidence, and reasoning at the expense of that procedure was to betray one's anti-Mississippi, left-leaning agenda.[9]

Editors at the *Delta Democrat-Times* did not try to demonize the leftist, out-of-town journalists, or Charles C. Diggs, Jr.; nor did they emphasize Swango's judiciousness nor call on the "bar of Heaven" to balance outstanding accounts. Instead, they went right to the heart of the matter: evidence brought forward by both the defense and prosecution—with a keen eye on Sheriff Strider, who famously remarked after the verdict, "Well I hope the Chicago niggers and the NAACP are satisfied." The twelve "open-collared, sun-burned farmers" were not derelict, in the opinion of the *Democrat-Times*, but the "law officials" were, those who had "attempted in such small measure to seek out evidence and to locate witnesses to firmly establish whoever was or was not guilty." In this the prosecution and defense were both culpable, especially given that the trial's most important witness, Willie Reed, had been located and compelled to testify only by the expert and perilous sleuthing of black journalists coordinated largely by T. R. M. Howard on the eve of the trial. The *Democrat-Times* expressed shock "at the quality of the investigation that preceded this most publicized trial in Mississippi history, and [shock] that the very man who was designated to lead an investigation into an obvious case of brutal murder, was busy most of the time inventing diverting fantasies as to how the whole thing could have been arranged by someone

"Forgotten as Quickly as Possible"? (September 24–September 30)

else." Missing only in name, Sheriff Strider's careful cover-up, "exposed as it was to the inquisitive eyes of the world, has been anything but covered up in reality." The pointed editorial closed with a direct rejoinder to the *Daily News*'s call to forget the victim, the verdict, and the defendants: "And Mississippi must now suffer for it for at least another generation." Three generations later and counting, Mississippi's "most publicized trial" has not been so quickly forgotten.[10]

Fifty miles north of Greenville, editors at the *Clarksdale Press Register* also singled out law enforcement for its investigatory missteps: "It was obvious that much was to be desired in the investigation of the case," they noted, but, unlike the *Democrat-Times*, concluded, "Correspondents appeared to be cognizant of the fact that law enforcement is also less than perfect elsewhere." The *Democrat-Times*'s specific indictment of Sheriff Strider was rendered as a fact of life in the law enforcement system, according to the *Register*. Like many of its peers, the paper also claimed that the "scrupulously fair trial" would accrue to Mississippi's benefit: "The state is likely to gain both in national respect and in its struggle to solve a perplexing problem." But the bulk of its editorial was devoted to "visiting [northern] journalists" and what they might write about the state's "racial problem"; the *Register* confessed that "Mississippians are curious about that." Judging by what the paper had read to date, the northern press had been "reliable and fair"—all, that is, save for the "Communist Daily Worker" and "Negro publications." "European newspapers," too, were singled out for their "biased and incorrect reports." We should keep in mind that the *Register*'s optimism (along with many other newspapers') about the state's reputation in the aftermath of the Till trial was expressed only on Monday following the verdict; it would take weeks and months before the northern press would weigh in on just what had happened in Sumner. That so many Mississippi papers moved with such dispatch to overdetermine northern news opinion in their favor belied a very real anxiety about the low esteem in which Mississippi and Mississippians were held; perhaps it also belied just a hint of guilt about the not guilty verdict.[11]

The *Tupelo Daily Journal*, much like the *Democrat-Times* and *Register*, fingered law enforcement for the outcome of the Till case. Barry Rutherford singled out "members of the sheriff's office who handled the investigation during its early stages," adding that poor "early detective work" had virtually guaranteed an acquittal in the case. Rutherford, though, quickly recovered his racial bona fides: in the future "a wave of crime committed by persons with above-average skill in such arts, coming possibly from outside the state [northern cities]" could force the shoe "on the other foot." In other words, urban black professional criminals with revenge on their minds, tak-

"Forgotten as Quickly as Possible"? (September 24–September 30)

ing advantage of Mississippi's underfunded and underqualified constabulary, could wreak havoc on "the white people of Mississippi—the people who elect the men who make the laws." Rutherford's was a curious balancing act: only increased resources for state law enforcement would lead to more just verdicts—be they involving white or black defendants and white or black victims.[12]

Balance, though, seemed to be on the wane in other parts of the state. Virgil Adams of the *Greenwood Morning Star* finally unleashed the term that seemed to be hovering in the interstices of nearly every Mississippi story on the case since at least September 2; it was done without equivocation and without a hint of any lexical vexations. In refusing the placement of an advertisement in his newspaper, Adams blithely referred to it as having "to do with the Till Rape Attempt case." In four brief weeks the playful "wolf-whistle" had morphed into the decidedly more grave phrase, attempted rape. If indeed "a choice of words is a choice of worlds," then Virgil Adams had finally loosed the animating trigger term for the South's way of life for more than sixty-five years. Thus does the defense's cynical and successful attempt to have Carolyn Bryant's nameless accusation written into the official record come into clearer focus. Instead of "the Till case," "the verdict at Sumner," the "wolf-whistle trial," or any other more mundane appellation, Adams's use of the term "rape" to describe an entire constellation of actions, grievances, hostilities, and ultimately verdicts—both legally and in the realm of public opinion—gave full rhetorical expression at long last to what had supposedly transpired on August 24 at the Bryant Grocery and Meat Market. It took four weeks to enter public discourse—not private—only because Carolyn Bryant, at the behest of Sumner's bar, remained silent until the afternoon of September 22. Of course, the issue was not evidentiary—Till's purported physical contact with her hand and waist hardly constituted an attempted rape—but historical and imagined: interracial sex was the animating and constitutive force of black men, or "husky lads" on the verge of manhood, in the 1955 southern worldview. The threat of black-on-white rape was ever present because of ontology, not sociology, and that threat had legislated race relations in the Deep South for at least eighty years. Mississippians would also learn in less than three weeks that Emmett Till's "attempted rape" of Carolyn Bryant had more familial and genetic antecedents.[13]

Adams made the link between black-on-white rape and segregation in an editorial the very next day. Again referring to the Till case as a "rape attempt case," Adams disclosed to readers that he had received a particularly "vicious" letter from Washington state; it contained "threats" that Mississippians "would have a great deal of intermarriage between the races, and that

"Forgotten as Quickly as Possible"? (September 24–September 30)

the races are destined to be mongrelized within a relatively short time." The unsigned letter writer's racist promise had taken on a new and urgent reality in the wake of the just-completed case: "Until this rape attempt case came up, many of us thought the writings of some of our better informed people about the danger which the Supreme Court decision brought to the nation were greatly exaggerated. If you still maintain that idea," Adams concluded, "perhaps reading this letter your editor received today will serve to help wake you up." In other words, the consequences of *Brown* were already upon the state—Emmett Till proved it; integration's dire sexual consequences had already found criminal, but predictable, residence because the Supreme Court's grand experiment in sociology simply ran afoul of black male biology. But Adams's use of the temporal qualification "Until this rape case came up" is particularly insidious: Till's act of racial atavism in Money nipped an incipient southern liberalism in the bud; his actions, in Adams's view, proved once and for all that *Brown's* critics had not exaggerated. Decontextualized, Emmett Till's daring flirtation with Carolyn Bryant had now been troped: his actions were a synecdochic expression for what many southerners thought black men and boys wanted, even needed, to do to white women—beauty queens and homely shopkeepers.[14]

Black-on-white sex also figured in the pages of the black *Jackson Advocate* following the verdict. In an article headlined above the fold "State Negroes Not Surprised at Till Verdict," the paper predictably vilified the NAACP for prompting the not guilty verdict at Sumner: "Negroes of the state see the verdict as having been dictated not by the facts and the law but by the southern tradition of the sacredness of white womanhood, now being revived in all of its violence[-]provoking fervor because of the NAACP drive for mixing of the South's and Mississippi's public education." Percy Greene was not disagreeing with Virgil Adams: fears of racial "intermingling" because of the *Brown* decision were to blame for the predictable Till verdict; furthermore, those fears were not altogether unjustified, according to the paper whose publisher would in a few short months become a paid informant for the racially retrograde Mississippi Sovereignty Commission. Even so, the conservative Greene could not help but side with the prosecution: given the "world wide reaction to the verdict," there were "times when the strict letter and interpretation of the law must give way to the demands of the higher virtues of justice, morality, right and christianity [sic]." For Greene, this was one of those times, but white Mississippians need not fret the unjust outcome: Black Mississippians would "remain tranquil, secured by the knowledge that they and their cause have been helped, rather than hurt, by the 'not guilty' ver-

"Forgotten as Quickly as Possible"? (September 24–September 30)

dict in the case." Centuries of such intimate "knowledge" of white-on-black injustice apparently mattered little to Greene.[15]

Rural Mississippi weeklies got their first chance to comment editorially on the trial's outcome only on September 29, almost a full week after the verdict; perhaps not surprisingly, many had taken their cue from editorials in the dailies. Near the Alabama border in the northeast part of the state, the *Aberdeen Examiner* chastised Congressman Diggs for labeling Mississippi a "jungle" and for not tending "to the 'Michigan jungle.'" And, even though the editor deemed the trial "an inglorious moment in Mississippi history," criticizing the verdict was "to assail every tenet upon which America was founded"; it would also play into "the hands of the Communists." Tom Alewine of the *Brandon News*, near Jackson, agreed: if Bryant and Milam had been convicted, "it would have been as much a miscariage [*sic*] of justice as the rabble-rousers claim the acquittal was." The editor at the nearby *Simpson County News* was one of the few to express uncertainty over the verdict: "The Lord only knows if justice was done"; even so, local blacks would "do well to burn any NAACP literature that falls into their hands . . . and they will do well by turning a deaf ear to anyone who tries to stir up racial strife." A diffident H. S. of the *Tate County Democrat* near the Tennessee line didn't "have too much to say," but he was still angry that negative publicity from the case "has injured Mississippi and the South for many years to come." Just north and east of New Orleans, the editor at the *Picayune Item* expressed his ire at southern dailies for not reporting a black-on-white rape story out of Chicago, "particularly after the 'Wolf-Whistle' incident." So angry was the editor that the *Item* reprinted a story on the rape and issued a challenge: "See if you think it was a weaker story than the Till murder trial." He was also angry with other rhetorical choices made by the same papers; specifically with "all the 'Mrs.' that prefixed the name of Mamie Bradley in our Southern Dailies, you would think you were reading a newspaper published in the heart of Harlem." He had less ennobling epithets in mind: "With the little journalism we know, we can think of more than a dozen ways we could have identified her as the mother of the slain boy without using even one 'Mrs.'"[16]

While many Mississippi newspapers offered some editorial comment on the verdict and its aftermath, news accounts kept the story on the front pages and back pages; the Till story and its many characters had become something of a phenomenon in four short weeks and the press was eager to feed the appetite it had created. Readers quickly learned that the sixty-seven-minute verdict had been punctuated by three votes: nine for and three undecided, ten for and two undecided, and finally a unanimous verdict. As

"Forgotten as Quickly as Possible"? (September 24–September 30)

for persuasive testimony and evidence, Willie Reed and Mamie Till had not fared well with the white, all-male jurors. Jury foreman J. A. Shaw claimed that the "gangling" youth was "ignored" by the jury and that the "plump" and "pudgy" mother had left the jury "unimpressed." Jurors claimed to be impressed, however, with the evidence offered by Strider, Otken, and Malone. Juryman Jim Pennington revealed that "generally everyone reached the conclusion that the body was not definitely identified." Of the twelve jurors, only Shaw and Pennington offered any public comment on their verdict. The NAACP and its leader Roy Wilkins was also conspicuously absent in the aftermath of the verdict. Perhaps because of his earlier inflammatory remarks, Wilkins and his board had agreed that he would not comment publicly on the case. Instead, board chairman Channing H. Tobias, while complimenting the prosecution and Judge Swango, ramified the closing remarks made by special prosecutor Smith: "The verdict is as shameful as it is shocking. The jurors who returned it deserve a medal from the Kremlin for meritorious service in communism's war against democracy."[17]

As for the fate of Roy Bryant and J. W. Milam, Swango agreed to Chatham's request to drop the kidnapping charges in Tallahatchie County. The two men were immediately bound over to Leflore County Sheriff (and good friend) George Smith, who would hold them on kidnapping charges committed in his jurisdiction. District Attorney Stanny Sanders told reporters that he would convene a grand jury in early November to hear the evidence; he and Leflore County attorney John Fraiser would present the case to Circuit Judge Arthur Jordan of Greenwood. The *Clarion-Ledger* also reported that the inmates had been unable to arrange bond "in order to spend the weekend with their pretty wives and children"; they would have to cool their feet in the Greenwood lock-up for a few more days. Carolyn Bryant, whose pretty, attractive, petite, and brunette features had been seared into the minds of Mississippians, was "very happy" with the outcome. "I feel a lot better than I did yesterday on the witness stand," she said. Her "muscular, handsome 26-year-old [sic]" husband offered a laconic "I'm not making any statement." His half-brother, who had remarked famously during the trial that the stifling heat was enough to make him "mean," said he was "well satisfied with the verdict. That's all I will say." His "unusually attractive" wife claimed to be "scared" as jurors deliberated her husband's fate. Sheriff Strider, though on his way out of office, promised to continue the investigation.[18]

From T. R. M. Howard's well-fortified estate in Mound Bayou, a beleaguered Mamie Till said, "I wasn't surprised. I had considered the possibility of an acquittal." She also admitted that she "didn't want to be there when it happened." The next morning, Saturday, September 24, she boarded a

"Forgotten as Quickly as Possible"? (September 24–September 30)

plane in Memphis headed north to Chicago. She had two unexpected travel companions, several newspapers reported: Willie Reed and Amanda Bradley would move permanently to Chicago where Congressman Diggs promised to help them start their lives over. Left unstated was why the eighteen-year-old Reed and the fifty-year-old Bradley would want to leave their native state. Only later would readers learn that the two eyewitnesses to Emmett Till's beating were fleeing in fear for their lives. Newspapers also reported that Moses Wright was headed north—not to Chicago, but to Middle Island, New York—the "sturdy, straight little figure" had apparently been offered a "lifetime job" at the Baier Lustgarten Farms and Nurseries. Also absent in stories of "Old Man Mose's" immanent departure was why the sixty-four-year-old sharecropper was abandoning his home, his car, his chickens, and his beloved "mongrel" dog, Dallas, for the north. Wright, though, did promise to return in November in order to testify at the grand jury hearing. No doubt the plucky man, whom New York columnist Murray Kempton famously described as having the "hardest life possible for a human being in these United States," labored under the guilt of his great-nephew's abduction.[19]

While his niece Mamie Till knew that an acquittal was likely, she also was aware from Willie Reed's testimony that Milam and Bryant likely were not the only ones involved in the abduction and murder of her son. Back home in Chicago, she began a forty-seven-year quest for justice. Like Howard and others, she believed that two key witnesses, perhaps participants, to the murder were being held under different names in the Charleston, Mississippi, prison. Hugh Stephen Whitaker later confirmed through a local deputy sheriff that Leroy "Too Tight" Collins and Henry Lee Loggins had in fact been held in the Charleston jailhouse, home of Tallahatchie County's other county seat. Rumors spread that Collins and Loggins were imprisoned there to keep them away from prosecutors and the intrepid black journalists helping Howard. Only the *Clarion-Ledger* carried a very brief squib on the mother's accusation, but the story would not soon go away—either in Mississippi or in black newspapers around the country.[20]

While details of the sensational Till case and its aftermath continued to generate headlines around the state, it also began to infiltrate other, completely unrelated news stories. On its Sunday front page, for example, both the *Clarion-Ledger* and the *Jackson State Times* reported the details of an attempted black-on-white rape proximate to Sumner. The lead read, "Officers of two states Saturday sought a Negro plantation hand wanted in the attempted criminal assault of a 30-year-old white housewife at her home 15 miles from Sumner, scene of the sensational Till murder trial"; the assault reportedly occurred "shortly after" the acquittal "in the Till verdict." While

"Forgotten as Quickly as Possible"? (September 24–September 30)

the time and place might have been purely coincidental, the lead suggested a subtle yet pernicious pattern: young and menacing black men were eager to assault and rape unsuspecting white women—where they worked and/or where they lived. That the accused, twenty-seven-year-old Wilson Melton, reportedly only put a hand on the unnamed woman's lap did not seem to matter; the offense was still "attempted rape."[21]

The *Clarion-Ledger* also printed a long and extraordinary letter from one Webster McClary, a pastor in Kingstree, South Carolina, and it was not carried on the editorial or opinion page. Just how the newspaper got hold of the folksy yet articulate letter is unknown, but, given its clear segregationist bias, it did not take long for the epistle to appear in the state's largest-circulation daily. During the months of October and November, McClary's twenty-five-paragraph letter would run in almost every Mississippi newspaper—from the eight-page weekly to the multisectioned daily. The letter never mentioned Emmett Till nor the events just ended in Sumner. But given the black minister's anti-NAACP and anti-integration opprobrium, white Mississippians now had a forceful black ally in their fight against the Diggses, the Howards, the Wilkenses, and other such black leaders. That he was an "outsider" did not seem to matter. The contents of the letter could have come right out of a white Citizens' Council organizational meeting: McClary claimed "colored children don't learn as fast as whites"; his "white friends," not the NAACP, helped him out economically; blacks in the NAACP "had better get out while the getting is good"; three quarters of all blacks do not really want integrated schools; integrated schools would inevitably lead to race mixing, which went against "God Almighty's plan to have a White Race and a Negro Race"; and "Northern Big Shots in the NAACP" would quickly learn that their southern brother prefers his "white friends" when it comes to lending a hand and would soon abandon the organization. McClary's letter could not have come at a better time for Mississippi whites; the influx of northern media and an aggressive NAACP had shaken them and their most revered institution. Little wonder, then, that the lengthy prosegregation letter got such extended play in the state. Upstate in Laurel, the *Leader-Call*, which would eventually reprint the letter, echoed McClary: "As time passes, and the colored people become more aware of what integrity of race means and pride in their tradition and their people, they'll want segregation, too."[22]

Only four days passed before McClary's letter received opinion-page comment. In a letter to the editor of the *Lincoln County Advertiser*, M. C. Durr had high praise for its segregationist sentiments—a week before the *Advertiser* had even reprinted it. "Every colored man and woman in Mississippi should know that we your white friends want to see you have better homes and bet-

"Forgotten as Quickly as Possible"? (September 24–September 30)

ter schools," Durr wrote; more importantly, "you will get them much sooner if you cooperate with us who have lived with you down thru the ages of time than you will to go and join the NAACP—that communist inspired organization which is out to destroy you and us." Once again, Mississippi blacks were essentially being forced to cooperate with paternalistic whites who claimed to know what they wanted and when. Of course it was assumed by Durr and others that "better" homes and schools could never be integrated; rather, in the dominant Mississippi discourse, the term attached itself to strictly segregationist calculations.[23]

That Durr called publicly in late September for peaceful and paternal segregation in a Lincoln County newspaper could not have surprised many: the county was home to Brookhaven, site of the recent murder of Lamar Smith. But integration was also on the minds of residents farther north, in the Delta community of Tchula. Given the town's proximity to Greenwood, Emmett Till would be tied to any issue involving race there—whether germane or not. In the curious case of two white men, A. E. Cox and D. R. Minter, Till was decidedly irrelevant, but to the "crowd of 700 white men and women jammed into a high school gymnasium" on September 27, the allegedly wolf-whistling would-be rapist seemed to suffuse all contexts. Front-page articles in the *Meridian Star* and the *Jackson State Times* immediately linked "the racial views" of Minter and Cox to a possible "Emmett Till wolf whistle case." Their offense was "fostering [the] idea of integration" by operating a farm cooperative on Cox's 2,700-acre plantation, Providence Farms, on which "racial mingling" and "certain strange racial relations" were supposedly being practiced. State Representative-elect J. T. Love translated any white-black interracial "mingling" as leading to a potential "Sumner here." Town residents "invited" Cox and Minter to move away, but the two men were not heeding the invitation-warning. The specter of the murdered Chicago boy bulked large for white Tchulans: interracial cooperative farming could quickly degenerate into interracial sex—cooperative or not. Residents listened intently to a tape recording of a black youth who claimed that blacks and whites actually swam together and sat together during meetings. Again, the logic was synecdochic: Emmett Till stood in for all black men. That he was acting on a dare from his cousins only obscured the larger, more menacing point for Tchulans: surely hypersexed black-male desire for white maidens had to be checked by clearly demarcated and enforced separations. Rape must needs of prevention; so, too, pleasure.[24]

The *Clarion-Ledger* quickly picked up the Minter-Cox integration story the following day, featuring photographs of the men and an accompanying story on its front page written by Jay Milner. While both Minter and Cox

"Forgotten as Quickly as Possible"? (September 24–September 30)

denied espousing racial integration at the cooperative, residents remained suspicious. Readers also learned that the initial meeting had been prompted by remarks made by four Negroes; they had been charged with "unlawful use of vulgar and obscene language" in the "presence of a white high school girl." In fact one of the accused, nineteen-year-old Curtis Freeman, pleaded guilty to the charge and was sentenced to six months on the county farm. Perhaps not punishment for a "wolf-whistle," the severity of Freeman's sentence suggests that the interracial and cross-gendered "obscenities" in Money in late August had Tchulans on tenterhooks. At least Freeman's harsh sentence saved him from an early morning visit like Till's.[25]

Other newspapers were not nearly as eager to translate the Till case into race writ large; many, in fact, seemed eager to exhale upon emerging from the taut and overheated Sumner courtroom. The *Jackson State Times* was one of the few papers that attempted humor, though of an anthropological bent: in its television and society pages, the *Times* ran a small story with large headlines: "Where Women do the Wolf Whistling." Among the Kickapoe Indians of Mexico, young women had to learn to make whistle replies to overtures of courtship. Staff writer Ralph Hutto also described the lonely and littered Sumner courtroom nearly an hour after the verdict: stray journalists "wandered blankly through the halls, as if not quite convinced that it was actually over." By dusk "Sumner was beginning to regain its appearance as a sleepy Delta Town." That wistful transformation would never quite be complete. The *Times* columnist Bob Moulder's description seemed sexually allusive: the "climax" had left many Sumnerians overwrought from too much press coverage. Robert H. Denley of the *Columbus Commercial Dispatch* tried to make light of the northern newsmen, whose sophisticated sound equipment still could not pick up southern accents. The *Clarksdale Press Register* featured a white reporter for the black *Pittsburgh Courier*: Jim Boyack, while a "nervous wreck" from the trial, praised the people he had met for their kindness and hospitality. Even the *Clarion-Ledger* tried to take the edge off after a week that had inalterably changed Mississippi: late-night "bull sessions" among journalists had so "accumulated during the one-week trial to last a lifetime."[26]

But the Mississippi press' exhalation did not last long; there was simply too much new to report, and, after a solid month of heavy coverage, readers needed their daily or weekly fix. Most of the coverage would migrate north, along with many of the trial's principals, but some papers such as the *McComb Enterprise-Journal* took the pulse of local reaction. G. W. Hinant sent a tattered confederate flag to the *Memphis Commercial Appeal* with a note that he was seceding. From his New Orleans pulpit, Unitarian minister Albert

"Forgotten as Quickly as Possible"? (September 24–September 30)

D'Orlando condemned the verdict in his sermon, "Why We Still Need Do-Gooders." Greenville's *Delta Democrat-Times* also recorded hostile reaction to the verdict. Reverend E. E. H. Harrell of nearby Cleveland tried to get back to basics: "I think every right-thinking Negro in the state of Mississippi, and all white people that think right, will agree that it is not right for anybody to be murdered." The qualifiers were most telling. John Behall from New York City ended his letter, "Wake up, damn you! You can't all be animals." The *Clarksdale Press Register* noted that several of its citizens had an abiding personal interest in the case, including one Mrs. O. R. Reed of 839 Pecan Street. Carolyn Bryant's sister was said to be "delighted" with the verdict. Still other newspapers sought to correct important local matters of fact. The *Columbia-Progress*, for instance, rebutted Clark Porteous's claim that a white Mississippian had never been legally executed for the murder of a black person. In fact, not far from Greenwood, in Grenada, M. J. Cheatham had been hanged for killing Jim Tillman back in 1890.[27]

Even as papers such as the *Jackson Daily News* called for a timely "forgetting" and others rallied around Swango's observance of protocol and the prosecution and defense's fulfillment of legal duties, the Till story continued to mutate and generate headlines on Mississippi front pages. And if newspapers had carefully inventoried the many anathemas heaped upon the state and its citizens leading up to the trial, the accounting seemed to grow even more vigilant following the sixty-seven-minute verdict. In many ways that accounting was a function of what must have seemed obvious to outsiders: the press had made unwitting celebrities out of nearly everyone directly involved in the case. This, combined with the fact that the essentials of the murder case were without resolution, ensured that the story would remain in the public eye. Mamie Till, T. R. M. Howard, Willie Reed, Moses Wright, and Congressman Diggs immediately parlayed their outspoken and courageous testimony bearing on the case and its conduct into both political and remunerative rewards. Perhaps ironically, J. W. Milam and Roy Bryant would later transform their silence into initial pecuniary advantage as well. Their public and infamous confession, though, would work to deleterious ends.

But as October beckoned and the annual cotton crop was harvested, Mississippi's large dailies could neither forget the case nor ignore the carefully coordinated rhetorical fireworks taking place in Detroit, New York City, Chicago, and Baltimore. Before a crowd of two thousand in Chicago's Metropolitan Community Church, Willie Reed repeated his testimony to a far more sympathetic audience. The NAACP-sponsored event "called the White House to halt 'the wave of terror against Negro citizens of Mississippi.'" Before a crowd of more than six thousand in Detroit, Charles Diggs

"Forgotten as Quickly as Possible"? (September 24–September 30)

described the "jungles of Mississippi and its daily region of terror." The *Clarion-Ledger* recorded some of the congressman's more inflammatory remarks, including, "Mississippi represents a shameful and primitive symbol of disregard for the essential dignity of all persons which must be destroyed before it destroys all that Democracy represents." As for the trial, Diggs stated, "I have never witnessed such perjury and fantastic twisting of facts." He called on "milling but orderly negroes" to contribute to the NAACP. Just below coverage of Diggs's speech, The *Clarion-Ledger* also featured an article on Mamie Till's remarks at an event at the Williams Institutional Christian Methodist Church in Harlem sponsored jointly by the NAACP and the Brotherhood of Sleeping Car Porters: "What I saw of the trial was a shame before God and man.... Lynching is now in order," the crusading mother exclaimed to a crowd of ten thousand. Earl Brown, a black city councilman "urged that a 'Mississippi refugee committee' be set up to evacuate every Negro from the state." The meeting, which also featured remarks by erstwhile head Roy Wilkins, passed a resolution calling on President Eisenhower to convene a special session of Congress to create antilynching legislation and a resolution encouraging Mississippi governor Hugh White and U.S. Attorney General Herbert Brownell to investigate the disappearance of two possible witnesses to the murder, Leroy "Too Tight" Collins and Henry Lee Loggins. At an NAACP-sponsored event in Baltimore, T. R. M. Howard's two-hour speech was encapsulated in one provocative sentence: "Everytime they get ready to lynch a Negro in the South, it's got to be about a white woman." The Mississippi press even carried news of a protest rally in Paris, France, where more than a thousand people, meeting under the aegis of the International League against Racialism and Anti-Semitism, condemned the verdict.[28]

All of the well-attended rallies flummoxed at least one white Mississippi journalist. In a page-one article, Jay Milner tried to square what he had heard during "bull sessions" among the press during the trial with the posttrial reaction up north: "The rash of rallies breaking out up north in protest of a Mississippi jury's verdict in the Sumner 'wolf whistle' murder trial contradicts verbal opinions expressed at the scene by most newsmen from north of Dixie." Staff writers from Detroit, New York City, and Chicago—even the NAACP and Rob Hall of the *Daily Worker*—all seemed initially to agree that no jury would have convicted the men based on the evidence presented. Milner could only infer possible dissembling: reporters "didn't write what they thought, if the protest rallies stem from their accounts of the trial." Furthermore, they seemed impressed by Swango, the prosecutors, and the search for additional surprise witnesses. Like so many of his home-state colleagues, though, Milner's fixation with legal form and protocol was beside

"Forgotten as Quickly as Possible"? (September 24–September 30)

the point: a sixty-seven-minute verdict received with whoops of approbation, a plantation-owning sheriff who claimed medical expertise based on one case, the close friendships between the Leflore County police and Milam and Bryant, the evidence of Till's ring, the eyewitness testimony of Willie Reed, to say nothing of overwhelming local support for acquittal despite a general consensus of guilt—all of the important evidences bearing on the case were conveniently overlooked. Yet cunning duplicity, contra Milner, was not the issue; "Yankee writers" could see through the racial phantasmagoria in ways that most Mississippi journalists simply couldn't—or wouldn't—not in polite or public conversation anyway.[29]

Milner's superiors at the *Clarion-Ledger* were beyond flummoxed at the northern reaction to the verdict; judging by their adjectives in a lengthy Sunday editorial—titled "A Careful, Last Look"—they had quickly gone from nonplussed to frothing: "absolutely fantastic," "inflamed mob," "callous," "perversion," and "cynical" dotted the first few paragraphs in describing the rallies. "The speakers said one thing in Mississippi, where they were open to challenge by others who had seen the trial, and another where political expediency suggested denunciations of the trial's conduct and outcome," the article intoned. But the editorial rage did not extend only to those on the speaker's dais. "Our Northern brethren of the Fourth Estate are due for some serious soul-searching for their misrepresentations," it continued, adding, "It is still considered good form to lie about popular issues when the purpose can be justified with a fuzzy web of doubtful sociological logic." The northern press, in other words, purposefully misrepresented the events in Sumner to its readers in order to marshal more evidence for a sustained attack on segregation. At least Mississippians were "intellectually honest," the *Clarion-Ledger* editors averred, in feeling an "earnest distrust and deep fear of organizations seeking to impose radical change" on the region and its way of life; furthermore, the north's deceit and dishonesty only lent "another lie to the Communist line of the Big Lie." Thus had the Kremlin and its propaganda campaign been faithfully invoked by both sides. And once again, the events specific to Emmett Till had been transformed into a rhetorical pawn in a contest that pitted north versus south and the United States versus the Soviet Union. With the political stakes so ratcheted up, it is little wonder that Emmett Till's name became increasingly rare in such editorial contexts.[30]

Sheriff Strider exercised other rhetorical options in the face of the northern reaction. On Thursday, September 29, headlines around the state raised the ringing question, "Is Emmett Till Alive?" While Harold Foreman's front-page story in the *Jackson Daily News* feigned ignorance as to who or what triggered the rumors, the *Jackson State Times* was quick to allege that the

"Forgotten as Quickly as Possible"? (September 24–September 30)

Tallahatchie County sheriff was responsible for planting the sensational story. "I've contended all along," Strider stated, "that Emmett Till is alive. As far as knowing anything definite, I don't know it. I definitely believe he's somewhere, but don't know where." To the Till family, the somewhere in question was in the ground; Mamie Till even promised to exhume the body should the rumors persist. Publication of Strider's comments predictably churned the rumor mill: Deputy Sheriff John Ed Cothran, who had testified for the prosecution, said with exasperation, "You couldn't even investigate a cow killing without somebody telling you about a rumor they heard." Till had supposedly been spotted variously in "Detroit, Chicago, New York and even near Parchman State Penitentiary in Sunflower County."[31]

Till had also supposedly been seen in the Delta community of Greenville. The *Clarksdale Press Register* reported the very next day that Mozella Brady, "maid to Mr. and Mrs. John Henry Black, claimed that Till visited her on Sunday morning the 28th and went to a movie with her 14-year-old daughter in Greenville." Four days later the maid confessed that she had made the story up.[32]

Down south in Jackson, the *Daily News* seemed in no mood to "forget" the Till case; if anything, the paper was doing everything in its power, including ridicule and sarcasm, to keep the story and its many subplots on its pages. In a lengthy article by Bill Spell, logistics and costs were calculated for Councilman Brown's suggestion that all Negroes be airlifted out of Mississippi. The cost to "haul all our good negroes to the nawth" was $77,880,783 and 51¢. A sidebar story from Natchez reported on a telegram sent to Brown by the "Committee to Cooperate with Councilman Brown": "We wholeheartedly approve [the] proposal advanced by you . . . to create [a] Mississippi Refugee Committee to evacuate every Negro from Mississippi. You may depend upon our complete cooperation in accomplishing all of your wishes."[33]

Spell reported more hijinks for readers the very next day. It had earlier been reported that the transplanted Willie Reed pined for his fifteen-year-old girlfriend, Ella Mae Stubbs, and his cotton patch back in the Delta. Spell reported on two offers to send Ella Mae and her mother north to Chicago, but "as of now, no one has come up with the answer to solve Willie's longing for a cotton patch." In one of its four front-page stories the following day— captioned "Ella Mae Shuns Willie"—Stubbs's father reportedly refused the funds to send his family north as they were "satisfied in Mississippi." The *Daily News* also made light of the twenty-four-hour police protection given to both Reed and Mamie Till back in Chicago, asking, If they were now safe from the impending violence in Mississippi, why the need for round-the-

"Forgotten as Quickly as Possible"? (September 24–September 30)

clock security? The *Daily News* also felt compelled to give the street addresses for both. Moses Wright came in for ridicule, too: Just what cemetery was he forced to hide out in for fear of his life? Who was in the three carloads that supposedly visited his house?[34]

The Friday stories were framed by a new picture of J. W. Milam and Roy Bryant. Bound over to Leflore County Sheriff George Smith after the trial, the half-brothers had not been seen since lighting cigars and kissing their "lovely" wives a week earlier after their acquittal. But after posting ten-thousand-dollar bonds, they had their first taste of freedom in thirty-three days. The bond money had been put up by "wealthy planters." Deputy Ernest Stowers bragged that "they could have gotten up to a million dollars in bond if they needed it." Neither man was met by his spouse as they were shown exiting the Leflore County Courthouse by a side entrance. Milam told reporters that he had cotton picking to do back home near Glendora. Bryant revealed plans to reopen his store in Money after he rested up. Both men were "congratulated" upon release by none other than Sheriff Smith, admitted close friend to Roy Bryant. Ed Milam, J. W.'s brother from nearby Itta Bena, ferried the defendants back home. They would never spend another day in jail for the kidnapping and murder of Emmett Till. But if the two men had entertained any thoughts of returning home, they would have been badly mistaken. While the rich alluvial plain of the Delta bore no cracks or fissures, the lives they had once lived—and by most accounts enjoyed—had ended with the seismic events of the past month. Near death almost forty years later, Roy Bryant could state without a hint of irony that Emmett Till had "ruined his life."[35]

Seven

"Like Father—Like Son"
(October 1955–January 1956)

Many Mississippi newspapers did not take the postverdict northern reaction lightly, and, while the *Jackson Daily News* was a prime example of the southern response, other papers followed their lead. Just east of Greenwood, in Winona, the local paper reprinted a story from the *Daily News* that featured the words of archsegregationist and powerful senator James O. Eastland, whose family owned and operated a large plantation not far from Sumner. Without mentioning the name Emmett Till, Eastland urged all white residents of the capital to sign up for the Jackson Citizens' Council. Not surprisingly, the senator used the language of warfare to describe the stakes: "The choice is between victory and defeat. Defeat means death, the death of Southern culture and our aspirations as an Anglo-Saxon people." In Eastland's description, the stakes over segregation did not constitute much of a choice, but he was sanguine about the regional battle: "With strong leadership and the loyalty and fortitude of a great people, we will climb the heights. Generations of Southerners yet unborn will cherish our memory because they will realize that the fight we now wage will have preserved for them their untainted racial heritage, their culture, and the institutions of the Anglo-Saxon race." Thus do rumors of "mingling" and interracial "swimming" in Tchula come into sharper relief. And with the NAACP's appropriation of the Till verdict as civil-rights rallying cry, Eastland hoped to capitalize on antiintegration fears. If the NAACP could use the Till case to catalyze its membership drive, so too the Citizens' Councils.[1]

The *Daily News*'s coverage of a speech by Eastland delivered in Jackson certainly was not anything out of the ordinary. Far more surprising were the lengths to which the paper went in trying to expose the NAACP's supposed manipulation and imprisonment of three key trial witnesses: Amanda Bradley, Willie Reed, and Moses Wright. Recall that they had been spirited out of Mississippi after the trial because of safety concerns; furthermore, each had been assigned round-the-clock police protection out of fear of possible retribution. Based on its reporting, it is clear that the *Daily News* took

"Like Father—Like Son" (October 1955–January 1956)

the stories of threat quite personally. And, in reporting on that threat, the *News* became the news.

On Sunday, October 2, in his front-page digest of news and opinion, Frederick Sullens foreshadowed much of what was to come that week: "Chicago police, working in three shifts, guard the home of Mary Bradley [*sic*] and the house where Willie Reed, . . . is staying. And that's just about the climax of police asininity." Neither person was in danger—in Chicago or Mississippi, asserted Sullens; the protection was merely "stage stuff" choreographed by the NAACP. The newspaper's charges grew exponentially by Wednesday when the first in a series of three features ran explosive claims that the NAACP was holding Bradley, Reed, and Wright against their will. *Daily News* reporter Bill Spell flew north to Chicago to try to interview each of the principals.[2]

The first part of Spell's exclusive ran on Wednesday, October 5. Printed above the newspaper's masthead on page one, the huge headlines blared, "State Negroes Held 'Captive' in Chicago." Conducted under the rationale of getting to the truth about conflicting reports, Spell "dared to penetrate" the city's south side. That there were no conflicting reports did not seem to matter. It also did not seem to matter that Willie Reed stated that he was not being held "captive" in the "deepest part of Chicago's south-side Negro section by the National Association for the Advancement of Colored People." In a notably personal first-person account of his travels and interviews, Spell found Willie Reed at Michael Reece Hospital "retching" when he entered the room. Despite police protection by a "six foot plus Negro detective," Reed answered Spell's questions without hesitation: yes, he'd fled Mississippi because of the "hard" looks he'd received at the trial from J. W. Milam; no, he had not been directly threatened by anyone; yes, he would rather stay in Chicago even though it forced him to leave his girlfriend, Ella Mae, behind. The brief interview apparently ended without Spell even asking the question about charges of NAACP-imposed captivity—the stated reason for his travels in the first place. Far more likely was that Reed had in fact answered the question—no, he was not a captive—and Spell chose not to mention it in the printed interview. But beyond speculation, more remarkable was the *Daily News*'s headline that the witnesses were in fact "held 'captive.'" Willie Reed betrayed not a hint of forced isolation.[3]

Neither did Amanda Bradley. "Deep in the heart of Chicago's South Side," began Spell, he found the fifty-year-old "heavy" domestic. Like the previous day's article, the second "exclusive" appeared above the masthead on page 1; the headline declared, "Woman Witness Told to Keep Silent." Spell was

"Like Father—Like Son" (October 1955–January 1956)

allowed entrance to a house on Lawrence Avenue—in fact it was Mamie Till's residence—by a black policeman. In response to the questions, and like Reed, she confessed to being afraid of Milam (and Bryant), though no one had threatened her. But she did claim that her husband, Alonzo Bradley, "got beat up and run out of Mississippi." At this point, Spell recited dramatically, the interview was cut off by Emmett Till's grandmother Alma Spearman, who warned Bradley against talking further. "It was at this point that I first encountered the NAACP," Spell claimed, "and learned that Mandy Bradley is under the complete domination of the NAACP." As day two of the "exclusive" drew to a lackluster close, it was perhaps more clear that Bill Spell was the one being dominated by racially motivated conspiracy theories of anti-Mississippi collusion.[4]

But Spell was not the only *Daily News* writer attempting to stretch racial innuendo into conspiratorial fact. In a front-page article that same day, W. C. Shoemaker teamed up with Spell to report that Amanda Bradley's husband denied being beaten by white men on the Leslie Milam–managed plantation near Drew. Alonzo Bradley's denial "proved" the existence of an NAACP-conspiracy against the state—since it seemed to Spell and Shoemaker that the NAACP had put both Amanda Bradley and Charles C. Diggs up to the allegations of violence. Perhaps the *Daily News* was still under the illusion that local blacks told the truth about white-on-black violence—even if that violence was bound up with the recent race-revenge killing of a young black boy. As an aside the *Daily News* did reveal that Bradley had been run off the plantation by Leslie Milam. Spell and Shoemaker found further proof of a NAACP conspiracy in Amanda Bradley's actions: that she had been "whisked" north to Chicago before she could tell her husband where she was going, let alone give him a goodbye, "substantiated a story published in the *Jackson Daily News* on Wednesday that Mandy Bradley is held 'captive' in Chicago by a Negro organization and used to spread world-wide hate against the state of Mississippi." Her actions, coupled with the Alma Spearman incident, were clear signs of a conspiracy—such was the frenzied logic of a newspaper and a state on the defensive.[5]

Spell's third and final exclusive ran the next day, Friday, October 7; it, too, was featured above the *Daily News*'s masthead with the headline "How the NAACP Network Operates." In summarizing his interviews with Reed and Bradley, Spell claimed that his work "had proved that neither the Reed boy nor Mandy Bradley had been harmed in Mississippi as was reported." Spell was exaggerating: nobody had reported that Reed or Bradley had been harmed; their move north had been prompted by threats and intimidation, not actual physical violence. Spell never got to talk directly with Moses

"Like Father—Like Son" (October 1955–January 1956)

Wright, as he was forced to go through a middleman to get his question answered. He wanted to ask whether Wright had been forced to hide out all night in a nearby cemetery because of the threat of white violence. The middleman never returned Spell's calls and, when contacted later, did not have Wright's answers. With his story in tatters, Spell took to reporting about the insidious NAACP network, how stealthily and rapidly the group had grown in Chicago and how it controlled huge blocks of votes. Moreover, that Wright could not be reached by Spell or by the AP was further proof to Spell of NAACP attempts to keep him quiet.[6]

Spell's main contention had been proven false: the NAACP was not holding any of the witnesses against their will. While not admitting as much to his readers, Spell closed his exclusive with unfounded claims: "One thing has been accomplished. Much of the propaganda which supposedly came from the lips of these three witnesses have [sic] been quieted by some facts." Unable to detail just what these facts were, Spell resorted to a rhetorical trick: the facts existed because they had been labeled "facts." The only facts uncovered in Spell's exposé were that Reed and Bradley (and later Wright) had left Mississippi because they no longer felt safe there and that police were giving them protection.[7]

As Bill Spell's journey north suggests, many white Mississippians' defensiveness in the wake of the trial's verdict shaded into paranoia. In their view, carefully coordinated attacks on the state could only be the consequence of northern black aggression aimed at undoing segregation and besmirching the good name of Mississippi. In many ways, Spell's incredulity was but the latest manifestation of an increasingly fevered white paternalism: surely our good Negroes would never leave the state of their own free will; surely "propaganda" of threats and intimidation was coming from NAACP headquarters, and when the reportorial facts do not align with this paternalism, claim that they do. The *Jackson Daily News* could not heed its own editorial counsel: How could it "forget" the Till case when Jim Crow's assumptions were daily being repudiated or called into question? Hubris may have also exerted a palpable influence on the *News*'s reporting: having sided with J. W. Milam and Roy Bryant, they could not backtrack at this point without admitting an error in judgment and recognizing the larger possibility that race relations might be festering under segregation. And so the *Daily News* did what most do when cultural verities are in doubt: proclaim them with even more certainty.

Fallout from Spell's exclusive was immediate: already on October 7 the *Daily News*—of all papers—ran a front-page story in which the Hearst-owned *Chicago American* disputed his charges that the three witnesses were being held captive. Said Amanda Bradley, "That's the most fantastic story I've heard yet. Nobody is keeping me here." Wright also expressed amazement at the charges, "Well, now I guess I have heard everything." Put on the defensive in his own newspaper, Spell revealed his reportorial motives: "I do not believe they left because they were afraid of their lives and somebody should defend Mississippi against the wave of propaganda the NAACP is directing toward my state." But in the wake of outright refutation of his claims, Spell modified his charges: NAACP intervention in his interviews—no NAACP intervention can be located in the record of his actual interviews—"is further proof that these Mississippi Negroes are held mental captive if not physical captives." Bill Spell could see through the fog of false racial consciousness—even as he prevaricated about the NAACP's involvement in his own reporting.[8]

The *Daily News*, perhaps with some ambivalence, sided with its staffer on the "captivity" exclusives. On its Saturday, October 8, front page, the paper ran a story of Moses Wright's account of sleeping in the Church of God in Christ cemetery on the night of September 23; the next morning a neighbor told him that men had come to the house bearing flashlights. On its face, the story completely refuted Spell's charges, but the headline insinuated NAACP intervention: "Mose Tells of Sleeping in Cemetery but 'Middle Man' Attended Interview." Inserted in the report by Felix B. Wold was a parenthetical editor's note that claimed both Reed and Bradley "would tell one version when interviewed alone and a different account when a representative of the NAACP was there to prompt 'captive' answers."[9]

That note was pure fiction. Not only had their stories not changed, but neither Reed nor Bradley had been interviewed in the presence of NAACP minders; the discrepancy awaited further accounts. Also on the front page that day was an article bearing the suggestive caption "Is Mandy Held a Captive?" In yet another article attempting to vindicate his wounded Mississippi pride, Bill Spell went to great lengths trying to phone Bradley to inquire as to the whereabouts and wishes of her erstwhile husband. His "attempt to reunite the two" ended when Bradley, whose voice did not sound to Spell like the Bradley he had interviewed days earlier in Chicago, hung up the phone. That an unnamed white reporter from the *Jackson Daily News* who claimed to bear residency information and messages from her family back in Mississippi—she should return home—thought he could get an interview is risible. The termination of the phone call raised the question to Spell, "Is Mandy Bradley a free person who can speak without censorship or is she a mental 'captive'?" As Spell's game of shadows, innuendo, and specula-

"Like Father—Like Son" (October 1955–January 1956)

tion played out, it was clear just who the captive was—and what he was captive to.[10]

Next to the story was a report of a black man who had allegedly raped "an attractive 21-year old."[11]

Other Mississippi newspapers were not quite sure what to make of Spell's exclusive for the *Daily News*—even as they carried it on their front pages. The *Natchez Democrat*, for example, headlined its article "Jackson News Says NAACP Holds Negroes Captive." An equally plausible headline might have read, "NAACP Denies Holding Negroes Captive." Two days later, however, the *Democrat* did report on "a conflict of newspaper accounts" between the *Chicago American* and the *Jackson Daily News*. That story also added a new twist to Spell's reporting: the *American* reported that Spell had posed as a police officer in Chicago and had traveled to the city "in an airplane of the Mississippi National Guard." While Spell denied the former charge, the *Daily News* claimed that Spell was a member of the Guard and that the plane was "making a scheduled instrument training flight." The *American* also added further fuel to the smoldering embers by quoting from Governor Hugh White. Recall that White had sent a private letter on September 12 in which he expressed fears that a just verdict would not be forthcoming. Those fears had now been confirmed: "Agitation by the NAACP did a whole lot to get the jury to set them free. . . . The NAACP overdid it, that's all. They created sentiment in favor of the defendants," claimed the outgoing Governor. "You can't convict people when sentiment is aroused." In other words, the blame lay not with "aroused" jurors who had rallied around the defendants but with excessive "agitation."[12]

If Governor White could reprise his earlier claims about justice in the Till case, so too could Roy Wilkins. The NAACP leader's conspicuous silence on the case ended on October 7. Before the Virginia state conference of the NAACP meeting in Charlottesville, Wilkins echoed his September 1 comments: "The people of Mississippi had created, or had sat by and acquiesced in the creating of, an atmosphere of physical violence directed at Negroes." While the carefully phrased statement was more nuanced than his earlier verbal blast, his wholesale indictment of the state only added to the racially roiling waters; it also did not help matters as the grand jury kidnap hearing loomed. Then again, perhaps like many others, Wilkins had simply dismissed the possibility that a Mississippi court could or would seek justice in a white-on-black kidnapping case.[13]

The *Vicksburg Evening Post* also reported on Spell's exclusive, but, instead of pitting the *Daily News* against the *Chicago American*, the *Post* featured a

"Like Father—Like Son" (October 1955–January 1956)

staunch denial by Enoch Waters, executive editor of the *Chicago Defender*. Recall that the *Defender* had come in for harsh critique by Mississippi newspapers, not only for its anti-Mississippi editorials but for running the infamous post-mortem of Emmett Till's corpse. Waters claimed that Bradley, Reed, and Wright had fled north to Chicago "of their own volition" and were not being held captive. Waters's newspaper made additional news the same week when it was revealed that the *Defender* had shepherded Leroy "Too Tight" Collins out of the Delta to Chicago for two days of careful questioning. Rumors persisted that Collins, along with fellow field hand on the Sheridan plantation Henry Lee Loggins, had been in the pick-up truck with Emmett Till early on Sunday morning, August 28. Collins denied the allegations, claiming that he and Loggins had been in Greenwood "visiting some girls" on the night in question. For undisclosed reasons, Waters revealed that a possible meeting between Collins and the hospitalized Reed had been "unsuccessful." Such a meeting might have provided further evidence as to the identity of the mystery black people riding in the back of J. W. Milam's truck.[14]

The Spell exclusive, along with counterarges from Chicago, the "mingling" furor in Tchula, Roy Wilkins's mass indictment, and the interracial rape trial near Laurel combined to make for very raw race relations in Mississippi. Some editors seized on the sentiment. Tom Alewine at the *Brandon News* wondered aloud whether "we should form an organization for the protection of white people, not just for their advancement." Looming racial violence was stoked further by "The Big Yick" in the *Oxford Eagle*, who wrote that, if the NAACP and its Communist allies want to march in Mississippi, "they won't be marching when they leave." Other editors decried the violence that the NAACP was supposedly trying to incite with its claims of lynching and a "wave of terror." The *Kosciusko Star-Herald* opined that a call for federal troops to occupy the state was not just "stupid" but would also create more interracial violence. In the small southwestern town of Poplarville, future site of the lynching of Mack Charles Parker in 1959, the editor of the *Weekly Democrat* railed against the NAACP "in its drive to cram racial integration down the throats of the people of the Southland." In nearby Picayune, the editor at the *Item* feared "that our South will be forced back into mob law." That mob was directly tied in the report to the NAACP and television programs such as "Ten Feet Tall," which had depicted an interracial marriage—and the white bride had hailed from New Orleans: "Never a day passes but that we read of some crime committed by Negroes who undoubtedly are seeing such rot on TV.... With a mongrel race, without morals our enterprising nation will fall as so many nations have." It was assumed

"Like Father—Like Son" (October 1955–January 1956)

that interracial couples—in the Mississippi imaginary, always a white woman and black man—lacked all moral scruples on account of their coupling; the inevitable "mongrel" offspring would also ensure the end of American supremacy. Thus was intrarace marriage also a profoundly patriotic act in this view. White Mississippi's anger boiled over in Alewine's weekly column from Brandon: "What the NAACP wants is a license for any negro to do anything to anybody he wants to . . . and a death penalty for any white person who asks to see the license." He counseled his black readers against joining or listening "to the 'big niggers' of the NAACP."[15]

Others pleaded for calm. From Natchez, Elliott Trimble urged local blacks not to fear whites as they had "lived side by side for decades without trouble." Race relations must not be arbitrated by "hotheads," he added, but by "intelligent calm people where they live." He called for an atmosphere of "friendliness and understanding" in order to preserve racial custom. In West Point, the editor claimed that progress "will be made if the Negro citizens of the state meet every radical NAACP claim with cool heads and clear thinking." From the "Tung Oil Center of the World," in Picayune, local black pastor F. Bunn of St. John Baptist Church offered thirteen reasons for maintaining segregation, number six of which read, "in any show-down of strength, we will always be the greatest sufferers." In nearby McComb, editor Oliver Emmerich encouraged readers not to be baited by insults from the north. Whites and blacks cannot let "hatred replace good relations in Mississippi and the South," he admonished. At the *Clarksdale Press Register* interracial good will was emphasized by reprising the story of little Dianne Kearney, who had saved her nurse, Jimmie Abrams, from drowning in the Tallahatchie River.[16]

In the midst of this torrent of editorializing, Mississippi papers also continued to reprint Reverend McClary's lengthy anti-integration, anti-NAACP letter; somehow it offered hope that reasonable southern black people might see the error of the NAACP's ways. Not even the nine Supreme Court justices, perceived as adjudicating in a haze of sociology and politics, had engendered this discourse at this volume. And that volume was about to get much louder with lurid revelations first published in the *Jackson Daily News* in mid-October.[17]

Before that revelation was published, Mississippi newspapers carried yet more incendiary policy proposals directed at the state. In addition to calls for the federal government to occupy and administer the state, the NAACP also picketed the U.S. Customs House in Chicago where a subcommittee of the Senate Internal Security Committee was meeting. They charged that human rights were being denied to black people in Mississippi. Punctuating

"Like Father—Like Son" (October 1955–January 1956)

the frenzied activism was Harlem's flamboyant Congressman Adam Clayton Powell's call on October 10 for Americans to boycott all products made in Mississippi. To a lunchtime Harlem crowd of twenty thousand people, Powell also called on President Eisenhower, who was just then recovering from a heart attack, to call a special session of Congress. During that session, Powell promised to propose legislation which would have barred seating congressional representatives from states that barred black people from voting "without fear of lynching or coercion of any kind."[18]

While Powell, Wilkins, and others were making open calls for federal intervention, behind the scenes, Mississippi's powerful senators James O. Eastland and John Stennis had been looking carefully at the Till family, specifically the little-known father of the murdered boy, Louis Till. Other than being the original owner of the silver signet ring found on Emmett's body when it came out of the river, very little had been said publicly about the Army private who had died while serving in World War II. Mamie Till revealed only that she had received a letter from the Army informing her that he had died in Italy in 1945; the cause was "willful misconduct." She tried investigating his death further in 1948, but satisfactory answers were not forthcoming. Perhaps because Mamie Till and her husband were separated at the time, the widow let the "willful misconduct" charge lie. But the charge sprung to life on October 14, 1955.[19]

The senators' search of highly classified military records revealed that Private Louis Till of the Army's 177th Port Company, 397th Port Battalion, had been executed on July 2, 1945, for having been found guilty of raping two Italian women and murdering a third. His execution order had been signed by then-General Eisenhower. He had been found guilty on February 17, 1945, after a military trial in Leghorn, Italy. For killing Anna Zanchi and raping Benni Lucretzia and Frieda Mari on June 27, 1944, in Civitavecchia, Italy, Private Till was hanged; he was later buried in a military cemetery in France. Without the death of his son nearly ten years later, the twenty-three-year-old private's war records would have remained sealed, kept forever from public scrutiny. But as the grand jury hearing loomed in early November and as the NAACP and its allies grew increasingly vocal about "jungle justice" in Mississippi, Louis Till became a most important rhetorical pawn in the high-stakes game of north versus south, black versus white, NAACP versus Citizens' Councils.

Details of his death were leaked by the senators to the *Jackson Daily News*; the lurid story would remain on Mississippi's front pages for the next several weeks. Unlike the Spell exposé that turned up nothing and was treated with some skepticism even by Mississippi newspapers, news of Louis Till's death

"Like Father—Like Son" (October 1955–January 1956)

redeemed claims of northern press bias even as it spoke directly and dramatically to black-on-white rape. As far as news value went, the story had none: Louis Till simply did not matter to the murder, the trial, or the aftermath; he was but an inconsequential footnote. But as far as rhetorical value went, the Louis Till story was a blockbuster. The immediate response, one even mentioned by Mamie Till, was something on the order of "like father-like son." Surely Emmett Till's misogynist attitude displayed in the Bryant Grocery and Meat Market had antecedents in his dead father's; he was merely playing out a set of instincts hardwired from birth. Perhaps for many Mississippians Virgil Adams had been proved right: Emmett Till had attempted to rape Carolyn Bryant. Of course, the story also vouchsafed the comely twenty-one-year-old's testimony. News of Louis Till's deplorable past begged for retroactive reinterpretation of Emmett Till's actions of August 24, especially for those seeking to do so.

The *Daily News* announced the story with all-capital headlines that stretched across its front page, and those headlines already indicated how the story would play out: "Till's Dad Raped 2 Women, Murdered a Third in Italy." First and foremost, in the *Daily News*, this story was about Emmett Till, but because of its negligible news value bearing on the case, the *Daily News* recontextualized the otherwise sordid story in its lead: "Shocking new information gathered by the Jackson Daily News [*sic*] Saturday further debunked some of the 'hate Mississippi' propaganda used by the nation's press following the Till trial at Sumner." Where Bill Spell had largely failed in his efforts to vindicate white Mississippians and their beliefs about press bias, the Louis Till story promised to redeem the *Daily News*. That the newspaper was featured so prominently in the article suggests that such redemption was indeed at stake. That the paper also misrepresented its role in the investigation is also suggestive—as is the telling adverb "further."[20]

To help readers fully appreciate the announcement of Louis Till's actions by "Mississippi's Greatest Newspaper" and understand the stakes of the perceived interracial danger, the newspaper offered a telling visual. Sandwiched immediately between the front-page editorial and the hard news of Louis Till's death, was a large picture of "pretty Carolyn Fountain." The picture of the woman with prominent breasts advertised that it was "Sweater Season in the Southland"; more to the point of the "news value" of the photograph, "the city's male population [would] get . . . a five month long eyeful." Jackson readers could have hardly missed the implication: the voluptuous and "pretty" Carolyns of the Southland were quite literally surrounded by menacing black rapists and murderers. In fact it is hard not to read the two Till stories without assuming that the pictured woman had been raped

"Like Father—Like Son" (October 1955–January 1956)

and/or murdered by the executed private. That she was "pretty" and also a "Carolyn" rounded out the message. Readers might suppose that an "eyeful" of Carolyn Bryant had triggered a crime in the son like those of his father.[21]

Two patterns of editorial reaction followed swiftly upon the story breaking: one claimed that the NAACP specifically and northern journalists generally had purposefully lied about Louis Till; the other attempted to link father and son. Regarding the former, several journalists immediately pounced on a short article that had appeared in the October 10 issue of *Life* magazine. That article contextualized Louis Till's World War II service (and death) as a heroic example of patriotic valor: Emmett Till "had only his life to lose, and many others have done that, including his soldier-father who was killed in France fighting for the American proposition that all men are created equal." The unattributed and obviously erroneous story was immediately deemed an NAACP plant; the organization, according to papers like the *Grenada Daily Sentinel-Star*, had been "portraying the youth's father as a World War II hero who died fighting for his country." The NAACP had done nothing of the sort; in fact, the only "heroic" public attributions heaped on Private Till came from the *Life* article. But in the rhetorical volley of attack, defend, and counterattack, details of authorship were largely beside the point: the Mississippi press had a new and explosive card to play, one that went to the heart of its anti-integration and antimiscegenation fears.[22]

Even as it broke the sensational story, the *Daily News* tried to take something of the high road; in so doing, the newspaper actually expressed agreement with the NAACP. In its front-page editorial titled "About Till's Father," the *Daily News*, like NAACP attorney William Huff, claimed that Louis Till's death had nothing to do with the circumstances surrounding his son's kidnapping and murder. But, the editorial went on, the real news in reports of Louis Till's ignominious execution was that the northern press "will publish rank Negro propaganda without even bothering to check the facts." As they saw it, the *Daily News* editors were merely fulfilling their civic role in publishing details of the execution since the northern press appeared to be in cahoots with the NAACP and its affiliates. This was a remarkable claim: even as a supposed "non-story," the paper clearly knew that it would exacerbate the state's volatile racial climate. Furthermore, to claim that the "northern press" was collectively guilty of lionizing Louis Till was to confuse the part for the whole. The illogic of *Life* magazine standing in for all northern journalists and press outlets somehow got lost in the details of Private Till's interracial and transcontinental sexual crime. The *News* concluded that Missis-

"Like Father—Like Son" (October 1955–January 1956)

sippians were "willing to stand on the facts, if they can find a publication outside the South willing to tell them."[23]

The *Daily News*'s neighbor to the north, the *Madison County Herald*, was trying to turn a deaf ear and a blind eye to the coverage. In an editorial titled "To [*sic*] Much Angry Shouting . . ." the newspaper wagged its finger at the Jackson paper: "We are unable to understand why certain of our daily newspapers think it necessary to print so many articles and use so many black headlines about some of the Negroes who were prominent in the Till case and are now in Chicago," including dead husbands. Like the *Daily News*'s editorial of September 24, the *Herald* stated it "would rather forget" the Till case, but the press simply would not "quiet down." It was a polite if quaint call for a truce, southern in sensibility and typical of many small weeklies that simply gave little attention to the case; it had little investment in the inventorying of racial slights. But at this late date, "forgetting" was simply out of the question.[24]

The Madison County newspaper was not alone in calling for mnemonicide. Further north, at the *Tupelo Daily Journal*, in a long and careful editorial on the Till case, the editor claimed it was time to "forget" it, but the *Daily Journal* went much further in elaborating why it thought the case should be forgotten: with news of Louis Till's life and death, Mississippians might get "unduly excited" and seek revenge on local black people. Such bitterness and anger, it elaborated, would only play into the Communist's hands, who would then further exploit such racial violence. As the *Herald* had pointed out, the basic problem was a journalistic one: carrying the story of Louis Till brought with it the likelihood of violence. A call to forget the case, the two papers seem to agree, even if justice may "have gone astray," was in essence a call for peace; Mississippi's many and continuing "black headlines" did not augur well for racial reconciliation.[25]

At least one of the lawyers directly involved in the case was in no mood for forgetting. In a letter to the editor published in the *Daily News* on October 19, J. J. Breland congratulated the newspaper on "digging up" the truth about Louis Till; such truth telling and publicity went to the heart of the state's present problems. That is, if the state would spend one million dollars publicizing Mississippi up north, the Supreme Court would not have had the "gall to try to enforce this decision [*Brown*] upon the white folks of the South." Not unlike his race-baiting closing statements to the jury, Breland suggested that publicity featuring black-on-white violence would force the Court to rethink its sociology; rape and attempted rape was the predictable outcome of school integration.[26]

"Like Father—Like Son" (October 1955–January 1956)

Positive publicity was also on the mind of Hazel Brannon Smith, who would win the Pulitzer Prize for editorial writing in 1964. In her weekly "Through Hazel Eyes" column in the October 20 *Lexington Advertiser*, Smith praised a recent speech by Senator Eastland in which he called for a sustained campaign against the NAACP's propaganda. Smith, who would also later win wide acclaim for her progressive views on Mississippi race relations, praised the archsegregationist for his proposal to "set up an organization to give the facts to the American public, using state funds to do so." Five months later, the Mississippi legislature created the State Sovereignty Commission, an organization that would use its considerable powers to enforce the racial status quo in the state for the next twenty years.[27]

What Breland only hinted at was made much more explicit by Wade Milam. Not a relative of the now-infamous Milam clan, the hostile letter was sent to *Life* magazine and also published in the *Daily News*. News of Louis Till's actions had clearly changed things: Emmett was now a "big 14-year-old brute," who had acted in true "like father-like son" fashion, in Wade Milam's description. The rapist's pedigree, combined with news of "two black boys raping a white woman in Louisiana the year before," had forced Milam and Bryant's hand, he argued; they were simply and justifiably defending imperiled white womanhood. This, it seems, is precisely the conclusion that defense attorneys hoped jurors would reach back in September: an attempted rape, coupled with recent history, transformed the kidnap and killing into a heroic defense provoked in the first place by the *Brown* decision, which had only "enhanced these crimes against white women." Such a scenario cast Milam and Bryant as counterhegemonic heroes forced into action by a Supreme Court that simply did not understand the black male mind. "No white woman," Wade Milam explained, "can be considered as safe in the city, town, or open country when left alone as there is always the possibility of a lurking Negro rapist, who may be aware of such conditions."[28]

The *Daily News* was not yet done publishing racist letters from its considerable readership. No doubt buoyed by its blockbuster on Private Till, on October 20 the paper published a letter by Jackson's A. S. Coody. The anti-Semitic letter actually argued for interracial coupling since all Negroes "who have attained distinction are mulattoes or octoroons." Only white blood, in Coody's eyes, had redeemed an irredeemable race. It was also telling to Coody that the NAACP was led not by a Negro but by a "Russian Jew," Arthur Spingarn, who "has a lengthy list of Negro (Mulatto) agitators, probably some of the Doctors here are part of that group." Most insidiously, he believed, Spingarn was "working for the Kremlin." Coody's missive marked

"Like Father—Like Son" (October 1955–January 1956)

one of the first instances when overt anti-Semitism entered public discourse on the Till case; perhaps given the cold war stakes at issue, such a late date is indeed surprising. As the next decade would reveal, the leftist Jewish bogeyman would prove a potent trope, especially in the federal government's own proxy war on civil-rights leaders. Two days after Coody's letter, the *Natchez Democrat* ran a page-one story on a report issued by the American Jewish Committee. Headlined "Till Murder Case Hurts US Prestige," the report claimed that "enormous damage" was done to the country's reputation in the six nations surveyed—nations "not limited to Communist or Communist-controlled groups."[29]

Editorializing on the *Daily News*'s discovery of Louis Till's past came quickly from the hinterlands. From Brandon, Tom Alewine gloated that "wishes—aided by a little hard work—do come true." The NAACP and the northern press' "hate Mississippi" campaign, Alewine hoped, had effectively ended with news of Louis Till's execution; finally the "hot potato" had been dropped. W. H. Anderson of the *Ripley Southern Sentinel* deemed that "campaign of hate" the most virulent "since the pre-Civil War period." Sid Harris of the *Houston (MS) Times-Post* commented wryly that "young Till might well have inherited his art of using the 'wolf whistle'" and that had the NAACP known of the father's exploits it might not have publicized the case from the beginning. From Collins, Jimmy Arrington, who had earlier called on Senator Eastland to criminalize collecting funds from the display of a corpse, poked fun at the northern press: "We bet the wimmen folks in Italy are glad that all American soldiers were not the kind of 'hero' that Emmett Till's father was." The *Kosciusko Star-Herald* editorialized that white Mississippians should thank the *Daily News* for exposing Till's father as a "rapist-murderer." Mississippians did "officially" thank the newspaper. The *Greenwood Commonwealth* noted on October 18 that the Mississippi Association of County Supervisors officially commended the *Daily News* and its editor, Major Fred Sullens, at its Jackson meeting.[30]

Meanwhile, the paper that broke the story kept a careful, if selective, accounting of reaction to its offending publication. An October 25 *Daily News* editorial reported that the *Memphis Commercial Appeal* had made light of the fact that *Life* magazine had yet to issue any sort of retraction. Minus an apology or note of explanation, the *Daily News* subtly pressed its propaganda claims even further: "National publications are so convinced of the truth of the NAACP that they don't even check their facts." The presumed anti-Mississippi conspiracy had now grown to include all national press outlets—regardless of geography it seemed.[31]

"Like Father—Like Son" (October 1955–January 1956)

Perhaps more bald-faced was the assertion that all national and northern outlets were dupes of the NAACP. Proof that the organization had celebrated Louis Till's war service was not forthcoming—primarily because there was not any. And yet, papers such as the *Winona Times* published a widely circulated wire story that the NAACP had "been busily portraying the youth's father as a World War II hero who died fighting for his country in France in 1945." Mamie Till certainly had not, even though she had been working with the organization; she knew that a death carrying the "willful misconduct" label, however indeterminate, was not a rhetorically advantageous one. In fact, in her posthumously published memoir, Mamie Till recounted that Roy Wilkins expressed relief that he had not "gotten caught in that 'Louis Till trap.'" The closest the executive secretary ever came to lauding Louis Till's military service was in a future speech—praise that never took place after the *Daily News*'s sensational disclosure.[32]

The lack of evidence for the NAACP's disingenuousness was likely lost in the explosive aftermath of the Louis Till story. "The South" had caught "the North" in a lie meant to disparage Mississippians. This truth functioned rhetorically for a much larger one: that national and northern journalists had it in for the state and its way of life. Evidence to the contrary was beside the point.

At least one white Mississippian tried to reason with a local editor on the inflammatory issue. In the October 27 weekly issue of the *Picayune Item*, editor and publisher C. H. Cole, in his column "Hardly a Column by Chance," ridiculed and belittled one Marguerite Holmes. The former Mississippi resident decried the curtailment of freedom of speech sustained by the editor's "racialism." She continued, "Can you be so shortsighted as not to see that this is just what the enemies of Democracy want—little good it does you to hide behind the gossamer curtain of Southern loyalty." She was both a Mississippian and white, "but," she stated, "I'm no longer proud of the former, and thankful to God for the latter." As to Cole's racial views, she added, "Only the blind will deny that a time of equality will come. The propaganda you spread is contrary to the love of God, to the concept of Democracy, and to a man's loyalty unto himself. And certainly, surely, it must be contrary to the ethics of a newsman." Cole could only respond by doubting the identity of Marguerite Holmes—surely a white Mississippian, and a woman no less, would never utter such racial "rot"—and dismissing her with a telling ad hominem remark: "We doubt if even one Negro whom you are trying to tell that you are so interested in will believe that you are sincere.... Our sane colored people know your kind, you cannot fool them into believing that kind of rot." The racial issue for Cole need not involve evidence, reasoning,

"Like Father—Like Son" (October 1955–January 1956)

good public policy, or even Biblical precept; rather, the real crux of the matter was sincerity. In one sense, Cole was right: most Mississippi blacks were likely very circumspect regarding self-proclaimed racially progressive Mississippi whites. But to dismiss Marguerite Holmes on the dual grounds of authenticity and sincerity spoke volumes about public discourse on race: premises and claims could not even be debated when arguments about race had been reduced to the ontological grounds of who the arguer was. The politics of identity was indeed a "gossamer curtain" on an issue that beckoned desperately for reasoned discussion and debate.[33]

Others argued that sincerity and authority were beside the point; God alone had sanctioned separation of the races. In a letter published in the *Drew Leader*, not far from where Willie Reed claimed to have seen Emmett Till in J. W. Milam's truck, Reverend Charles C. Jones from Mendenhall divined God's mandate for segregation in the first chapter of Genesis. In the act of creating, God was also "separating, or segregating things that were different"; thus was Yahweh the original segregationist. Jones's creative reading of Genesis encompassed far more than just the Pentateuch: "There is no law in the Bible for indiscriminately mixing, or mongrelizing of the races of mankind." Jones's theology was almost as inconsistent as his reasoning: the New Testament redeemed the law of Moses by divine incarnation. The preacher carefully steered clear of Christ's travels through Samaria and Paul's letter to the church at Galatia. Theological specifics were apparently beside the point when southern tradition was at stake; retrofitting the Bible for supremacist ends promised a bigger audience for the Citizens' Council in Mendenhall. A proud member, Jones urged his readers to join.[34]

Nearly three weeks after the *Daily News* published the Louis Till revelations, Virgil Adams of the *Greenwood Morning Star* expressed a feeling of vindication for his posttrial assessment that Emmett Till's transgression had in fact constituted attempted rape. The supposed vindication was borne of the father's transgressions: "We are glad to note that the 'wolf whistle' angle of the case is getting less attention. If this case had always been referred to in the papers as an 'attempted rape' case, it would have been considered in a different light by the thinking people of the nation." No doubt Adams's rhetorical criticism was on the mark: "attempted rape" signifies very differently than does whistling—whatever the predator. Left at the level of suggestion was the conclusion that Carolyn Bryant's testimony coupled with Louis Till's transgressions made Emmett Till's offense "attempted rape." The like-father-like-son indictment was now firmly fixed in Adams's mind—and no doubt in the minds of many of his readers as well.[35]

The *Daily News* finally got what it apparently wanted in *Life's* October 31 issue: an admission of error. But, the *News* editorialized, it was "a mighty magre [*sic*] correction for such a glaring error." Then again, no apology or correction that *Life* magazine might have made would have sufficed. Errors of fact were largely beside the point, especially when the entire northern press establishment could be fingered as complicit in the "hate Mississippi" propaganda.[36]

As it turns out, Tom Alewine and others were quite wrong about the effect of the Louis Till story; instead of dropping the story "like a hot potato," the NAACP continued to orchestrate speaking tours for T.R.M. Howard, Mamie Till, and Congressman Diggs. Before large audiences in Des Moines, Pittsburgh, and Mobile, each castigated Mississippi as "ignorant," loaded with "bigotry and race hatred," and ruled by a "reign of terror." A back-pages AP story in the *Vicksburg Evening Post* highlighted the NAACP's involvement in the coordinated attacks on the state and the call for federal involvement. Representative Diggs's remarks received the most notice. "I regret that it took the death of a 14-year-old boy to bring out this crowd," he intoned. "I am here because of the tremendous interest in the situation in Mississippi and what it symbolizes."[37]

The *Post* appeared to play off of Diggs's remark; just three days later it ran an editorial titled "Murder of Four Boys." The *Post*'s logic had been seen before: How was it that one murdered boy in Mississippi gets infinitely more attention than three murdered boys in Illinois? The murder of Emmett Till had become "a national, yes international issue, while the wholesale murder of the three is regarded only as a local incident." The *Post*'s explanation for the appearance of the national and international headlines was simple: the story "furnished the fuse to ignite the greatest explosion of hate this country has witnessed. Mississippi has been denounced as a state, her people maligned, her good name sullied by the dispensers of venom." In other words, hatred for Mississippi and its way of life had fueled the systematic and widespread press bias.[38]

Even at this late date, many in the Mississippi press still did not seem to understand that the Till case was first and foremost about race and the state's oppressive, occasionally deadly, white supremacy. Lumping together murder victims—thus "Four Boys"—transcended specifics in favor of generic vagueness: murder was murder regardless of skin color, age, and geography. Such a rhetorical repositioning was then leveraged to argue for equality: the murders were "just as bad" in other states. Thus, for the out-of-state press to treat Mississippi with such collective invidiousness was a marker of hate in the minds of Mississippi journalists. As long as the Mississippi press did not acknowledge its supremacist politics and culture, it would translate any criti-

"Like Father—Like Son" (October 1955–January 1956)

cism as leading to federal usurpation or forced mongrelization—both of which served the same end, namely Communism. The self-sealing system provided ready rhetorical topoi for a state and a people thrust on the defensive.

For those outside the state, hope remained in the form of possible kidnapping indictments. Immediately upon announcing the verdict on September 23, Judge Swango had bound over Milam and Bryant to Sheriff George Smith of Leflore County. District Attorney Stanny Sanders would convene a grand jury on November 7 to hear evidence for the kidnapping charge in Greenwood. Free on ten-thousand-dollar bonds, Milam was reportedly busy hiring out mechanical cotton pickers while his half-brother tried to sell the infamous grocery store; it was first advertised in the October 19 *Greenwood Morning Star*. Bryant had been effectively forced into selling the store because of a boycott by local black people.

That thin veneer of hope might have easily shattered based on an AP story published around the state on November 9. The opening paragraph began, "The Leflore County grand jury pondered today whether two white men will stand trial on charges of kidnapping Emmett Till, 14-year-old Chicago Negro boy who disappeared while vacationing in Mississippi." Remarkably, any factual references to Till's murder and kidnapping had been entirely expunged; he had simply "disappeared," as if he had run away from home. Whether the rumors of Till being alive spread by Sheriff Strider had taken hold or whether the anonymous writer had so contorted his prose in order to appear unbiased, the farther one got from August 28, it seemed, the farther one also got from the rotting corpse with the silver signet ring hauled out of the muddy Tallahatchie River—to say nothing of the dual kidnap confessions. What had been a body with a name initially identified by Sheriff Strider had become an unraced palimpsest in less than three short months.[39]

The *Jackson State Times* was also not very hopeful about a possible grand jury indictment. On November 6, the newspaper ran a lengthy article that originally appeared in the *New York Times*. Authored by John Popham, who had attended the murder trial in Sumner, it noted that in the past month public opinion had shifted away from the likelihood of indictments. Several factors had caused the change in sentiment, but none had a more "powerful impact" on public opinion than the Louis Till story. And even if the grand jury chose to indict the half-brothers, most figured that another acquittal was likely. As with the murder trial, evidence and testimony seemed to be largely beside the point.[40]

While news of the grand jury hearing made headlines around the state,

"Like Father—Like Son" (October 1955–January 1956)

the number of stories about the Till case had decreased significantly. Other than recapping the testimony of Reed, Wright, Smith, and Cothran bearing on the kidnapping, the only news as the hearing approached was District Attorney Sanders's announcement that he might empanel some black people to serve on the grand jury. As it turned out, Sanders selected twenty white men from Leflore County. Willie Reed and Moses Wright traveled south from Chicago to testify; Wright for twenty-one minutes and Reed for nineteen. The two admitted friends of the defendants, Sheriff Smith and Deputy John Ed Cothran, also testified. Recall that both Smith and Cothran disclosed that Milam and Bryant had confessed to the August 28 kidnapping. Those confessions, along with Reed and Wright's eyewitness accounts, mattered little. On Wednesday, November 9, Circuit Judge Arthur Jordan declared, "Gentlemen, in the case you are interested in there was a no[-]bill returned." Jury foreman June Broadway revealed that he wanted to make a statement, but a six-month no-disclosure pledge prevented him from doing so. District Attorney Sanders did not seem particularly contrite about the verdict: "As far as I know, the case is closed."[41]

The verdict did not come as a surprise to Roy Wilkins. From New York, the executive secretary of the NAACP said the no-bill was in keeping "with the administration of justice in Mississippi." But from Chicago, Mamie Till expressed the opposite: "I didn't think they would ever be sentenced. But I was positive they would be indicted on the basis of their own admission. It never dawned on me that they wouldn't." Sheriff Smith was quick to point the finger, not at the twenty men but at two mothers directly involved in the search for material witnesses: Elizabeth Wright and Mamie Till. Both, he contended, refused to cooperate by not allowing family members present in the Wright home on August 28 to testify before the grand jury. Their refusal was not related to personal safety but to a larger conspiracy alleged by Smith, who imagined that "the material witnesses didn't want the defendants indicted or convicted. They wanted them freed . . . so they can attack 'injustice down here.'" Given such an attitude, we can only wonder what Sheriff Smith testified to about his "friends." Given that the grand jury statements would remain secret, we can only surmise that some things had changed since his testimony of September 22.[42]

Whereas the September 23 not guilty verdict engendered editorializing from around the state, the no-bill announcement received relatively scant editorial comment. Whether that was because of the state's collective embarrassment or because there was less public discourse surrounding the grand jury's meeting, the case was now "over" in the eyes of most Mississippians—white and black. Perhaps because they felt it was over, editors who had earlier

"Like Father—Like Son" (October 1955–January 1956)

professed a hope to see justice done in the case—especially in small towns scattered around the state—let it fade from public consciousness. Yet, unlike the relatively one-sided editorial comment immediately after the murder trial, the few editors registering a public opinion were sharply divided once the reality of J. W. Milam and Roy Bryant's freedom from punishment had become a reality.

Predictably, Virgil Adams of the *Greenwood Morning Star* continued to promote the justifiable homicide defense. He defended the grand jurors as "men who know justice and are capable of making the right decision." Furthermore, he asserted, "Till attempted to molest Mrs. Bryant, grabbed her and made indecent proposals. Where is there a husband worthy of the name who would not protect his wife?" Adams's contrary-to-fact conditional meant only one thing: "Had Bryant been present and slain Till on the spot there would not be a grand jury in the South who would have indicted him . . . and not many in the nation." Adams was clearly still writing post-mortems on the trial in Sumner, not Greenwood; after all, the grand jury was investigating kidnap charges, not murder. Too, J. W. Milam was conspicuously absent from Adams's nostalgic defense of white southern womanhood—and white manhood. Racial decorum, it seemed, stipulated killing or kidnapping—or both.[43]

While the *Jackson Daily News* did not go as far as Adams in stoking the white male Mississippi racial imagination, the newspaper claimed that the state's principal witnesses had been "discredited" and that their grand jury testimony was "rambling, incoherent and often contradictory." Did this include police officers Smith and Cothran? Did the *Daily News* have access to the secret proceedings? Were they claiming that Wright and Reed's testimony was irrelevant to adjudicating the case? Despite the earlier kidnapping confessions, the newspaper confidently concluded, "There was no miscarriage of justice."[44]

Recall that several Mississippi newspapers had adopted a wait-and-see posture after the first trial; if the body was not in fact Till's, then perhaps the jurors had made the proper judgment. Since the half-brothers had confessed to the kidnapping, so these papers reasoned, justice surely would be meted out at a later date regardless of corpus delicti. But once the grand jury returned a no-bill, the justice-delayed argument swiftly became justice denied. Both the *Delta Democrat-Times* and the *Jackson State Times* registered strongly worded disapprobation of grand jury's outcome; they also seemed to understand something of its consequences: "A Leflore County grand jury has told the world that white men in Mississippi may remove Negroes from their homes against their will to punish them or worse, without fear of

"Like Father—Like Son" (October 1955–January 1956)

punishment for themselves." Hodding Carter, who perhaps more than any other editor could see through much of the state's racial phantasmagoria, understood that the kidnapping confession "meant nothing to the grand jury. Unfortunately, it is going to mean a great deal to Mississippi and none of it will be good." Even more problematic, he argued, was that the grand jury's inaction represented only the latest in a sustained and systemic way of life; furthermore, the state's dwindling population and its depressed economics were structurally tied to the fact that "racially-inspired terror" was the Mississippi status quo. With a "curse" on the state, Carter could only conclude that "[i]t will be a long time before Mississippi recovers from the injury the Leflore County grand jury has done to our state and to humanity." Unlike many editors, Carter connected race relations with economics and ethos and understood that a protracted stand-off with the NAACP or northern journalists would get Mississippi nowhere.[45]

Norman Bradley of the *Jackson State Times*, in an editorial synthesizing all that Emmett Till had imported to the state and, in turn, exported to the world, expressed the same sentiment but with different imagery:

> The unfortunate truth is that the Till case ceased to be a hideous crime for which a solution had to be found and punishment meted. Instead it became a symbol of the white-hot determination of Mississippians to conduct their affairs as they pleased. For a great many residents of the state, however, the symbol was ill chosen, the battle waged against the wrong foe, because it took the course of blind opposition to 'outside interference' rather than to an obvious injustice. Mississippi was caught up in a rebellion against its detractors who stooped to falsehood and calumny in their abuse of the state and its people. Its determination to do anything which smacked of acceding to the demands of outsiders led it into a blind alley from which there was no honorable exit. In so doing, it has betrayed its own sense of decency and its own cause of independence in the management of its own affairs. We showed the world, all right, that Mississippi does not bow to the dictates of the NAACP, but the NAACP is not the loser. Justice is the real loser, and when that is true, Mississippi suffers. For justice is not what shrill[-]voiced propagandists say it is; justice is what is right, and when we swerve from a course serving the ends of justice, we harm only ourselves.

While some of the particulars had changed, the ends were eerily reminiscent of the outbreak of the Civil War in 1861.[46]

Bradley's remarkably apt summary of the Till case resonated with at least one prominent Mississippi editor. In the southwestern city of McComb, a place that would later see even the advance guard of civil-rights activists

147
"Like Father—Like Son" (October 1955–January 1956)

flee in fear, Oliver Emmerich quoted extensively from Bradley's editorial. He could only conclude that "we can but be ashamed of our conduct." That sense of shame had one principal source: "When justice appears in the role of a farce and people generally are afraid to assert themselves, then we, the people ourselves because of cowardice, become parties to the crimes." In other words, the rhetoric coming out of Jackson, Greenwood, Picayune, and Branden was nothing but the tactics of the coward turned bully. And, as with most bullies, the state had fallen hard for a group most expert, Emmerich believed, in the arts of cunning indirection: "We fell for a divergent attack. We approached the Till cases as if we had succeeded in placing the NAACP on trial." Emmerich continued, "By failing to find and convict the murderers and kidnapers we assumed that the NAACP was getting a kick in the teeth. The truth is that we supplied that organization with propaganda material which has been used to defame our state in every country of the globe." For those willing to look through the racial haze of the state, such as Carter, Bradley, and Emmerich, their transnational gaze returned always to the inevitable mirror; the corrective to "blind opposition" demanded it. The mythical scales of justice were still absent from a state so aware of the colors of race.[47]

In one important sense, Stanny Sanders was right: with the November 9 grand jury verdict the Till case was "over." The federal government maintained that federal laws had not been violated, and the state laws of Mississippi had reached their end. Mamie Till's remaining legal hope was that the NAACP would file a civil suit, but with frayed relations over a proposed West Coast speaking tour—Wilkins refused her request for five thousand dollars—further legal maneuvers were not likely. But in a less narrow sense, Sanders was quite wrong: Mississippi would never be "over" with Emmett Till; the state's newspapers had inadvertently seen to that. Two concluding stories illustrate the generative influence of the Till case.

On Saturday evening, December 3, 1955, white thirty-five-year-old Elmer Kimball pulled up to a gasoline pump in Glendora, Mississippi. On duty that evening was the station owner, Lee McGarrh and his trusted employee of ten years, Clinton Melton, a black father of four. Melton filled up the 1955 green and white Chevrolet with gas. Kimball, who had been drinking, was furious; he had wanted only two dollars worth of gas. He vowed to return to the gas station with his shotgun. He did. He killed Melton with two shotgun blasts to the head. Kimball's best friend, as it turned out, was J. W. Milam, whose green and white Chevrolet he was driving and with whom he had been hunting and drinking that afternoon.[48]

Before the press could even say the name Emmett Till, local white citizens

"Like Father—Like Son" (October 1955–January 1956)

rallied around the grieving Melton family. The Glendora Lions Club rushed into print a letter drafted collectively on December 6. Two days later, the *Sumner Sentinel* featured the open letter above the fold on its front page. Though his name was not invoked, Emmett Till was clearly still on everyone's mind. Beneath headlines that announced the reopening of the Tomahawk Tavern was the open letter. "We, the men of the Glendora Lions Club, hereby wish to make known our convictions, feelings and intentions with regard to the regrettable tragedy perpetrated on the night of December 3, 1955, which claimed the life of one of the finest members of the Negro race in this community," the letter opened. "We consider the taking of the life of Clinton Melton an outrage against him, against all the people of Glendora, against the people of Mississippi as well as against the entire human family. We deplore the irreparable hurt and harm done to the wife and five children [*sic*] of Clinton Melton. We intend to see to it that the forces of justice and right prevail in the wake of this woeful evil." The matter of race could not be overlooked:

> We deeply regret that such an outburst should shatter the relationship of the two races in this community. It is our sincere purpose and plan of action that all the people of the Glendora community may live together in peace and harmony with liberty and justice for all. We extend to Beulah Melton, widow of the deceased, and her five children [*sic*] our deepest sympathy in sharing their great loss and sorrow and our helping hand in this time of serious trouble and heartache; this we do in the name of humanity and in the name of God the Father who commands us to visit the fatherless and the widows in their affliction. We humbly confess in repentance for having so lived as a community that such an evil occurance [*sic*] could happen here, and we offer ourselves to be used in bringing to pass a better realization of the justice, righteousness and peace which is the will of God for human society.

The letter was sent to newspapers in Sumner, Charleston, Greenwood, and Clarksdale.[49]

The swift communal rallying around the Melton family no doubt was influenced by several positive factors: Clinton Melton had been a life-long resident of Glendora; he had gotten along with local whites; and he had been a hard-working supporter of the status quo. The case differed from Till's in several important ways: Clinton Melton had not been from the North; he had not gotten fresh with a white woman; and, despite a visit from the new Mississippi field secretary, Medgar Evers, Beulah Melton did not want the NAACP to intervene. With such local support, it seemed that Glendora's

"Like Father—Like Son" (October 1955–January 1956)

whites hoped to rewrite race relations in the Mississippi Delta—even if the national press was not watching.

Despite the initial outpouring of rhetorical support, though, things quickly reverted to pre-Till racial realities. On December 21, Beulah Melton was killed in a car accident. Many would later claim that the grieving but justice-seeking widow was forced off the road and into a bayou by local whites for her involvement in Kimball's pending prosecution. Kimball was tried in the spring of 1956, and, despite three eyewitnesses to the shooting, including the respected white storeowner McGarrh, the cotton gin operator was acquitted by an all-white and male Tallahatchie County jury; it took the jury four hours and nineteen minutes to return a verdict—much longer deliberation than the sixty-seven minutes of September 23. Once again Clarence Strider testified for the defense. J. W. Kellum reprised almost verbatim his closing remarks in the Till case. Kimball's son sat next to his father for jurors to see. And the judge—not Swango, who had taken ill—conducted the trial in a decorous manner. Perhaps most telling, though, were prosecuting attorney Hamilton Caldwell's final words to the jury: "Regardless of whether a man's white or black, you've got to be impartial. A nigger's a human being. He's got life." The telling epithet—and reminder—might have even coaxed a smile from the surly "Big" Milam, an interested observer in the very same courtroom where he and his half-brother had been tried six months earlier. Hodding Carter was one of the very few to editorialize on the outcome: "So another 'not guilty' verdict was written at Sumner this week. And it served to cement the opinion of the world that no matter how strong the evidence, nor how flagrant is the apparent crime, a white man cannot be convicted in Mississippi for killing a negro." Carter's conclusion commented retroactively on the Till case: for all the public discourse about miscegenation, corpus delicti, the NAACP and its ties to Communism, the alleged attempted rape of a white woman, and northern press bias, the Till verdict came down to only one germane fact—white Mississippians would not convict one of their own when race was at issue. This the Clinton Melton case seemed to have decisively proved.[50]

Milam factored far more prominently in the second story—a story so inflammatory that it would prove to be the half-brothers' undoing among local whites. On January 9, 1956, both the *Delta Democrat-Times* and the *Jackson State Times* broke the story on their front pages: according to an article to be published in the January 24 issue of *Look* magazine and authored by the Alabama reporter William Bradford Huie, Milam and Bryant had confessed to murdering Emmett Till. Both newspapers featured extensive quotes from the *Look* article, including the words that supposedly sealed Till's fate. Asked

"Like Father—Like Son" (October 1955–January 1956)

by Milam if the boy was still as good as him, Till said "yeah." Questioned if he had still "had" white women, Till answered "yeah," and Milam supposedly waxed sociopolitical: "Chicago boy, I'm tired of 'em sending your kind down here to stir up trouble. Goddam you, I'm going to make an example of you—just so everybody can know how me and my folks stand." The World War II veteran then squeezed the trigger on his Colt .45, killing Till in the early dawn along the banks of the Tallahatchie River. He defended the murder to Huie: "We never was able to scare him. They had just filled him so full of that poison he was hopeless."[51]

Many Mississippians were incredulous—and perhaps with good reason. First, surely Milam and Bryant would not confess to the crime, even if they did it, especially not in the mere span of two months since the kidnapping charges had been dropped. Second, Huie was a known "dramatist," and given his penchant for the sensational, surely this was another manifestation of his talents—even if he did hail from Alabama. And third, both men staunchly denied that they had confessed to the killing, let alone meeting someone named William Bradford Huie. Milam was so aggrieved that he claimed that he had enlisted his attorney, John Whitten, to inquire about the prospects of a libel case. Careful readers might have also been skeptical of Milam's ostensible rhetorical talents. It would take a degree of intellectual abstraction to situate and articulate what he was about to do in the context of a post-*Brown* world—to say nothing of doing it with a loaded pistol, while under the influence, and with a rapidly rising summer sun. By all accounts, Big Milam was not one for abstraction or careful rationalization; no, his talents, by his own admission, were in killing and in working negroes.[52]

As the shocking story registered with readers in Mississippi, both Milam and Bryant continued to plead ignorance. Milam was quoted in the January 14 edition of the *Clarion-Ledger*: "I don't know a damn thing about it, and you can quote me on that. . . . I never saw anyone named William Bradford Huie that I know of. . . . I've never made statements like that to anyone." Bryant was less loquacious: "It's false." Even as Congressman Diggs entered the story into the *Congressional Record*, Huie and *Look*'s general counsel John F. Harding stood staunchly by the story's accuracy. Huie would not reveal his sources for the story, but he did claim to have talked with all the "important sources" in the state.[53]

As it turns out, J. W. Milam was not adept at lying. Interviewed by Jay Milner the following day, Milam revealed that Huie "didn't quote me direct." He was also clearly reveling in celebrity-murderer status: "I'll say one thing for the article," Milam grinned, "It was written from a Mississippi viewpoint. I've gotten a lot of letters from people complimenting me for what Look said

"Like Father—Like Son" (October 1955–January 1956)

I did." As he showed Milner that day's mail—fourteen letters—Milam also revealed that two movie companies had contacted him. He was also pleased that news of Reverend George W. Lee's May 7, 1955, murder in Belzoni was finally dying down; too many race-based murders in the state was bad for business: "I think our's [sic] will get publicity for at least five more years. My lawyer said there'd be more publicity about us from now on than before."[54]

Not even in his wildest imagination could J. W. Milam have predicted that his run of fame would last more than fifty years. The story that he and his half-brother sold to Huie also had a considerable shelf life. Free from double jeopardy and even freer from the likelihood of conviction from his Mississippi peers, the story they told Huie was both fantastic and southern. It might go something like the following. Two white men with only a bit of corporal punishment on their minds had effectively been forced into action. Little did the half-brothers know when they took him from Moses Wright's residence that Emmett Till was filled with such "poison" and contempt for the southern way. They had not set out with murder on their minds, only a bit of roughhouse meant to frighten the Chicago boy. If only Till had said "no sir" with enough conviction in response to Milam's final questions, the half-brothers might well have let him find his way back to his great-uncle's home.

Such a flattering self-portrait—flattering at least to some white southerners—raised the hackles of many others, including Roy Wilkins. In a letter to the editor of *Look*, he wrote, "Look's story of the Till murder in Mississippi carries the material covering the alleged remarks and acts of the dead boy as 'facts.' Who stands by these 'facts'?" That Wilkins felt compelled to defend Emmett Till spoke volumes about the South and motive; in fact, Milam would later confess to Huie his surprise that their January 24 *Look* confession did not engender greener pastures—or a bigger cotton yield.[55]

Increasingly do we now realize that Huie had been bamboozled and *Look* hoodwinked. Thanks largely to the investigative work of filmmaker Keith Beauchamp and the FBI, the half-brothers' heroized confessional and impromptu defense of the southern way was pure hooey, so to speak. Chances are we will never know with compelling certainty what happened to Emmett Till in the early morning hours of August 28, 1955. In brazenly going public with their motives for the killing, J. W. Milam and Roy Bryant sought to defend their actions—and to reap the rewards—for killing a person whom they saw as a belligerent northern child-man intent on making a mockery of the culture's abiding premise. Who can blame their logic? They had read about such a scenario in many Mississippi newspapers for the better part of four months.

"Like Father—Like Son" (October 1955–January 1956)

At some point Mississippians accepted the fact that J. W. Milam and Roy Bryant killed Emmett Till—accepted, that is, in a strictly factual sense. Harry Dogan did, too. In the tens of thousands of pages that comprise the Mississippi State Sovereignty Commission Papers, housed at the Mississippi Department of Archives and History in Jackson and available online, sits a rather terse and curious document. The centered, all-capitals title—"Tallahatchie County"—is followed by four carefully spaced and neatly typed names appearing in table form—Melton, Clinton; Leggett, Ed; Outlaw, Clara Mae; and Till, Emmett Louis. All are listed as "Non-white," followed by the dates and causes of their deaths. The cause of Till's death is listed as "Other means." In a second neatly typed table is a list of the "persons [who] committed the homicides" listed above. Bearing not a hint of uncertainty, the document lists "J. W. Milam and Roy Bryant, White" as the killers. The document is dated somewhat officially, "This 3rd. day of October, 1956." It bears the signature of H. H. Dogan, sheriff of Tallahatchie County.

Minus even the hint of an explanation, this laconic text provides a fitting close to this part of our study. Perhaps we may also consider it the urtext of Mississippi's protracted and ongoing efforts to come to terms with its racist past. The identity of the corpse is not in doubt. Based on the condition of that corpse, Emmett certainly died by "other means" than a gunshot. J. W. Milam and Roy Bryant unequivocally committed the murder. Race likely played a role. And, most importantly, the signature of Sheriff Strider's successor transforms the document from a banal table to a state document. A list converted to official acknowledgment, perhaps even, in its recalcitrant margins, a confession of culpability—perhaps.

Eight

Retrospective Prospects

With the gallons of ink spilled in Mississippi on the Emmett Till case, it is easy to forget that it all started with some playful adolescent boasts among friends and family on a hot summer evening near a ribbon of road in a nowhere southern town. It is also easy to forget the awful tragedy that ensued: turning Emmett Till into an object of discourse is to transform him into something more and something less than what he was. He was a slightly heavy fourteen-year-old boy who looked forward to the eighth grade, loved baseball, nice clothes, his adoring mother, and others' attention. He hated picking cotton and found the Jim Crow south a strange place. Clearly, he did not fully recognize what it meant to have black skin in the Mississippi Delta in 1955; he was too busy having a good time. Somehow these important flesh-and-blood details get obscured following the events of August 28. In spilling our own ink on those events, we acknowledge our own complicity in the inexorable depersonalization that language can perform.

The Mississippi press quickly transformed Emmett Till and the details of his kidnap and murder for its own rhetorical ends. The story was a local kidnap-murder case for all of three days; in less than three weeks it became a regional, national, and international story. But nowhere was the story more discussed, analyzed, and fought over than in Mississippi; in so many different ways it is a uniquely Mississippi story. Given such intense scrutiny leading up to the trial, to say nothing of the involvement by the outgoing governor, Hugh White, we might logically conclude that justice would have been forthcoming. Such a conclusion, of course, misses the point entirely: as the press discourse surrounding the case grew more fevered, it became clear that white (and some black) Mississippians and a way of life were on trial. Milam and Bryant just happened to be proxies; they realized this rather quickly as they attempted to cash in on their celebrity and supposed "good looks." *Brown* had punctured a region's way of life created nearly sixty years earlier by Black Codes, Homer Plessy's seating preferences, and a prosegregation Supreme Court. Little wonder that a stout black kid with a slight stuttering problem could become, for southerners, the face of the perceived northern black menace in a single, though rather attenuated, news cycle.

Retrospective Prospects

One of the important rhetorical outcomes of the Mississippi press' defense of a system whose foundation was built with the bricks and mortar of white supremacy was exposure; that is, with each editorial and letter to the editor, others could glimpse the tortured logic and insidious assumptions of a way of life that ran counter to America's most powerful and enduring myths. It is hardly surprising that many in the Mississippi press called belatedly for a collective forgetting when it came to the Till case and its aftermath; all the talk exposed a way of life paternalistic at best and genocidal at worst. That such talk occurred within the volatile context of the cold war only called unwanted attention to Mississippi's caste system. Much more was exposed than just a nude corpse when it came out of the Tallahatchie River on August 31. With the Mississippi press as unwitting accomplices, Emmett got his revenge, eventually.

After the sensational revelations in William Bradford Huie's *Look* piece and a follow-up one year later, the Emmett Till story remained relatively fallow for decades. Aside from an occasional mention or an anniversary article, the media, Mississippi's included, moved on to other civil-rights events—Autherine Lucy's attempt to integrate the University of Alabama, the ongoing bus boycott in Montgomery led by a young, eloquent Baptist preacher, which had also inspired a similar boycott in Florida's capital city of Tallahassee, and school integration in places such as Sturgis and Clay, Kentucky, and Clinton, Tennessee. Still later, the news media would fan out into southern cities such as Little Rock, Nashville, Atlanta, Greensboro, Oxford, Danville, Jackson, Birmingham, Albany, and Selma. Gradually, the many disparate stories about race and the struggle for equality were grouped under the labels "civil-rights movement" or "black freedom movement." To this day, the years between 1954 and 1968 are designated by such terms, as if the many events during this period were part of a larger, carefully orchestrated series of strategies and tactics.

Most historians of the period understand the singular term "movement" as a convenient, if misleading, fiction; its use suggests a coherence and coordination when in fact incoherence and a lack of coordination are hallmarks of the period. But even to use the term "period" is to fall victim to the same logic. What then becomes of pioneers such as Frederick Douglass, Booker T. Washington, W. E. B. DuBois, Ida Wells, James Weldon Johnson, Marcus Garvey, and A. Philip Randolph? Were they not part of a movement for civil rights? And what of leaders such as Elijah Muhammad and Malcolm X and organizations such as the Deacons for Defense? Does a method of nonviolent resistance disqualify them as movement participants?

Retrospective Prospects

A movement for civil rights, in sum, has beginnings and endings, heroes and villains, defeats and triumphs. These are rhetorical conventions, less the stuff of "objective" history and more the staples of compelling drama. In the last twenty years and for the foreseeable future, a black fourteen-year-old boy stands uncontested at the head of the civil-rights movement. These days, Emmett Till has become something of an historiographical cliché: he was the "spark" or "catalyst" for what would become the civil-rights movement. What better way to begin a story of a nation's—not just the South's—redemption than with the brutal violence inflicted upon an unsuspecting black boy visiting relatives? *Brown* was but text; Emmett was flesh and blood. As Mamie Till would later proclaim in her memoir's subtitle, her son's murder had "changed America."[1]

We do not think so. Nor do we think that Emmett Till "sparked" the movement. The metaphor answers the need of many to locate a source of the movement, for without a spark there is no fire and without Emmett Till, so the logic goes, the civil-rights "movement" must await some other founding origin, or perhaps it does not begin at all. But by elevating Emmett Till to the status of founding cause we redeem an injustice, we right an awful wrong. In so doing, we should also realize that a nation's collective memory, however belatedly, is simultaneously being shaped. We would certainly agree that the massive media coverage of the murder and trial and the lack of justice in the case have contributed significantly to its appeal; in fact, it is hard to imagine contemporary documentary work bearing on the trial if it weren't for the extensive film footage shot in Sumner. Even so, we are left with the rather inconvenient fact that for thirty years the story did not hold much interest for scholars, playwrights, poets, and especially politicians. Somewhere in that thirty years the facts bearing on the case did not change. We did, though.

The modification in civil-rights memory to feature Till's murder lacks a single cause; rather, the change is a result of a three-tiered transformation, a series of partially linked trends centered on a reinterpretation of history and a desire for belated justice. These include the somewhat recent acknowledgment of Emmett Till's significance within academia, the attempts by several government entities to rectify complicity with civil-rights-era violence, and, finally, the spread of Emmett Till public memorials. While each of these has played an important role in the process of writing and rewriting Till into history, the memorials to Till are most in need of careful examination. Memorials often sneak under the radar of explicit analysis; their role as purveyors of official "truth" and "history" is often neglected. Yet a careful look at

Retrospective Prospects

public memorials also demonstrates important complexities and contingencies bearing on the case. They also tell us something of ourselves in relation to a troubled past.

Many of the memorials to Emmett Till are symbolic namings and renamings. Similar to the rhetorical work performed by more traditional forms of public memory enacted in bricks and mortar, such naming projects not only call our attention to a person and a past but can also "stand in" for others who might have suffered a similar fate; in this sense are they synecdochic—and thus very partial representations of a complicated history. For example, in the summer of 2005, the U.S. Senate passed a resolution apologizing for not having approved antilynching legislation in the past. The Senate had multiple opportunities to pass such legislation in the twentieth century, but the attempts were typically blocked by southern Senators. Ida B. Wells, the NAACP, and many others lobbied Congress tirelessly, only to see their efforts thwarted. The Senate's apology brought Emmett Till's name to the center: one of the featured speakers in the Senate hall during the presentation of the resolution to the media was none other than Simeon Wright, cousin of Emmett Till and the person with whom Till shared a bed on the night of August 28, 1955. Wright's presence was symbolic, as the remembrance of Till revivified the hope of reconciliation; it also reminded the audience that these lynching horrors of the past took place within living memory. But why not a member of Mack Charles Parker's family, a Mississippian brutally lynched in Poplarville, Mississippi, in 1959? Why not relatives of Mickey Schwerner, Andrew Goodman, or James Chaney, murdered by a police-Klan cabal in June of 1964? Was Simeon Wright's presence a proxy for Emmett Till, or did his appearance coincide from the Justice Department's new interest in the case?

The memorial-filled summer of 2005 did not end with the Senate's apology. The new evidence from Keith Beauchamp's documentary *The Untold Story of Emmett Louis Till*, the Justice Department's actions, and the ensuing exhumation of Till's body from Burr Oak Cemetery led two Senators to successfully sponsor the appropriately named "Till Bill," legislation designed to create an Unresolved Crimes Section of the Civil Rights Division in the Department of Justice. Emmett's name would now come to embody the hope and possibility of renewed justice, perhaps against the odds. Again, similar questions arise: Why not the Henry Dee and Charles Moore Bill, referring to two black men murdered by the Klan near Natchez in May of 1964? Or, why not the Hubert Orsby (Herbert Oarsby?) Bill for the headless youth found wearing a CORE T-shirt in the Big Black River in the summer of 1964?

On a broader scale, the case of Emmett Till is one of many attempts by the

Retrospective Prospects

federal government at working towards the resolution of, and reconciliation for, horrific crimes of the civil-rights era. More specifically, Till has come to embody many of the complications of contemporary racial reconciliation: potentially clashing notions of forgiveness, hope, justice, and truth. His repeated memorialization in contemporary reconciliation discourse has helped make him a civil-rights celebrity of the twenty-first century, thus elevating his status in public memory. As the public becomes more familiar with Emmett vis-à-vis contemporary calls for justice, knowledge of him and what took place in Leflore and Tallahatchie Counties in the summer of 1955 takes root; retrospectively it educates a new generation as to the horrors of the Jim Crow South.

Justice for civil-rights-era crimes is not the only component of the public memory puzzle. Another means of rewriting Till into the dominant civil-rights narrative has been sculptures recalling the deceased Emmett. For some time, the only Till memorial was in Colorado. This memorial, in the form of a sculpture of Till with Martin Luther King, resided in Denver for twenty-six years before being moved to the Pueblo, Colorado, Martin Luther King Cultural Center. Emmett Till's name, along with those of thirty-nine others, also appears on Maya Lin's national civil-rights memorial in Montgomery, Alabama.

As we noted earlier, in February of 2005, the Mississippi state legislature approved a bill that included renaming a thirty-two-mile portion of U.S. Highway 49 East as the Emmett Till Memorial Highway. Additionally, there is a movement underway by several Mississippians for the creation of a "Till Trail," which would lead tourists to sites related to the kidnap, murder, and trial, spurring the restoration of dilapidated structures such as the Bryant Grocery and Meat Market. The Leflore County supervisors have also agreed to establish an Emmett Till memorial on the county courthouse lawn—the same lawn where local lawmen protected J. W. Milam and Roy Bryant in September of 1955. Such belated dedications to Till are not confined to the Magnolia State. Emmett's hometown of Chicago has several Till memorials, including the naming and dedication of Emmett Till Road, the Emmett Till Bridge, and the Emmett Till Math and Science Academy. The most recent memorial includes a modest brick church on South State Street—the site where Emmett's mutilated corpse was so famously put on display.

The relatively recent spate of Till memorials is a significant indicator of a shift in the rhetorical landscape of civil-rights history. The memorials parallel the other means of writing Till into public memory—academic inquiry and belated justice. One Till memorial in particular helps us untangle some of the complexities that these memorials embody and reproduce. On

Retrospective Prospects

February 10, 2005, the conservative Mississippi State Senate unanimously approved a bill that would rename a portion of Mississippi 19 South as the Chaney, Goodman, and Schwerner Memorial Highway, along with the portion of U.S. Highway 49 East to be named the Emmett Till Memorial Highway. These civil-rights memorials were amendments to a larger piece of highway legislation. Unanimous Senate passage prompted Lieutenant Governor Amy Tuck to exclaim, "It will go a long way in promoting race relations in our state." Similarly, Senator Gloria Williamson of Philadelphia, Mississippi, stated, "They gave their lives for freedom. This is part of our way of acknowledging that we are sorry that it happened." Likewise, Jewel McDonald of the Philadelphia Coalition commented that "this is the first time something has been done in their honor. This shows me Mississippi is ready to move on." While many accounts paint such memorials as signs of honor and tribute, they also signify a larger rhetorical process: an attempt at reconciliation.[2]

Reconciliation is still a highly contested concept. This is especially true in relation to reconciliation for American racism. Where varying interpretations of history exist and many parties are interested in "leaving the past in the past," achieving reconciliation is no small feat. More than fifty years later, Mississippi is still struggling to "move on" from the brutal murder of Till and the ensuing legal injustice. Proponents of the highway memorial claim that it represents a crucial step by Mississippi to apologize, or reconcile, this racial injustice. But does a civil-rights memorial truly constitute reconciliation? Can it? The discursive landscape and pragmatic considerations of Mississippi politics threaten to undermine the sincerity of reconciliation. In short, creation of the Emmett Till Memorial Highway is commendable; however, it is not nearly enough to bring the kind of closure on the Till case that many advocates seem to be seeking.[3]

The Till Memorial Highway exemplifies a victory for previously counter-hegemonic conceptions of history. Although Till's murderers confessed to the killing, the state of Mississippi never issued an official apology; the landscape of the Delta region was absent a form of *memorial* acknowledgement of Till's murder until the highway sign. By formally inserting Till's name into the landscape, African-Americans of Mississippi assert a place of physical ownership in a landscape where this has traditionally been prohibited. The sign is a demonstration of black political strength in a former "place-of-trauma." It signifies that African-Americans have appropriated authority over space and place in the region. Additionally, the placement of the sign in traditionally white space challenges the "privileged status of white history."[4]

The Emmett Till Memorial Highway simultaneously authorizes a once-

Retrospective Prospects

contested interpretation of history and reminds Mississippians of the reality of the not-so-distant past. It also refutes the rhetoric of those who would continue to deny or even question the events of Till's abduction and murder. As Paul Hendrickson notes in his book *Sons of Mississippi*, many locals continue to deny that the body found in the Tallahatchie was that of Till. A local commented to Hendrickson in Money, "I was a year out of high school. I was walking past my grandmama's bridge game. I just overheard one of the women say to the others that when Emmett Till's mama . . . went into the mortuary for the first time to look at the body, she started screaming before she even got inside the door, 'That's my baby! That's my baby!' Now I know that's true." Thus, the highway memorial represents a form of state-sanctioned autobiography of Mississippi where Till is written into the landscape, finally writing over vestiges of Jim Crow "local knowledge." Public memory theorist Edward S. Casey surmises that state memorializations such as the Till Highway are significant due to their location in public space. The Emmett Till Memorial Highway is public, thus signifying "that it is out in the open, in the *koinos cosmos* where discussion with others is possible—whether on the basis of chance encounters or planned meetings—but also where one is exposed and vulnerable, where one's limitations and fallibilities are all too apparent." This openness on the landscape disables individual and collective amnesia, whether deliberate or accidental.[5]

The positive discourse surrounding the outcome of the Senate bill to create the Emmett Till Memorial Highway and its unanimous passage suggests that a degree of forgiveness and apology must have occurred by various stakeholders. But after conducting a phone interview with Mississippi State Senator Robert Jackson, we became aware that the bill's passage was a bit more complicated, perhaps even disappointing. He noted that the passage was a "fluke kind of deal" that capitalized on chance timing. Nevertheless, he expressed a significant degree of optimism and enthusiasm for the legislation, noting that it was more reconciliation than concerned Mississippians could have hoped for.[6]

The Memorial is a symbolic reparation, with significance intensified by its placement on a racialized landscape, proximate to the terrain of Emmett's brutal murder in the summer of 1955. While this inference would certainly make for an easy closure for reconciliation, the reality is far from being this simple. Political considerations, sustained white hegemony in Mississippi, and other factors complicate the Till Memorial as *coherent* reconciliation.

As to political considerations, it should come as no surprise that the Mississippi state legislature could have alternative motives for memorializing Till. The obvious objection is that memorials confine racism to the past rather

Retrospective Prospects

than acknowledging its contemporary manifestations. Southern historian W. Fitzhugh Brundage is optimistic about the changing southern landscape; however, he cautions that it is difficult to measure the sincerity behind the opening of black spaces in the South: "Pragmatic political considerations, as well as economic interests, provided the impetus for the revision of southern promotional strategies. For white politicians eager to put the tumult and recriminations of the civil rights struggle behind them, the promotion of 'heritage' tourism was of a piece with their efforts to publicize the 'New' Sunbelt South. They pointed to the commercialization of black history as a gesture of reconciliation and progress." Brundage's point about tourism should not be overlooked; many southern states have begun to incorporate civil-rights landmarks into the landscape as a means of attracting tourists. Brundage even notes that "survey data, which revealed that blacks spend more money than other tourists, caught the eye of public officials eager to use tourism to revitalize depressed communities across the South's hinterland." Owen Dwyer has also shown how large memorials in the South have been strategically placed in segregated communities—and with tourism on the political agenda.[7]

Applied to the Till Memorial, this politicoeconomic interpretation seems apt. Perhaps the memorial is a way of capitalizing on the growing awareness of Till, a means of bringing tourists into the surrounding impoverished counties. Even Senator David Jordan, who represents nearby Greenwood and was one of the amendment's sponsors, acknowledges that the dilapidated Bryant store already receives regular tourists (including us). But tourism alone hardly seems like a reason to discard the hope of reconciliation. In defense against this political tourism challenge, perhaps one could say that the memorial "kills two birds with one stone": Till is honored and the region gets a much-needed economic boost. Reconciliation in the context of increased tourism may depend on the benefactors of civil-rights tourism with regard to race, class, and provenance (local or "foreign").[8]

A second challenge to symbolic reparation for the Till case is a resistive or "non-authorized" reading of the highway memorial. Given that Till's murderers were acquitted, his death arguably symbolizes unresolved violence and a form of white power. The sign could be read as a warning about race relations to passers-by. Additionally, there is no guarantee that visitors or locals will interpret the sign in the empowering and eulogizing manner that its supporters clearly intended. As Karen Till acknowledges, "The recent popularity of places of memory as tourist sites does not indicate that visitors accept the narratives exhibited, or that they share uniform interpretations and experiences of these places." This compromises the coherence of the symbolic reparation itself; there is simply no guarantee that every traveler will interpret the memorial as a form of restitution or commemoration. Furthermore, the Till Memorial Highway differs from other, more traditional memorials in that "visitors" do not travel to a site for the sole purpose of experiencing it. Not a few people with racist views probably still live between Tutwiler and Greenwood and are therefore effectively coerced into a rhetorical exchange of which they want no part.[9]

Given such considerations, it is hardly surprising that a Till Memorial Highway sign was recently defaced. In June of 2006 someone registered a counterreading of the state's authorized memory project: the vandal spray-painted a red "KKK" on the prominent blue sign. This defacement demonstrates more than just a cowardly act of racism. Just as the sign molds public memory by praising a martyr, the acronym suggests that some are unwilling to accept Emmett Till on the still-racialized Mississippi landscape. A stealthy minority does not want to embrace the new, officially sanctioned history and wants to make this known.[10]

Another challenge to reconciliation is tied to the contemporary conception of *forgiveness*. In the case of Emmett Till, forgiveness is complicated for several reasons. The most apparent reason lies in the extreme brutality wrought upon Till at the age of fourteen. The visual display of Emmett's battered face was incredibly jarring, leaving a permanent scar for many. Additionally, scholars frequently refer to Till as a martyr, a "sacrificial lamb" of the civil-rights movement. Similarly, the Reverend Jesse Jackson asserts that Emmett Till's death was the "big bang" of the civil-rights movement. The memory of his death is a unique blend of horror at the atrocity and injustice of Mississippi racism and awareness that his death was an important "spark" that galvanized black America in the 1950s. By rhetorically constructing Till as a martyr for the movement, the violent offenders are not absolved of their violent acts, but it can be argued that reconciliation over a martyr requires less forgiveness, as the ends in "20/20 hindsight" implicitly destabilize objections to the means. That is, the outcome of erosion of Jim Crow, increased civil rights for African Americans, and other advancements could enable a form of forgiveness for the Till murder and state-sanctioned complicity.[11]

One final challenge to the reconciliatory potential of the Emmett Till Memorial Highway is the scope of the audience. At the local level, the establishment of the memorial received a considerable amount of news coverage. In the national news, the memorial's creation was overshadowed by the exhumation and the FBI's reopening of the investigation. The psychological violence inflicted upon black America outside of Mississippi did not reap the rewards of the reconciliation effort of the Mississippi legislature. With the

Retrospective Prospects

exception of tourists driving through the Delta on the proposed "Till Trail," the memorialization is a highly localized event.

This issue of audience for the Till memorial is also linked to different group expectations about appropriate responses. In their analysis of the Truth and Reconciliation Commission of South Africa, Adam and Adam identify two broad categories of abuses and their expected reconciliatory outcomes: historical injustice and contemporary abuses. The former entails violence from "a long time ago . . . [where] the best way of doing justice to the collective legacy is by keeping the memory of the injustice alive and mourning the victims through political education about the historical crime." The Mississippi legislators that passed the Till Memorial amendment treated the decision as such: something of the *past* that needs to be recognized. Contemporary abuses, not surprisingly, demand some form of "justice through legal recourse, as well as the development of new institutions to facilitate reconciliation . . . or peaceful coexistence." The fact that the excitement about the potential prosecution of Carolyn Bryant—now Carolyn Donham—and others was so strong suggests that these proponents treat reconciliation as a blend of historical and contemporary abuses, rather than solely historical. Because possible parties to the crime are still alive and free problematizes the notion that Till's murder is *only* a historical injustice. Thus, these two different frameworks for understanding abuse and proper restitution may create cleavages in reconciliation. For example, many white Mississippians may be reluctant to embrace the necessity of *contemporary* justice, because they see Till's murder as a regrettable event of the past. If these competing frameworks split down black-white racial lines, reconciliation will be dealt another blow.[12]

As an isolated act, the Emmett Till Memorial Highway represents a significant stride toward reconciling a traumatic act of violence and the ensuing state complicity. The memorial is a powerful symbolic reparation as it inserts counterhegemonic black memories into a traditionally white-dominated landscape. However, as demonstrated by these challenges to reconciliation, the issue is infused with complexities that threaten to strip the reparation of its sincerity. Reconciliation of this civil-rights-era race-based murder is complicated by its status as a national trauma. Regardless of the challenges to reconciliation, the criticisms lodged against the memorial are ultimately displaced by the symbolic power of the sign. It functions as visual and state-sanctioned confirmation of the formerly displaced memories born in 1955. We are not suggesting that a highway sign is enough to close the Till case and move on. To the contrary, the memorial's significance lies in its ability to foster a public dialogue about what happened to Emmett Till—and, more

Retrospective Prospects

important, the conditions under which it could have happened. Mississippi's willingness to expose its Jim Crow skeletons for all to see is indeed a bold maneuver.

Back in Webb, Mississippi, Emmett Till once again intersects with Sheriff H. C. Strider, who "welcomed" the few African-American journalists covering the Till murder trial with a "good morning, niggers." From the perspective of racial reconciliation in the American South, the Till and Strider highway memorials' intersection could not be more appropriate. It captures the contradictions between history and memory, and the revisioning process in the face of sociopolitical changes. In short, public memory is exposed as an active and dynamic process that is susceptible to an array of social forces, rather than an objective and static phenomenon.[13]

The manifestations of Emmett Till's rebirth into the American conscience —academic interest, the government's recent attempts at justice and reconciliation, and public memorials—are undeniably interdependent. The reopening of the Till case creates the potential for greater academic examination of the murder. Academic interest in the form of books, journal articles, and conferences, has spawned public knowledge about a race-based murder that many never knew happened. Greater public awareness of Till makes public memorials more likely as new generations gain an appreciation for his unique role in stirring the sentiments of an emerging civil-rights movement. As Till's rebirth continues to develop, the likelihood that he will enjoy a privileged space in civil-rights history only grows.

In Montgomery, Alabama, the national Civil Rights Memorial designed by Maya Lin in front of the Southern Poverty Law Center also tells a narrative of civil-rights history. The forty most significant martyrs of the civil-rights movement are engraved into this attractive yet simple memorial. Emmett Till made the list. But whether it is a blue highway sign in Minter City or majestic black granite in Montgomery, the point about history—namely, civil-rights history—should be clear: the dominant historical narrative of this movement highlights a few key persons or events, while others remain in a representational void. Many stories of struggle, perseverance, and even death remain untold. Some of the best-known chapters in the civil-rights movement—those concerning *Brown v. Board of Education*, Rosa Parks, and Martin Luther King, Jr.—may get revised. The public's memory of the kidnapping and murder of Emmett Till continues to grow as the spotlight on his importance shines brighter. The bloated corpse has been pulled out of the Tallahatchie River once again as a new readership shows a willingness to revisit a murder so many hoped to forget.

Finally, what of the Mississippi press? Perhaps it should come as no surprise that given the outcome of the legal proceedings and the *Look* confessions, many simply wanted to avoid the subject of Emmett Till. In one of the first "anniversary" newspaper articles about the case, *Jackson State Times* reporter Al Kuettner tried to interview some of the Mississippi protagonists. Few apparently wanted to talk, and, of those who did, former Leflore County Sheriff George Smith offered remarks that were particularly revelatory about what the case had already come to mean just two years after the murder: "I hate to even mention the case. . . . Don't quote me on anything. I don't want my name ever printed again in connection with the people involved in this case." Smith's striking nonquote links to the state's contemporary profusion of Emmett Till memorialization projects. Given a past unwillingness to talk publicly about the case—many principals have never said a public word after the trial—the state's verbosity on the subject of Emmett Till today makes sense. Suppressed discourse can remain suppressed only for so long; taboo subjects are eventually relieved of that status by a new generation, one perhaps not freighted with the guilt, anger, and resentment of its parents.[14]

The changes more than fifty years later are breathtaking. To invoke even the designation "white Mississippi press" is a quaint anachronism. Reporters and editors are interracial. Editors such as the *Greenwood Commonwealth's* Tim Kalich write forcefully on the sins of the newspaper even as they celebrate the lessons of Emmett Till. At the *Clarion-Ledger*, which long ago merged with the *Jackson Daily News*, reporters such as Jerry Mitchell not only report on the state's civil-rights past but provide important investigatory details crucial in prosecuting the likes of Byron de la Beckwith and Edgar Ray Killen. Mitchell was also key in getting a posthumous exoneration for Clyde Kennard, falsely imprisoned for nearly four years over a twenty-five-dollar bag of chicken feed when in fact his real offense was applying to the all-white Mississippi Southern College (now the University of Southern Mississippi). Gone are the race-baiting likes of Thomas Alewine, Fred Sullens, Virgil Adams, David Bready, Bill Spell, and C. H. Cole. Gone, too, are the carefully segregated sections of newspapers that featured "colored news" and news from "colored circles." And gone are the suggestive shots of young and white southern belles.

If the Mississippi press has changed dramatically, so too have its educational institutions; in fact, no other state can boast of the historical resources related to race relations in quite the way that Mississippi can. In Oxford is the William Winter Institute for Racial Reconciliation. Also on the Ole Miss campus, the university's special collections department houses myriad civil-rights holdings, including the recently opened papers of James H. Meredith and James O. Eastland. In Jackson, the Mississippi Department of Archives

Retrospective Prospects

and History has innumerable holdings bearing on the state's racial past, perhaps none more valuable than the State Sovereignty Commission Papers; it also recently opened the Medgar and Myrlie Evers Collection. And downstate in Hattiesburg, at the University of Southern Mississippi, the McCain Library and Archives has made a vast collection of civil-rights-related oral histories available online.

Of course a Chicago boy was not alone in changing Mississippi's racial landscape; he had help from local people spread across the state, including racist whites and prosegregation blacks. And yet it is Emmett Till who still draws "outsiders" like us to gaze upon and trespass the sacred ruins of the Bryant Grocery and Meat Market still hard by the railroad tracks in depopulated Money, straining to hear the voice of the "big talkin'" Bobo and to holler a warning about what awaited him inside.

Notes

Introduction

1. Paul Hendrickson, *Sons of Mississippi: A Story of Race and Its Legacy* (New York: Vintage, 2004), 5–6.

2. *Eyes on the Prize's* opening segment, "Awakenings," begins in earnest with the Emmett Till case; it was broadcast on PBS in 1987 and rebroadcast in the fall of 2006. Whitfield's book was published by the Free Press in 1988. Other books bearing directly on the case include Clenora Hudson-Weems, *Emmett Till: The Sacrificial Lamb of the Civil Rights Movement*, 3rd ed. (Troy, MI: Bedford, 2000); Mamie Till-Mobley and Christopher Benson, *Death of Innocence: The Story of the Hate Crime That Changed America* (New York: One World, 2003); Chris Crowe, *Getting Away with Murder: The True Story of the Emmett Till Case* (New York: Fogelman, 2003); Marilyn Nelson, *A Wreath for Emmett Till* (Boston: Houghton Mifflin, 2005); and Christopher Metress, ed., *The Lynching of Emmett Till: A Documentary Narrative* (Charlottesville, VA: University of Virginia Press, 2002). There are very recent, very public disputes over scholarship and the Till case. Clenora Hudson-Weems, in *The Definitive Emmett Till: Passion and Battle of a Woman for Intellectual Justice* (Bloomington, IN: Authorhouse, 2006), claims that many scholars have plagiarized from her work; she also claims to be the most important scholar writing on the Till case. She remains adamant that no black men participated in the Till lynching—despite Keith Beauchamp's painstaking and intrepid detective work and despite the fact that she actually claims Leroy "Too Tight" Collins accompanied Milam and Bryant to the Wright house on August 28; see Hudson-Weems, *Emmett Till*, 3rd ed., 39.

3. Throughout the book we will refer to Emmett Till's mother as Mamie Till; this is to avoid confusion with her legal married name during the trial—Mamie Bradley—and her later legal married name of Mamie Till-Mobley.

4. John Dittmer, *Local People: The Struggle for Civil Rights in Mississippi* (Champagne, IL: University of Illinois Press, 1994); Steven R. Goldzwig, "Multiculturalism, Rhetoric, and the Twenty-first Century," *Southern Communication Journal* 63 (1998): 273–90.

5. Davis W. Houck, "Killing Emmett," *Rhetoric and Public Affairs* 8 (2005): 225–62. We were able to assemble this broad array of newspaper coverage from the excellent archive at the Mississippi Department of Archives and History (MDAH) in Jackson. While they did not have a microfilm record of every state newspaper, the MDAH is without peer in archiving and preserving Mississippi's written journalism. For a narrative of the case using several Mississippi and Memphis-area newspapers, see William M. Simpson, "Reflections on a Murder: The Emmett Till Case," in *Southern Miscellany: Essays in History in Honor of Glover Moore*, ed. Frank Allen Dennis, (Jackson, MS: University Press of Mississippi, 1981), 177–200. For additional analyses of press coverage of the Till case, see Warren Breed, "Comparative Newspaper Handling of the Emmett Till Case," *Journalism Quarterly* 35 (1958): 291–98; and John Craig Flournoy, "Reporting the Movement in Black and White: The Emmett Till Lynching and the Montgomery Bus Boycott" (PhD diss., Louisiana State

Notes

University, 2003). For the televisual importance of the Till case, see Sasha Torres, *Black, White, and In Color: Television and Black Civil Rights* (Princeton, NJ: Princeton University Press, 2003), 1–35. For a recollection of three reporters who covered the trial, see John R. Tisdale, "Different Assignments, Different Perspectives: How Reporters Reconstruct the Emmett Till Civil Rights Murder Trial," *Oral History Review* 29 (2002): 39–58.

6. For an excellent history of the black press in Mississippi, see Julius E. Thompson, *The Black Press in Mississippi, 1865–1985* (Gainesville, FL: University Press of Florida, 1993). For details of Percy Greene and the *Jackson Advocate*, see Julius E. Thompson, *Percy Greene and the Jackson Advocate: The Life and Times of a Radical Conservative Black Newspaperman, 1897–1977* (Jefferson, NC: McFarland, 1994); and Caryl A. Cooper, "Percy Greene and the *Jackson Advocate*," in *The Press and Race: Mississippi Journalists Confront the Movement*, ed. David R. Davies (Jackson, MS: University Press of Mississippi, 2001), 54–83.

7. For an analysis of photographs bearing on the case, see Jacqueline Goldsby, "The High and Low Tech of It: The Meaning of Lynching and the Death of Emmett Till," *Yale Journal of Criticism* 9 (1996): 245–82.

8. Kenneth Burke, *A Grammar of Motives* (Berkeley, CA: University of California Press, 1968), 59. For Burke's discussion of terministic screens, see Kenneth Burke, *Language as Symbolic Action: Essays on Life, Literature, and Method* (Berkeley, CA: University of California Press, 1966), 44–62.

Chapter 1. "Sowing Seeds of Hatred" (August 28–September 1)

1. Clark Porteous, "Grand Jury to Get Case of Slain Negro Boy Monday," *Memphis Press-Scimitar*, September 1, 1955, 1+.

2. Moses Wright quoted in "328 Attend 'Protest' of Till Killing," *Arizona Republic*, November 20, 1955, n.p.

3. In her memoir, Peggy Morgan recounts life growing up in the impoverished Albritton family of Greenwood, Mississippi. Interspersed with the details of spousal abuse, alcoholism, petty crime, and poverty is the hint of an affair between her father, Gene, and Carolyn Bryant. Morgan also claims that her mother's mental problems stemmed from her insider knowledge of the Till murder. See Carolyn Haines, *My Mother's Witness* (Fairbanks, AK: River City Press, 2003).

4. "Chicago Negro Youth Abducted by Three White Men at Money," *Greenwood Commonwealth*, August 28, 1955, 1; "White Orders Boy's Death Investigated; Woman's Arrest Ordered in Tallahatchie County," *Clarksdale Press Register*, September 1, 1955, 1+; "Negro Youth's Slaying Slated for Grand Jury Monday while NAACP Pours Wrath on State," *Laurel Leader-Call*, September 1, 1955, 1+.

5. Details of the dialogue in the Wright house emerged during and after the trial. One of the best sources on what transpired in the house comes from a tape-recorded statement that Moses Wright made on October 25, 1955. See "I Saw Them Take Emmett Till," *Inside Detective*, February 1956, 26+. We are grateful to Devery Anderson for sharing this source with us.

6. "White Storekeeper Held in Abduction of Negro Youth," *Jackson Daily News*, August 29, 1955, 1; "Two Greenwood Men Arrested Monday on Kidnapping Charges,"

Notes

Grenada Daily Sentinel-Star, August 30, 1955, 1; "Unable to Find Young Negro Boy," *Biloxi Daily Herald*, August 30, 1955, 17.

7. Crawford makes this controversial claim in the DVD release of Keith Beauchamp's documentary *The Untold Story of Emmett Louis Till* (New York: Till Freedom Come Productions, THINKFilm, 2005).

8. Dittmer, *Local People*, 1–18.

9. "Chicago Negro Youth," 1.

10. "White Man Held in Abduction of Negro Youth," *Hattiesburg American*, August 29, 1955, 9; "White Storekeeper Held," 1; "Charged Greenwood Storekeeper with Abducting Youth," *Delta Democrat-Times*, August 29, 1955, 2.

11. "Claim Release Boy Unharmed," *Meridian Star*, August 30, 1955, 1; "Two White Men Charged with Kidnaping Negro," *Delta Democrat-Times*, August 30, 1955, 1; "Parents and Relatives Keep Silent in Case of Boy Charged with Ugly Remarks to Storekeeper[']s Wife," *Jackson Advocate*, September 3, 1955, 1+.

12. "Kidnap-Murder Case Will Be Transferred to Tallahatchie," *Greenwood Commonwealth*, September 1, 1955, 1; "Find Missing Youth's Body; Blow On Head Killed Him," *Clarksdale Press Register*, August 31, 1955, 1; "Negro Boy's Slaying to Grand Jury," *Biloxi Daily Herald*, September 1, 1955, 1+; "Find Body Of Missing Boy in State River," *Meridian Star*, August 31, 1955, 1+. In her memoir, Mamie Till states that her relative Rayfield Mooty was instrumental in securing political and press interest in the case. See Mamie Till-Mobley and Christopher Benson, *Death of Innocence: The Story of the Hate Crime That Changed America* (New York: One World, 2003), 147. In commenting on the media's interest in the story, editors at the *Southern Patriot*, the newspaper arm of the Southern Conference Education Fund (SCEF), stated, "As bitter as it may sound, there seems little reason to doubt that if a Mississippi boy, and not a Chicago boy, had been the victim of the outrage, the incident would not have gained notice beyond the state borders and very little notice within." See "Mississippi: Many Share the Guilt," *Southern Patriot*, October 1955, 1+.

13. The picture appears in section 2, page 12 of the September 1, 1955, edition of the *Jackson Daily News*; the caption reads, "Here is 14-year-old Emmitt [sic] Louis Till of Chicago with his mother. The youth's body was found floating in the Tallahatchie River near Greenwood Wednesday." The same picture appeared in the September 2, 1955, edition of the *Vicksburg Evening Post*; it appears on the front-page. A cropped version of the photograph sits atop Till's headstone in Burr Oak Cemetery near Chicago; it is also the same image that appears on the cover of Mamie Till's memoir. For a fine reading of the theme of motherhood as it played out in reporting on the Till case, see Ruth Feldstein's *Motherhood in Black and White: Race and Sex in American Liberalism, 1930–1965* (Ithaca, NY: Cornell University Press, 2000), 86–110. For additional readings see, Susan Brownmiller, *Against Our Will: Men, Women and Rape* (New York: Simon and Schuster, 1975), 245–48; Angela Davis, *Women, Race and Class* (New York: Random House, 1981), 172–201.

14. "White Orders Boy's Death Investigated," 1+; "A Brutal Murder," *Clarksdale Press Register*, September 1, 1955, 4. For the later editorial, see "Fair Trial Fairly Reported," *Clarksdale Press Register*, September 26, 1955, 4.

15. Robert H. Brumfield, "Mississippians Are Urged to Stand, Be Counted in Actions Local Doctor Says 'White Trash' Is Perpetrating," *McComb Enterprise-Journal*,

Notes

September 1, 1955, 1. For a discussion of Emmerich and the state's racial politics, see David R. Davies, "J. Oliver Emmerich and the *McComb Enterprise-Journal*," in *The Press and Race: Mississippi Journalists Confront the Movement*, ed. Davies (Jackson, MS: University Press of Mississippi, 2001), 111–34.

16. James Featherston, "White Orders Investigation in Slaying Of Delta Negro," *Jackson Daily News*, September 1, 1955, 1; "Murder Charges against Deltans in Case of Slain Negro Boy, 14 Will Go Swiftly to Grand Jurors," *McComb Enterprise-Journal*, September 1, 1955, 1+; Prentiss Cox, "Jury to Probe Boy's Murder," *Jackson State Times*, September 1, 1955, 1A+; "Kidnap-Murder Case Will Be Transferred," 1; "NAACP Officials Launch Bitter Attack on State," *Clarion-Ledger*, September 1, 1955, 1+.

17. "NAACP Officials Launch Bitter Attack," 1+; Till-Mobley and Benson, *Death of Innocence*, 130.

18. "NAACP Charges Lynch, Council Sends Regrets," *Meridian Star*, September 1, 1955, 1.

19. "NAACP Officials Launch Bitter Attack," 1+; "Missing Negro's Body Discovered in River," *Tupelo Daily Journal*, September 1, 1955, 1; "Negro Lad's Slaying Attributed to Whistle," *Hattiesburg American*, September 1, 1955, 1; "Negro Boy's Slaying to Grand Jury," 1+; "Bryant and Milan [*sic*] Face Murder Charge in Slaying of 15 [*sic*] Year Old Negro Boy," *Greenwood Morning Star*, September 1, 1955, 1; "Negro Youth's Slaying," 1+; "Gov. Hugh White Asks Full Probe on Murder Kidnapping, Greenwood," *Delta Democrat-Times*, September 1, 1955, 1+; "'A Den Of Snakes' Youth's Mother Calls Mississippi," *Delta Democrat-Times*, September 1, 1955, 1.

20. Roy Wilkins, telegram to Hugh White, August 31, 1955 and Hugh White, telegram to Roy Wilkins, September 1, 1955, in the J. P. Coleman Papers, Box 23, Folder 3, Mississippi Department of Archives and History, Jackson, Mississippi. In its monthly publication, *The Crisis*, the NAACP voiced its more drastic condemnation: "It is a hard conclusion. But the facts make it difficult to evade. The white people of Mississippi are directly responsible for this hideous crime. It is one more casualty in their campaign of reprisal being waged against the NAACP and Negro advancement." It is also clear that this editorialist had not been reading Mississippi newspapers in the days following the abduction: "But where are they [good people]? Excepting the novelist William Faulkner, no responsible citizen has spoken out in rage and indignation." See, "Mississippi Barbarism," *Crisis*, October 1955, 480–81.

21. "NAACP Officials Launch Bitter Attack," 1+; "Gov. Hugh White Asks Full Probe," 1+; "'A Den Of Snakes,'" 1; Hugh Stephen Whitaker, "A Case Study in Southern Justice: The Murder and Trial of Emmett Till," *Rhetoric and Public Affairs* 8 (2005): 189-224.

22. "Justice Is the Answer," *Jackson State Times*, September 2, 1955, 4A.

Chapter 2. "Comely Carolyn" (September 2–September 6)

1. "Youth's Killing Labelled Murder by Governor; Full Investigation Called For in State, Elsewhere," *McComb Enterprise-Journal*, September 2, 1955, 1; "Drowsy State Delta Stirs Uneasily as 2 Governors Ask Probe in Negro Death," *Laurel Leader-Call*, September 2, 1955, 1+; "White Calls Boy's Death 'Murder; Not Lynching,'" *Jackson Daily News*, September 2, 1955, 14; "Kidnap-Murder Stirs Delta," *Clarksdale Press Register*, September 2, 1955, 1+; "Governors Ask Probe of Slaying," *Biloxi Daily Herald*,

Notes

September 2, 1955, 1+; "White Says No Lynching," *West Point Daily Times Leader*, September 2, 1955, 1.

2. "Designed to Inflame," *Jackson Daily News*, September 2, 1955, 8.

3. "Irresponsible Statement," *Laurel Leader-Call*, September 2, 1955, 4; "A Brutal Slaying," *Delta Democrat-Times*, September 2, 1955, 4; "A Just Appraisal," *Greenwood Commonwealth*, September 2, 1955, 1.

4. "Just Appraisal," 1.

5. "Mother Vows to Stand By 2 Accused Sons," *Meridian Star*, September 2, 1955, 1.

6. Robert H. Brumfield, letter to the editor, *McComb Enterprise-Journal*, September 2, 1955, 2. The photographs ran above the fold on the *Clarion-Ledger's* September 2, 1955, front page. "White Says No Lynching," 1.

7. "Mother of Pair Accused in Delta Slaying 'Will Stand By Them,'" *Jackson Daily News*, September 2, 1955, 14; "White Demands Full Probe into Murder; Mom Stands By Sons," *Delta Democrat-Times*, September 2, 1955, 1; "Mother of Accused Men Promises to Stand By Them; Dead Boy's Mother and Chicago Mayor Write President," *Grenada Daily Sentinel-Star*, September 2, 1955, 1; "'Full Prosecution' Ordered in Slaying of Negro Youth," *Tupelo Daily Journal*, September 2, 1955, 1; "Mother Vows to Stand By 2 Accused Sons," 1.

8. "Officers Hunt Evidence to Support Charges of Murder," *Meridian Star*, September 3, 1955, 1+; "Halt Hunt for Woman in Slaying," *Biloxi Daily Herald*, September 3, 1955, 1.

9. See page 1 of the *Clarion-Ledger*, September 3, 1955.

10. "'Cannot Condone' Killing," *Clarion-Ledger*, September 3, 1955, 4.

11. Till-Mobley and Benson, *Death of Innocence*, 134, 135, 139.

12. David Smothers, "Killing of Boy in Mississippi Called 'Atrocity,'" *Jackson Daily News*, September 3, 1955, 1; "Mourners, Curious Mingle at Till Rites; Abandon Search for Woman Who Figured in Case," *Clarksdale Press Register*, September 3, 1955, 1; "15,000 Attend Funeral," *Biloxi Daily Herald*, September 3, 1955, 2.

13. Smothers, "Killing of Boy", 1; "Officers Hunt Evidence," 1+.

14. "Try to Determine Spot Where Negro Was Slain," *Greenwood Morning Star*, September 3, 1955, 1.

15. "Mississippi Editors Unanimous in Deploring Delta Kidnap and Murder," *Laurel Leader-Call*, September 3, 1955, 5; "Slaying, NAACP Methods Rapped by Newspapers," *Biloxi Daily Herald*, September 3, 1955, 8.

16. "Sheriff Doubts Body That of Emmitt [sic] Till," *Jackson Daily News*, September 4, 1955, 1.

17. "P. S. To NAACP," *Jackson Daily News*, September 4, 1955, 6.

18. William Middlebrooks, "Sheriff Says Body Thousands Viewed May Not Be Till's," *Delta Democrat-Times*, September 4, 1955, 1+; "Mississippi Sheriff Voices Doubt Body Was That of Till," *Greenwood Morning Star*, September 4, 1955, 1.

19. "Sheriff Doubts Identity of Boy," *Columbus Commercial Dispatch*, September 4, 1955, 1; "Grand Jury Calls Several Witnesses in Till Murder Case; More Due to Testify; Guards at Courthouse," *Greenwood Morning Star*, September 6, 1955, 1.

20. "Officer Fears Actions Build Up Resentment," *Jackson Daily News*, September 4, 1955, 1.

21. "Doubts Body Found in River Is Till's," *Meridian Star*, September 4, 1955, 1+;

Notes

Jay Milner, "Chicago Hysteria Called Hinderance [sic] in Delta Slaying; Arrest of Negroes on Speeding Charge Sets Off Wild Rumor," *Clarion-Ledger*, September 4, 1955, 1; "Mississippi Sheriff Voices Doubt," 1.

22. "Officer Fears Actions Build Up Resentment," *Jackson Daily News*, 1; "Officer Fears Actions Build Up Resentment," *Clarion-Ledger*, September 4, 1955, 1.

23. "Troops Guarding Pair Charged with Kidnap-Murder of Negro Lad," *Delta Democrat-Times*, September 5, 1955, 1; "National Guard Called to Protect Accused Men after Outside Threats," *Greenwood Commonwealth*, September 5, 1955, 1; "Says Usual Thing for Negroes to Visit Relatives in Delta," *Jackson State Times*, September 4, 1955, 1. A photograph on the front page of the September 5 *Greenwood Commonwealth* shows John Ed Cothran at the ready with a rifle while Captain Joe Heard of the National Guard looks on.

24. "Dr. T.R.M. Howard in Chicago Limelight after Till Slaying," *Jackson Advocate*, September 10, 1955, 1+. This story carried a September 5 byline.

25. "Negro Mass March Called Rumor; Discount Doubts of Till's Identity," *Jackson State Times*, September 4, 1955, 1A; "Grand Jury Calls Several Witnesses," 1; "Guard Pair at Greenwood against Mob," *Biloxi Daily Herald*, September 5, 1955, 1+; "Kidnap-Murder Case Grand Jury to Report Today," *Natchez Democrat*, September 6, 1955, 1+.

26. "Officers Offer Different Opinions in Race Slaying; Delta Sheriff Links Murder with N.A.A.C.P.," *Tupelo Daily Journal*, September 5, 1955, 1.

27. "Officers Offer Different Opinions," 1.

28. "Troops Guarding Pair Charged," 1.

29. "Grand Jury to Call 5 More Witnesses in Kidnap-Slaying Case," *Delta Democrat-Times*, September 6, 1955, 1+; "Pair Indicted in Race Slaying," *Jackson State Times*, September 6, 1955, 1A; "Two White Men Indicted for Murder; Grand Jury Takes Action in Slaying of Chicago Negro," *Vicksburg Evening Post*, September 6, 1955, 1; "Two White Men Plead Innocent to Murder of Negro Youth," *Natchez Democrat*, September 7, 1955, 1+; "Bryant, Milam Indicted for Murder, Kidnaping by Jury in Tallahatchie," *Daily Times Leader*, September 6, 1955, 1.

30. Chester Marshall and James McBroom, "Delta Pair Indicted for Murdering Negro," *Jackson Daily News*, September 6, 1955, 1+.

31. Jay Milner, "Doctor's Testimony May Alter Inquiry," *Clarion-Ledger*, September 6, 1955, 1+.

32. The caption of the September 6 photograph in the *Clarion-Ledger* reads, "Victim of Alleged Wolf-Whistle." Emmett Till was "reported" to have done the whistling. The picture is accompanied with the statement "A body believed to be Till's was found in [the] Tallahatchie [R]iver on Aug. 31."

33. Henry Harris, "Pencil Shavings," *West Point Daily Times Leader*, September 6, 1955, 4.

34. "Lynching Post-Facto," *Delta Democrat-Times*, September 6, 1955, 4; "Meddling in Local Case Creates Problems," *Greenwood Morning Star*, September 6, 1955, 4. John R. Tisdale claims that Hodding Carter did not write this or other Till editorials in September as he was on vacation in Maine. See Tisdale, "Different Assignments, Different Perspectives," 44 n14.

35. "Indict 2 Men Charged with Youth's Death," *Meridian Star*, September 6, 1955, 1.

Notes

36. Robert B. Patterson, letter to the editor, *McComb Enterprise-Journal*, September 6, 1955, 1+; J. Morris Jones, letter to the editor, *McComb Enterprise-Journal*, September 6, 1955, n.p.

37. "Speedy Trial Planned in Kidnap-Slaying Case," *Greenwood Commonwealth*, September 7, 1955, 1; Phil Stroupe, "Delta Residents Expected Indictments and Want Justice Done in Till Case but Outside Interference Resented," *Jackson Daily News*, September 7, 1955, 2:3.

Chapter 3. "Resentful of the Slant" (September 7–September 9)

1. The Milam-Bryant picture appears under the front-page headline "Murder Trial Of Deltans Expected Later In Month," in the September 7, 1955, *Clarion-Ledger*. Carolyn Bryant's picture appears on the bottom front page of the September 7, 1955, *Hattiesburg American*.

2. Juxtaposed with the "conference" that Milam and Bryant were conducting with Kellum, the caption of the funeral photograph drew attention to the "large crowd" gathered outside of the "Roberts Temple Church of God in Christ on the south side of Chicago"; see the *Clarion-Ledger*, September 7, 1955, 1. "Accused White Men Plead Innocent of Murder and Kidnap; To Set Trial Date Thursday; Guard Removed," *Greenwood Morning Star*, September 7, 1955, 1.

3. "Why Didn't They Get the Same Publicity?" *Greenwood Morning Star*, September 7, 1955, 4.

4. "As It Is in Chicago," *Jackson Daily News*, September 7, 1955, 8.

5. Stroupe, "Delta Residents Expected Indictments," 2:3.

6. Henry Harris, "Pencil Shavings," *West Point Daily Times Leader*, September 7, 1955, 6.

7. "Innocent Pleas Entered by 2 Indicted in Slaying of Negro Youth; Early Trial Predicted," *Laurel Leader-Call*, September 7, 1955, 1+.

8. "Random Thoughts by the Editor," *Yazoo City Herald*, September 8, 1955, 1.

9. "Unfortunate and Regretable [sic]," *Kosciusko Star-Herald*, September 8, 1955, 2:4.

10. "Mullen Musings: Let's Not Change," *Madison County Herald*, September 8, 1955, 3.

11. Dave Langford, editorial, *Lincoln County Advertiser*, September 8, 1955, 1.

12. Sid R. Harris, "The 'Wolf Whistle' Murder Case," *Houston (MS) Times-Post*, September 8, 1955, 2.

13. James Skewes, "We Can't Condone Murder," *Meridian Star*, September 8, 1955, 4.

14. "An Even Bigger Crime," *Scott County Times*, September 8, 1955, 4.

15. Thomas M. Alewine, "Built for the NAACP," *Brandon News*, September 8, 1955, 2; Thomas M. Alewine, "They'd Better Stay Home," *Brandon News*, September 8, 1955, 2.

16. C. H. Cole, "Interference Will Injure . . ." *Picayune Item*, September 8, 1955, 2.

17. "Asks Law against Displaying Bodies to Collect Money," *Greenwood Commonwealth*, September 8, 1955, 1; Jimmy Arrington, "Random Remarks by Ye Editor," *Collins News-Commercial*, September 9, 1955, 1.

18. A. B. Ainsworth, letter to the editor," *Greenwood Commonwealth*, September 8,

Notes

1955, 8. The letter was reprinted in the town's other daily. See "Ainsworth Asks for Funds to Defend Milam and Bryant," *Greenwood Morning News*, September 9, 1955, 1.

19. "Bad News for NAACP," *Jackson Daily News*, September 8, 1955, 8.

20. Gwen Gibson, "Negroes Assured of Action If Probe Proves Violation of Civil Rights in State," *Jackson Daily News*, September 8, 1955, 2.

21. Tom Ethridge, "Mississippi Notebook," *Jackson Daily News*, September 9, 1955.

22. "Set Trial for Sept. 19 in Till Slaying," *Delta Democrat-Times*, September 9, 1955, 1; "Mother to Testify at Trial; May Set Date Today," *Greenwood Morning Star*, September 9, 1955, 1.

23. "Dianne Kearney to Receive Red Cross Award for Saving Nurse," *Greenwood Morning Star*, September 9, 1955, 1; "Dianne Kearney Given Certificate of Merit Award," *Greenwood Commonwealth*, September 9, 1955, 1.

24. "Many People Resentful over Coverage of Case," *Greenwood Morning Star*, September 9, 1955, 6; "Citizens Councils Are Given Unjust Criticism," *Greenwood Morning Star*, September 9, 1955, 6.

25. "Grenada Pastor Speaks 'Mind' on NAACP Remarks," *Grenada Daily Sentinel-Star*, September 9, 1955, n.p.

26. "'Spurs Fight,'" *Delta Democrat-Times*, September 9, 1955, 1.

27. The same picture appeared in all three newspapers on September 9. While the photograph in the *Grenada Daily Sentinel-Star* and the *Clarksdale Press Register* appeared on the front page, the *McComb Enterprise-Journal* featured it on page 9.

28. Marvin J. Barloon, "Till Kidnapping Challenges Right of American to Defend Household," *Delta Democrat-Times*, September 9, 1955, 7.

29. William Faulkner, "Faulkner Pictures Till Case as Test of Survival of White Man, America," *Jackson Daily News*, September 10, 1955, 1.

Chapter 4. "The World Is Watching"
(September 10–September 18)

1. "Coleman Names Assistant to Aid Delta Prosecution," *Clarion-Ledger*, September 10, 1955, 1; "Mother of Till Boy to Testify at Trial," *Clarion-Ledger*, September 11, 1955, 1+.

2. "On the Emmett Louis Till Incident," *Jackson Advocate*, September 10, 1955, 4.

3. "State Calls Special Counsel to Assist with Prosecution," *Clarksdale Press Register*, September 10, 1955, 1.

4. "State Calls Special Counsel," 1.

5. The photograph of Till laying on a bed with his chin resting on his right hand was cropped to menacing effect. The first appearance of the photograph appears to have been in the September 3 issue of the *Tupelo Daily Herald*; the picture is credited as an "NEA Telephoto."

6. "Panel of Jurors May Be Drawn for Till Case Today," *Daily Corinthian*, September 12, 1955, 1; "State Declines to Comment as to Whether It Will Ask for Death in Delta Trial," *Laurel Leader-Call*, September 12, 1955, 1+; "Drawing of Jury List Begins for Two White Men at Sumner," *Vicksburg Evening Post*, September 12, 1955, 1; "Prosecution Ready for Trial of Men," *Greenwood Commonwealth*, September 12, 1955,

Notes

1; "Half Brothers to Face Trial Later in Month," *Tupelo Daily Journal*, September 12, 1955, 1+; Mamie Till-Mobley and Christopher Benson, *Death of Innocence*, 179.

7. Hugh Stephen Whitaker, "A Case Study in Southern Justice: The Murder and Trial of Emmett Till," *Rhetoric and Public Affairs* 8 (2005): 189–224. Whitaker's essay is a shorter version of his master's thesis completed in 1962 at Florida State University. Whitaker's thesis is available online at http://etd.lib.fsu.edu/theses/available/etd-05272004-140932/unrestricted/whitaker_thesis.pdf.

8. "Prosecution Doesn't Say If Death Penalty Sought in Trial of White Men," *Jackson Daily News*, September 12, 1955, 1.

9. "For a Few Extra Nickles," *Greenwood Commonwealth*, September 13, 1955, 6.

10. Mrs. Charles Stewart, letter to the editor, *Greenwood Commonwealth*, September 13, 1955, 8.

11. Barry Rutherford, "Both Races Must Reject Hot-Headed Leaders," *Tupelo Daily Journal*, September 13, 1955, 11.

12. Editorial, *Jackson State Times*, September 13, 1955.

13. Hoover's confidential letter can be accessed at www.emmetttillmurder.com.

14. "Ironic Parallel," *Daily Corinthian*, September 14, 1955, 4.

15. Robert B. Patterson, letter to the editor, *Clarksdale Press Register*, September 14, 1955, 7.

16. "Kidnapping Near Columbus Brings FBI Probe; Stirs More NAACP Criticism," *Greenwood Morning Star*, September 14, 1955, 1.

17. M. C. Durr, "Open Forum," *Brookhaven Leader-Times*, September 14, 1955, 2.

18. "Chicago Has Its Troubles," 14.

19. Hugh White to Armis E. Hawkins, September 14, 1955, Box 23, Folder 3, J. P. Coleman Papers, Mississippi Department of Archives and History, Jackson, Mississippi.

20. W. H. Anderson, editorial, *Southern Sentinel*, September 15, 1955, n.p.

21. Sid R. Harris, "Nation Eyes Wolf-Whistle Murder Trial," *Houston (MS) Times-Post*, September 15, 1955, 2.

22. "Sordid Crime Has Even More Serious Aspects," *Clarion-Ledger*, September 16, 1955, 12.

23. "Publicity in the Big City Papers," *Greenwood Morning Star*, September 16, 1955, 4.

24. "Till's Mother, 'Wary Of Foes,' Keeping Her Route to Trial Secret," *Jackson Daily News*, September 16, 1955, 1; "Delta Veniremen Called; Mother to Attend Trial," *Clarion-Ledger*, September 16, 1955, 1; Lois J. Schultz, "Strolling—Around Clarksdale," *Clarksdale Press Register*, September 17, 1955, 1; "Arrival Expected at Clarksdale," *Jackson State Times*, September 18, 1955, 14A. In fact, Mamie Till traveled from Memphis to the Clarksdale home of Fulton Ford on the morning of September 17. See Till-Mobley and Benson, *Death of Innocence*, 152.

25. John Herbers, "Sumner Surprised by Way World Watching Pending Till Trial Today," *Delta Democrat-Times*, September 18, 1955, 1.

26. The side-by-side photographs appear prominently on page 4 of the September 18, 1955, edition of the *Clarion-Ledger*; the picture of Till is the same one that originally appeared in the September 3, 1955, edition of the *Biloxi Daily Herald*.

27. Sam Johnson, "Two White Men Go on Trial Monday for Slaying of Negro,"

Notes

Clarion-Ledger, September 18, 1955, 4; Sam Johnson, "Murder Trial at Sumner Opens Monday," *Natchez Democrat*, September 18, 1955, 1+.

28. "Defense Predicts State Cannot Prove Murder; Till Trial Opens Monday," *Greenwood Morning Star*, September 18, 1955, 1.

29. Tom Ethridge, "Mississippi Notebook," *Jackson Daily News*, September 18, 1955.

30. Whitaker, "Case Study in Southern Justice," 189–224.

Chapter 5. "Every Last Anglo-Saxon One of You" (September 19–September 23)

1. Jay Milner, "Negro's Funeral at Sumner Takes Spotlight from Trial," *Clarion-Ledger*, September 19, 1; "All Is Quiet at Sumner as Trial Begins," *Jackson State Times*, September 19, 1955, 8A.

2. The single best account of locating potential witnesses was written by James Hicks, a black reporter covering the trial for several black newspapers. His serialized reports can be found in Christopher Metress, ed., *The Lynching of Emmett Till: A Documentary Narrative* (Charlottesville, VA: University of Virginia Press, 2002), 155–77.

3. "Juror Selection Underway in Till Murder Trial," *Daily Corinthian*, September 19, 1955, 1; John Herbers, "Defendants Confident Acquittal Will Result in Trial at Sumner," *Grenada Daily Sentinel-Star*, September 19, 1955, 1. For Judge Swango's rules see Sam Johnson, "69 Covering Murder Trial in Mississippi," *Natchez Democrat*, September 19, 1955, 1.

4. John Herbers, "Till Trial Bogs Down in Jury-Picking Job," *Delta Democrat-Times*, September 19, 1955, 1+.

5. Arthur Everett, "Till Nearly Missed His Fatal Journey to Land of Cotton," *Clarion-Ledger*, September 19, 1955, 1+; Sam Johnson, "State Will Not Ask Death Penalty in Trial of White Men at Sumner," *Greenwood Commonwealth*, September 19, 1955, 1; Sam Johnson, "State Is Not Seeking Death Penalty for Men as Delta Trial Opens," *McComb Enterprise-Journal*, September 19, 1955, 1+.

6. James Featherston, "Delta Courtroom Is Packed as Murder Trial Opens; Evidence 'Circumstantial,'" *Jackson Daily News*, September 19, 1955, 1+; Everett, "Till Nearly Missed His Fatal Journey," 1+.

7. "Till Murder Trial at Sumner Got Underway Yesterday," *Natchez Democrat*, September 20, 1955, 1+.

8. The six pictures are framed under Sam Johnson's article, "State Tentatively Accepts Eleven Jurors in Trial of Bryant and Milam at Sumner," *Vicksburg Evening Post*, September 19, 1955, 1+.

9. The caption under Moses Wright's photograph in the September 19, 1955, *Vicksburg Evening Post* reads, "Boy's grandfather." Featherston, "Delta Courtroom Is Packed," 1+; Sam Johnson, "State Won't Ask Death Penalty," *Hattiesburg American*, September 19, 1955, 1; "Mother Won't Attend Trial," *Jackson State Times*, September 18, 1955, 14A; "Arrival Expected at Clarksdale," 14A.

10. "Impose Equal Justice," *Jackson Daily News*, September 19, 1955, 10.

11. Virgil Adams, "10 Jurors Accepted as Milam and Bryant Go on Trial at Sumner; Most Spectators Predict Acquittal," *Greenwood Morning Star*, September 20, 1955, 1. Adams's newspaper was the only one we noted that reported a burglary at the Bry-

Notes

ant Grocery and Meat Market on Saturday evening, September 17. See "Bryant's Store in Money Robbed Sat. Night; Boys Fire Guns," *Greenwood Morning Star*, September 20, 1955, 1.

12. "'Money' Jars for Defense Delay Trial," *Jackson State Times*, September 20, 1955, 2A; James Featherston, "Negro Congressman Eyes Trial—His Role Not Clear; Testimony Starts Today," *Jackson Daily News*, September 20, 1955, 1+; Till-Mobley and Benson, *Death of Innocence*, 165.

13. Featherston, "Negro Congressman Eyes Trial," 1+; Sam Johnson, "Jury Selected, State Summons 13—Till's Mother, Now at Sumner, Is Included as One Trial Witness," *McComb Enterprise-Journal*, September 20, 1955, 1+; "Arrival of Victim's Mother Causes Stir," *Jackson State Times*, September 20, 1955, 1A; "Judge Limits Sketching of Murder Trial," *Jackson State Times*, September 20, 1955, 2A.

14. "Cast in Impelling Court Drama Matches Movies," *Jackson Daily News*, September 20, 1955, 6.

15. Ralph Hutto, "Dynamic Personalities Form Till Trial Cast," *Jackson State Times*, September 20, 1955, 2A.

16. "Milam Is Pictured a War Hero Who Also Snatched Negro from Drowning," *Jackson Daily News*, September 20, 1955, 6; Jay Milner, "Bryant Didn't Mind His Negro Non-Com During Korean War," *Clarion-Ledger*, September 20, 1955, 1+. Milam was pictured playing with his sons on page 6 of the *Jackson Daily News*; similar pictures would appear frequently during and after the trial. See also "Lives of Two Negroes Saved by J. W. Milam," *Vicksburg Evening Post*, September 20, 1955, 1; "Milam Is Pictured a War Hero Who Snatched a Negro from Drowning," *Jackson Advocate*, September 24, 1955, 6.

17. Milner, "Bryant Didn't Mind His Negro Non-Com," 1+.

18. Sam Johnson, "Jury Completed in Sumner Trial; State Summons 13 Witnesses In Trial; Till's Mother Arrives," *Vicksburg Evening Post*, September 20, 1955, 1; "13 Witnesses Summoned in Murder Case," *Biloxi Daily Herald*, September 20, 1955, 1+; "Crowded Courtroom Causes Judge to Recess Sumner Trial Overnight," *Greenwood Commonwealth*, September 20, 1955, 1.

19. "Sidelights at Sumner Trial," *Greenwood Commonwealth*, September 20, 1955, 1.

20. Arthur Everett, "Sumner Trial Opens Briskly," *Clarion-Ledger*, September 20, 1955, 1+; Milner, "Bryant Didn't Mind His Negro Non-Com," 1+; John Herbers, "Testimony Opens Today in Till 'Wolf-Whistle' Murder Trial," *Delta Democrat-Times*, September 20, 1955, 1+.

21. Virgil Adams, "Bitterest Statements from Chicago," *Greenwood Morning Star*, September 20, 1955, 6.

22. Henry Harris, "Pencil Shavings," *West Point Daily Times Leader*, September 20, 1955, 4. While Halberstam did not cover the trial, he did visit Sumner twice to watch journalism's leading lights ply their craft. See David Halberstam, "The Real Founder of the New Journalism—Murray Kempton," *Washington Monthly*, April 1994, available online at http://www.thefreelibrary.com. Halberstam wrote about the seminal importance of the Till case to the modern civil-rights movement in his book *The Fifties* (New York: Villard, 1993), 429–41, but with some lapses in accuracy.

23. John Herbers, "Wright Tells of Kidnaping of Till Boy," *Delta Democrat-Times*, September 21, 1955, 1+; "Uncle of Victim Identifies Defendants as Abductors," *West Point Daily Times Leader*, September 21, 1955, 1+; John Herbers, "Contradictions

Notes

Develop as Testimony in Till Trial Begins; Negro Tells How Till Was Taken from Bed," *Greenwood Morning Star*, September 22, 1955, 1; John Herbers, "Uncle [sic] of Slain Boy Appears as First Witness," *Grenada Daily Sentinel-Star*, September 21, 1955, 1; John Herbers, "Uncle [sic] Identifies Boy's Abductors; Says One Had Gun And Light," *Jackson State Times*, September 21, 1955, 1A; Arthur Everett, "Defendants Admit Kidnaping Till Boy but Deny 'Murder,'" *Clarion-Ledger*, September 22, 1955, 1+; James Featherston, "Dim Light Casts Some Doubt on Identity of Till's Abductors; Slain Boy's Uncle [sic] Points Finger at Bryant, Milam but Admits Light Was Dim," *Jackson Daily News*, September 21, 1955, 1+; Sam Johnson, "Uncle [sic] of Till's Identifies Pair as Men Who Abducted Chicago Negro; State Hopes to Strengthen Case by Surprise Witnesses," *Greenwood Commonwealth*, September 21, 1955, 1.

24. Featherston, "Dim Light Casts Some Doubt," 1.

25. Jay Milner, "Sumner Folk Already Plenty Bored with All This Ruckus," *Clarion-Ledger*, September 21, 1955, 2.

26. "Undertaker's Story Heard," *Jackson State Times*, September 21, 1955, 1A+; Herbers, "Wright Tells of Kidnaping," 1+.

27. "New Witnesses May Take Till Murder Trial to Sunflower," *Delta Democrat-Times*, September 21, 1955, 1.

28. "New Story on Murder of Till," *Greenwood Commonwealth*, September 21, 1955, 1. For the original story, see Clark Porteous, "New Till Evidence: Reporter Finds It; Officers Work All Night on Searches," *Memphis Press-Scimitar*, September 21, 1955, 1+.

29. "Undertaker's Story Heard," 1A+.

30. Ibid.

31. Virgil Adams, "State Granted Recess to Produce New Witnesses in Till Case; Defense to Testify Attack Tried," *Greenwood Morning Star*, September 21, 1955, 1.

32. Adams, "State Granted Recess," 1; "Will the NAACP Accept Blame?" *Delta Democrat-Times*, September 21, 1955, 4.

33. "No Indictment Returned in Brookhaven Slaying," *Tupelo Daily Journal*, September 21, 1955, 1. The *Lincoln County Advertiser* quoted from the harshly worded statement of the grand jury meeting in the Smith case: "We think that it is impossible for people to be within 20 or 30 feet of a difficulty in which one party is shot and lost his life, in broad open day light, and nobody knows anything about it, or know who did it. . . . Most assuredly somebody had done a good job trying to cover up the evidence in this case and trying to prevent the parties guilty, therefore, from being brought to justice." "Not Enough Evidence Reports Grand Jury," *Lincoln County Advertiser*, September 22, 1955, 1. Though charged with the murder of Lamar Smith, Noah Smith, Mack Smith, and Charles Falvey were never indicted for the murder of the voting-rights activist.

34. "Till Witness Says Hears Beating, Cries; Claims Milam Wearing Gun; Seen with Boy," *Meridian Star*, September 22, 1955, 1+; Virgil Adams, "Resentment Rising against Radicals at Trial," *Greenwood Morning Star*, September 22, 1955, 6; John Herbers, "Cross-Burning at Sumner Went Almost Un-Noticed Yesterday," *Delta Democrat-Times*, September 22, 1955, 11.

35. Adams, "Resentment Rising Against Radicals," 6; Velma Taylor, "Just Ramblin'," *Holly Springs Southern Reporter*, September 22, 1955, 1; Sid R. Harris, "As Diggs Sows His Seeds of Ill Will," *Houston (MS) Times-Post*, September 22, 1955, 2; N. H. C.,

Notes

"Just Beating Around," *Simpson County News*, September 22, 1955, 1; Jay Milner, "Jittery News Men at Sumner Kept in a Dither by Rumors," *Clarion-Ledger*, September 22, 1955, 2.

36. Everett, "Defendants Admit Kidnaping," 1+.

37. For Smith and Cothran's testimony see, Ralph Hutto, "Mother, 'Surprise Witness' Give Dramatic Testimony; Mamie Bradley Says Corpse Was That of Her Slain Son," *Jackson State Times*, September 22, 1955, 2A. For Moses Wright's testimony, see Ralph Hutto, "Slain Boy's Uncle [sic] Identifies Bryant, Milam on Stand; But Moses Wright Admits He Never Saw Faces in Light," *Jackson State Times*, September 21, 1955, 8A.

38. Everett, "Defendants Admit Kidnaping," 1+; Hutto, "Mother, 'Surprise Witness' Give Dramatic Testimony," 2A.

39. Everett, "Defendants Admit Kidnaping," 1+.

40. Arthur Everett, "Jury Deliberations Expected to Begin Today in Till Case; Bryant's Wife Tells Incident," *Clarion-Ledger*, September 23, 1955, 1; James Featherston, "'Surprise' Witness Describes 'Hollering' in Sunflower Barn; Negro Youth Testifies He Saw Milam Armed at Barn, Says Till Boy Was There," *Jackson Daily News*, September 22, 1955, 1+; "Willie Reed, Negro Youth, Testifis [sic] about Seeing Pick-Up Truck and Hearing Hollering from Barn," *Jackson Daily News*, September 22, 1955, 8; Hutto, "Mother, 'Surprise Witness' Give Dramatic Testimony," 2A.

41. Sam Johnson, "Mother of Till Says Body That of Her Son—Negro Youth Testifies Four White Men Took Chicago Boy into Sunflower Plantation Barn," *McComb Enterprise-Journal*, September 22, 1955, 1+; John Herbers, "Witness Says He Saw Milam Take Lad into . . ." *Delta Democrat-Times*, September 22, 1955, 1+; Mamie Till-Bradley, "I Want You to Know What They Did to My Boy," *Afro-American*, November 12, 1955, 6+.

42. Featherston, "'Surprise' Witness Describes 'Hollering,'" 1+; Herbers, "Witness Says He Saw Milam," 1+; Dave Bready, "Sidelights of Trial at Sumner," *Greenwood Commonwealth*, September 22, 1955, 1; Thomas M. Alewine, "Time Out with the Editor," *Brandon News*, September 22, 1955, 1.

43. Alewine, "Time Out with the Editor," September 22, 1955, 1; "Trial at Sumner Draws Attention of Entire Nation," *Coffeeville Courier*, September 22, 1955, 1.

44. John Herbers, "Youth Testifies Saw Till Taken into Barn; Tells Jury of Hearing Screaming," *Jackson State Times*, September 22, 1955, 1A+; Featherston, "'Surprise' Witness Describes 'Hollering,'" 1+.

45. Herbers, "Youth Testifies Saw Till," 1A+.

46. Bready, "Sidelights Of Trial," 1; Herbers, "Youth Testifies Saw Till," 1A+.

47. W. C. Shoemaker, "Mrs. Bryant Won 2 Top Beauty Honors—Mother Loyally Stays at Trial," *Jackson Daily News*, September 22, 1955, 11. For a moving account of how black girls were made readily available to white men and the banality of cross-racial pedophilic rape, see Endesha Ida Mae Holland, *From the Mississippi Delta: A Memoir* (New York: Simon and Schuster, 1997).

48. "Judge Sends Jury out of Courtroom during Testimony of Defendant Roy Bryant's Wife," *Jackson State Times*, September 23, 1955, 2A.

49. Ibid.; "Mrs. Bryant Tells How Northern Negro Grabbed Her, 'Wolf-Whistled' in Store," *Jackson Daily News*, September 23, 1955, 9.

50. Till-Mobley and Benson, *Death of Innocence*, 185–86.

Notes

51. Arthur Everett, "Jury Deliberations Expected to Begin Today in Till Case; Bryant's Wife Tells Incident," *Clarion-Ledger*, September 23, 1955, 1; John Herbers, "Wolf Whistle Murder Case Goes to Jury in Sumner Circuit Court," *Delta Democrat-Times*, September 23, 1955, 1+.

52. The pictures in the *Clarion-Ledger* and *Greenwood Morning Star* ran on the front pages of each paper's September 23 edition. The page-one pictures in the *Jackson Daily News* appeared on September 21.

53. John Herbers, "Jury Absent as Mrs. Bryant Tells of Struggle with Till; Expect to Complete Case Today," *Greenwood Morning Star*, September 23, 1955, 1; James Featherston and W. C. Shoemaker, "Verdict Awaited in Till Trial; State Demands Conviction; Defense Says No Proof Presented, Asks Acquittal," *Jackson Daily News*, September 23, 1955, 1+.

54. "Sheriff Strider's Testimony Raises Doubt Body in River Was Till Youth," *Jackson Daily News*, September 23, 1955, 9.

55. Ibid.

56. "Negro Body Was in Water 10 Days, Witnesses Say," *Jackson Daily News*, September 23, 1955, 9; "Judge Sends Jury Out," 2A.

57. "Jury Acquits Bryant, Milam of Murder Charge as Trial Ends," *Clarksdale Press Register*, September 23, 1955, 1+; Dave Bready, "Sidelights at Sumner Trial," *Greenwood Commonwealth*, September 23, 1955, 1.

58. W. C. Shoemaker, "Reporter for Commies Relates How He Shifted to 'Left'— Says Trial 'Fair,'" *Jackson Daily News*, September 21, 1955, 14; Harry Marsh, "Communist Writer at Trial Lauds Citizens," *Delta Democrat-Times*, September 22, 1955, 1.

59. B. J. Skelton, "Testimony at Bryant-Milam Trial Has Left Many Questions Unanswered," *Clarksdale Press Register*, September 23, 1955, 7.

60. "Final Arguments Underway in Till Trial; Jury May Get Case Today," *Grenada Daily Sentinel-Star*, September 23, 1955, 1.

61. A composite of closing arguments, quoted in the following paragraphs, was culled from several sources: "Defense Urges Acquittal; State Asserts Defendants Guilty of Cowardly Crime," *Laurel Leader-Call*, September 23, 1955, 1+; "District Attorney Opens State's Final Arguments in Sumner Trial; Jury May Return Verdict Today," *Daily Corinthian*, September 23, 1955, 1; Herbers, "Wolf Whistle Murder Case," 1+; "Jury Returns Not Guilty Verdict in Till Trial, Deliberated One Hour," *Natchez Democrat*, September 24, 1955, 1+; Sam Johnson, "Jury Hears Defense and Prosecution Arguments as Testimony Ends in Kidnap-Slaying Case," *Greenwood Commonwealth*, September 23, 1955, 1; Featherston and Shoemaker, "Verdict Awaited in Till Trial," 1+; John Herbers, "State Asks Death or Life Sentence," *Jackson State Times*, September 23, 1955, 1A+. In an ironic historical twist, John Whitten's granddaughter, Ellen Whitten, wrote a thesis at Rhodes College in 2005 bearing on the case. See "Injustice Unearthed: Revisiting the Murder of Emmett Till," available online at www.olemiss.edu/winterinstitute/documents/till-whitten-paper.htm.

62. "Roman Circus," *Jackson Daily News*, September 22, 1955, 12; Harry Marsh, "Editors Eye Clock in Awaiting Verdict," *Delta Democrat-Times*, September 23, 1955, 1.

63. Jay Milner, "Till Case Defendants Freed by Jury on Third Ballot because of Doubt Concerning Identification of Body," *Clarion-Ledger*, September 24, 1955, 1+; Arthur Everett, "Trial in Leflore Must Await Action by Next Grand Jury," *Clarion-Ledger*, September 24, 1955, 1+.

Notes

64. Jay Milner, "Delta Town Welcomes Quiet Following in Wake of Sensational Murder Trial," *Clarion-Ledger*, September 25, 1955, 10.

Chapter 6. "Forgotten as Quickly as Possible"? (September 24–September 30)

1. "Milam, Bryant Face Leflore Kidnap Case," *Jackson State Times*, September 24, 1955, 1A; "The Truth Remains," *Jackson State Times*, September 24, 1955, 1A.

2. Virgil Adams, "Fair Trial Was Credit to Mississippi," *Greenwood Morning Star*, September 23, 1955, 4.

3. James Featherston, "Two Who 'Saw Milam, Till at Barn' Flown North by Congressman Diggs," *Jackson Daily News*, September 24, 1955, 1; "A Meddlesome Visitor," *Jackson Daily News*, September 24, 1955, 6.

4. "The Verdict at Sumner," *Jackson Daily News*, September 25, 1955, 8.

5. Ibid.

6. Ibid.

7. "Broad View of the Verdict in the Till Trial," *Natchez Democrat*, September 25, 1955, 6.

8. "As Time Passes," *The Laurel Leader-Call*, September 26, 1955, 4.

9. "It Was a Fair Trial," *Greenwood Commonwealth*, September 24, 1955, 4.

10. "Acquittal," *Delta Democrat-Times*, September 25, 1955, 4. Strider's comments were recorded in Milner, "Delta Town Welcomes Quiet," 10.

11. "Fair Trial Fairly Reported," 4.

12. Barry Rutherford, "Need of Trained Crime Investigators Mounts," *Tupelo Daily Journal*, September 26, 1955, 11.

13. Virgil Adams, "A New Wrinkle in the Vilification of Mississippi," *Greenwood Morning Star*, September 27, 1955, 6. That it was Adams who first publicly accused Till of attempted rape does not surprise us given the reminiscence of John Herbers. In a February 2000 letter sent to Paul Hendrickson, Herbers recounts a conversation he had had with the *Star's* publisher (whom he did not name in the letter, but who was Virgil Adams) about the guilt or innocence of Milam and Bryant: "He thought too much was being made of Till's tender age. 'He may have been only 14 but I'm told he had a dong on him like this,' elevating his forearm and dismissing any suggestion that the lynching was wrong." See Hendrickson, *Sons of Mississippi*, 319.

14. Virgil Adams, "More Vicious Threats," *Greenwood Morning Star*, September 28, 1955, 4.

15. "State Negroes Not Surprised at Till Verdict," *Jackson Advocate*, October 1, 1955, 1+; "The Till Case Verdict," *Jackson Advocate*, October 1, 1955, 4.

16. "By Striking at Till Jury's Verdict NAACP Plays in Communist Hands," *Aberdeen Examiner*, September 29, 1955, 4; Thomas M. Alewine, "Time Out with the Editor," *Brandon News*, September 29, 1955, 1; Royce Laughman, "Just Beating Around," *Simpson County News*, September 29, 1955, 1; H. S., "Hal-Lucinations," *Tate County Democrat*, September 29, 1955, 1; C. H. Cole, "Hardly a Column by Chance," *Picayune Item*, September 29, 1955, 1.

17. "Half-Brothers Found Innocent of Slaying," *Biloxi Daily Herald*, September 24, 1955, 1+; "Kidnap Counts Face 2 Freed in Till Trial," *Meridian Star*, September 24, 1955, 1; Sam Johnson "Bryant, Milam Freed in Till Slaying; Face Kidnap Charge,"

Hattiesburg American, September 24, 1955, 1+; "Half-Brothers Back in Jail," *West Point Daily Times Leader*, September 24, 1955, 1+; John Herbers, "Not Guilty Verdict in Wolf Whistle Murder," *Greenwood Morning Star*, September 24, 1955, 1; Arthur Everett, "Till Case Defendants Freed by Jury on Third Ballot Because of Doubt Concerning Identification of Body," *Clarion-Ledger*, September 24, 1955, 1+.

18. "Leflore Officials Delay Fixing Bond in Till Case," *Clarion-Ledger*, September 25, 1955, 1; James Featherston and W. C. Shoemaker, "Byrant [sic], Milam Still in Custody of Law to Face Kidnap Charges in Leflore after Acquittal of Murder at Sumner," *Jackson Daily News*, September 24, 1955, 1+.

19. James Featherston, "Mandy Bradley, Reed Boy Leave with Congressman after Testifying at Trial," *Jackson Daily News*, September 24, 1; Paul Burton, "'Old Man Mose' Sells Out, He'll Move to New York," *Clarion-Ledger*, September 26, 1. For Kempton's remarks, see Murray Kempton, "He Went All the Way," *New York Post*, September 22, 1955, reprinted in Christopher Metress, ed., *The Lynching of Emmett Till: A Documentary Narrative* (Charlottesville, VA: University of Virginia Press, 2002), 65–67.

20. "From Press Dispatches," *Clarion-Ledger*, September 25, 1955, 1. Whitaker claims that special prosecutor Robert B. Smith III and defense attorney J. J. Breland revealed to him that Collins and Loggins had both been kept under false names at the Charleston jail. See Hugh Stephen Whitaker, "Case Study in Southern Justice," 208–09.

21. "Attempted Rape of White Woman Occurs Near Marks," *Clarion-Ledger*, September 25, 1955, 1; "Assault Suspect Sought," *Jackson State Times*, September 25, 1955, 1A+.

22. Webster McClary, "Negro Pastor Declares: Neither Race Wants Mixing," *Clarion-Ledger*, September 25, 1955, 2:7; "As Time Passes," 4.

23. M. C. Durr, letter to the editor," *Lincoln County Advertiser*, September 29, 1955, n.p. The *Advertiser* carried McClary's letter on October 6.

24. "Accuse Men of Fostering Idea of Integration," *Meridian Star*, September 29, 1955, 1+; "2 White Men Censured in Protest Meet," *Jackson State Times*, September 29, 1955, 1A+.

25. Jay Milner, "2 Accused Deny Advocacy of Integration in Holmes," *Clarion-Ledger*, September 30, 1955, 1+.

26. "Where Women Do the Wolf Whistling," *Jackson State Times*, September 25, 1955, n.p.; Ralph Hutto, "Now Sumner Is Just Another Sleepy Delta Town," *Jackson State Times*, September 24, 1955, 1A; Bob Moulder, "Radio, Newspaper, TV Overplay Till Trial," *Jackson State Times*, September 25, 1955, 9B; Robert H. Denley, "Southern Accent Throws Newsmen at Till Trial," *Columbus Commercial Dispatch*, September 25, 1955, 1:6; B. J. Skelton, "Visiting Newsmen Pack Typewriters, Head for Homes," *Clarksdale Press Register*, September 24, 1955, 1; Milner, "Delta Town Welcomes Quiet," 10.

27. "Bryant, Milam Get Preliminary Hearing This Week on Kidnaping Charge Arising in State's Till Case—Expected Outcries Begin to Be Heard Up North," *McComb Enterprise-Journal*, September 26, 1955, 1+; "Till Case Is Still Helping to Fill Mailbox of Greenville Newspaper," *Delta Democrat-Times*, September 29, 1955, 10; "City Watches Trial Results," *Clarksdale Press Register*, September 26, 1955, 1; "White

Notes

Man Was Hanged 65 Years Ago in Grenada for Murdering Negro," *Columbia-Progress*, September 29, 1955, 2:2.

28. "Till Trial Acquittal Protested by Rallies," *Delta Democrat-Times*, September 26, 1955, 1+; "Rep. Diggs Blasts Mississippi Trial," *Clarion-Ledger*, September 26, 1955, 2:6; "Mamie Bradley Says Trial A 'Comedy,'" *Clarion-Ledger*, September 26, 1955, 2:6; "France Irate over Till Case," *Clarion-Ledger*, September 26, 1955, 2:6; "French Protest Till Verdict in Mass Meeting," *Jackson State Times*, September 29, 1955, 11A.

29. Jay Milner, "Newsmen Disagree on Protest Rallies," *Clarion-Ledger*, September 27, 1955, 1+.

30. "A Careful Last Look," *Clarion-Ledger*, October 2, 1955, 8.

31. Harold Foreman, "Reports Till Boy Alive in Detroit Bring 'Hoax' Comment from Mother," *Jackson Daily News*, September 29, 1955, 1; "Rumors Till Seen Alive Lack Basis," *Jackson State Times*, September 30, 1955, 1A; "Mother Denies Till Found Alive; Rumor in Detroit Held 'Cruel Hoax' by Mamie Bradley," *Vicksburg Evening Post*, September 29, 1955, 1; "Sheriff Repeats Belief That Till Is Still Alive," *Vicksburg Evening Post*, September, 29, 1955, 1; "Strider Believes Till Is Still Alive," *Greenwood Commonwealth*, September 29, 1955, 1; "Denies Definite Knowledge Till Is Found Alive," *Meridian Star*, September 29, 1955, 1; "Emmett Till Still Alive, Says Sheriff," *Biloxi Daily Herald*, September 29, 1955, 1+; "Till's Mother Denies Report He Is Alive," *Hattiesburg American*, September 29, 1955, 1; "Is Emmett Till Alive?" *Clarksdale Press Register*, September 29, 1955, 1.

32. Jack Stapleton, "Query Lingers: Is Till Dead?" *Clarksdale Press Register*, September 30, 1955, 1.

33. Bill Spell, "Would Take $77,880,783.51 to Haul All Our Good Negroes to the Nawth," *Jackson Daily News*, September 28, 1955, 5.

34. Bill Spell, "Daily News Readers Offer Help to Send Willie Reed's Girl Friend to Chicago," *Jackson Daily News*, September 29, 1955, 1; "Ella Mae Shuns Willie," *Jackson Daily News*, September 30, 1955, 1; "Reed Boy, Bradley Woman Fled State for 'Safety' but Police Guard Homes," *Jackson Daily News*, September 30, 1955, 1.

35. "Bryant, Milam Released under $10,000 Bonds in Emmett Till Kidnaping," *Jackson Daily News*, September 30, 1955, 1; Till-Mobley and Benson, *Death of Innocence*, 261.

Chapter 7. "Like Father–Like Son" (October 1955–January 1956)

1. "To All White Men and Women in Jackson," *Winona Times*, September 30, 1955, n.p.

2. Frederick Sullens, *Jackson Daily News*, October 2, 1955, 1.

3. Bill Spell, "State Negroes Held 'Captive' in Chicago," *Jackson Daily News*, October 5, 1955, 1+.

4. Bill Spell, "Woman Witness Told to Keep Silence," *Jackson Daily News*, October 6, 1955, 1+.

5. Bill Spell and W. C. Shoemaker, "'Missing' Negro Used in NAACP Propaganda Found; He's Not Able to Contact His Wife, Mandy Bradley," *Jackson Daily News*, October 6, 1955, 1.

Notes

6. Bill Spell, "How the NAACP Network Operates," *Jackson Daily News*, October 7, 1955, 1+.

7. Ibid., 4.

8. "Hearst Newspaper in Chicago Accuses Daily News of Slanting NAACP Stories," *Jackson Daily News*, October 7, 1955, 1.

9. Felix B. Wold, "Mose Tells of Sleeping in Cemetery but 'Middle Man' Attended Interview," *Jackson Daily News*, October 8, 1955, 1.

10. Bill Spell, "Effort to Tell Mandy of Her Husband Fails as Phone Connection Was Cut," *Jackson Daily News*, October 8, 1955, 1.

11. "Fate of Negro Accused of Raping White Woman Goes to Jury in Laurel," *Jackson Daily News*, October 8, 1955, 1.

12. "Jackson News Says NAACP Holds Negroes Captive," *Natchez Democrat*, October 6, 1955, 1+; "Much Conflict in Newspaper Report," *Natchez Democrat*, October 8, 1955, 1+.

13. "Entire State Is Blamed by Negro Leader," *Vicksburg Evening Post*, October 8, 1955, 1.

14. "Mose Wright Tells New York Paper He Fled for His Life," *Vicksburg Evening Post*, October 4, 1955, 1; "Negro Editor Denies Trio Held," *Vicksburg Evening Post*, October 6, 1955, 8.

15. Thomas M. Alewine, "Time Out with the Editor," *Brandon News*, October 6, 1955, 1; Big Yick, "Communists Are Stirring Strife," *Oxford Eagle*, October 6, 1955, 6; "NAACP Sows Seeds of Hate," *Kosciusko Star-Herald*, October 13, 1955, 4; Murphy Weir, "Ramblins," *Poplarville Weekly Democrat*, October 13, 1955, 1+; C. H. Cole, "Hardly a Column by Chance," *Picayune Item*, October 13, 1955, 1; Thomas M. Alewine, "Time Out with the Editor," *Brandon News*, October 13, 1955, 1.

16. Elliott Trimble, "Lamentable Aspects of Racial Propaganda," *Natchez Democrat*, October 7, 1955, 4; "No Change in Attitude," *West Point Daily Times Leader*, October 15, 1955, 4; "Negro Pastor Favors Voluntary Segregation," *Picayune Item*, October 6, 1955, 4; Oliver Emmerich, "A Trap Is Set . . . and Baited with Insults," *McComb Enterprise-Journal*, October 7, 1955, 1.

17. McClary's letter was a particular favorite of the rural Mississippi press; it ran in the *Picayune Item* on September 29, the *Winston County Journal* on September 30, the *Winona Times* on October 14, the *Drew Leader* on November 17, the *Brandon News* on October 6, and the *Grenada Daily Sentinel-Star* on September 26.

18. "NAACP Signs Rap Eastland," *Jackson State Times*, October 7, 1955, 1; "National Boycott of Mississippi Products Urged," *Vicksburg Evening Post*, October 11, 1955, 1.

19. Till-Mobley and Benson, *Death of Innocence*, 202–04.

20. "Till's Dad Raped 2 Women, Murdered a Third in Italy," *Jackson Daily News*, October 14, 1955, 1.

21. The photograph appears on the front page of the October 15, 1955, *Jackson Daily News*; it is captioned with "Sweater Season in Southland."

22. Morris Cunningham, "Father of Till Hanged in Italy for Attacks on 3 Women in 1944," *Grenada Daily Sentinel-Star*, October 17, 1955, 1+.

23. "About Till's Father," *Jackson Daily News*, October 15, 1955, 1.

24. "To [sic] Much Angry Shouting . . ." *Madison County Herald*, October 18, 1955, 3.

Notes

25. "Time for Us to Forget the Till Murder Case," *Tupelo Daily Journal*, October 18, 1955, 11.

26. J. J. Breland, letter to the editor, *Jackson Daily News*, October 20, 1955, 3.

27. Hazel Brannon Smith, "Through Hazel Eyes," *Lexington Advertiser*, October 20, 1955, 1. For an in-depth examination of the State Sovereignty Commission, see Yasuhiro Katagiri, *The Mississippi State Sovereignty Commission: Civil Rights and States' Rights* (Jackson, MS: University Press of Mississippi, 2001).

28. Wade Milam, letter to the editor, *Jackson Daily News*, October 19, 1955.

29. A. S. Coody, letter to the editor, *Jackson Daily News*, October 20, 1955; "Till Murder Case Hurts US Prestige," *Natchez Democrat*, October 22, 1955, 1.

30. Thomas M. Alewine, "Time Out with the Editor," *Brandon News*, October 20, 1955, 1; W. H. Anderson, editorial, *Southern Sentinel*, October 20, 1955, n.p.; Sid Harris, "Till's Father Executed for Rape-Murder in Italy," *Houston (MS) Times-Post*, October 20, 1955, 2; Jimmy Arrington, "Random Remarks," *Collins News-Commercial*, October 21, 1955, 1; "Vote of Thanks Due," *Kosciusko Star-Herald*, October 20, 1955, 4; "Sullens Praised for Till Exposure," *Greenwood Commonwealth*, October 18, 1955, 8.

31. Editorial, *Jackson Daily News*, October 25, 1955.

32. "Till's GI Dad Hanged in Italy for Women Attacks in 1944," *Winona Times*, October 28, 1955, 1; Till-Mobley and Benson, *Death of Innocence*, 203.

33. C. H. Cole, "Hardly a Column by Chance," *Picayune Item*, October 27, 1955, 1.

34. Charles C. Jones, "This Mendenhall Preacher Has the Right Ideas," *Drew Leader*, November 3, 1955, 1.

35. Virgil Adams, editorial, *Greenwood Morning Star*, November 6, 1955, 4.

36. "A Meagre Correction." *Jackson Daily News*, November 5, 1955, p. 6.

37. "Mississippi Gets New Rapping at NAACP Rallies," *Vicksburg Evening Post*, October 24, 1955, 12.

38. "Murder of Four Boys," *Vicksburg Evening Post*, October 27, 1955, 4.

39. "Grand Jury Now Considers Case of Two White Men," *Vicksburg Evening Post*, November 9, 1955, 1; Sam Johnson, "Grand Jury, Not Examined Witnesses in Till Kidnaping," *Greenwood Commonwealth*, November 8, 1955, 1.

40. John N. Popham, "Till Case Rocked by Many Factors," *Jackson State Times*, November 6, 1955, 5A.

41. Sam Johnson, "Grand Jury Empaneled Today, Expect Action in Kidnapping," *Greenwood Commonwealth*, November 7, 1955, 1; John Herbers, "'Case Closed' as Jury Fails to Indict Pair for Till Kidnapping," *Delta Democrat-Times*, November 10, 1955, 1.

42. John Herbers, "'Mississippi Justice' Draws Critics' Fire," *Jackson State Times*, November 10, 1955, 1A; "Mamie Bradley Wants NAACP to File Suit," *Jackson State Times*, November 10, 1955, 1A; Harry Marsh, "Sheriff Says He Got Little Cooperation," *Delta Democrat-Times*, November 10, 1955, 1.

43. Virgil Adams, quoted in Herbers, "Case Closed," 1.

44. Editorial, *Jackson Daily News*, November 13, 1955.

45. Hodding Carter, "Justice in Leflore County," *Delta Democrat-Times*, November 10, 1955, 4.

46. Norman Bradley, "The Real Loser," *Jackson State Times*, November 11, 1955, 4A.

47. Oliver Emmerich, quoted in "The Till Case in Retrospect," *Jackson State Times*, November 21, 1955, 4A.

Notes

48. Details of the Melton killing and ensuing trial come from David Halberstam, "Tallahatchie County Acquits a Peckerwood," *Reporter*, April 19, 1956, 26–30.

49. "An Open Letter from the Glendora Lions Club," *Sumner Sentinel*, December 8, 1955, 1.

50. Hamilton Caldwell, quoted in Halberstam, "Tallahatchie County Acquits," 29. Carter's remarks are quoted from http://themiddleoftheinternet.com/clinton_melton.html.

51. "Look Says It Has 'True Story' of Emmett Till Case," *Delta Democrat-Times*, January 9, 1956, 1; "'Look' Says Till's Boastful Defiance Spelled His Death," *Jackson State Times*, January 9, 1956, 1A. For the original story, see William Bradford Huie, "The Shocking Story of Approved Killing in Mississippi," *Look*, January 24, 1956, 46–50. Milam's reason for killing Till does not square with the fact that the half-brothers clearly did not want the body discovered. It is hard to make an "example" of someone—in this case to warn aggressive northern male negroes—without a body or motive. Far more likely is that Milam murdered the boy in an alcohol-fueled rage.

52. See, for example, "Bryant and Milam Deny Look Story," *Greenwood Commonwealth*, January 13, 1955, 1; "Bryant and Milam Deny Giving Story," *Clarion-Ledger*, January 10, 1956, 1; "Milam Denies Look Article Quotes; May Sue Magazine," *Delta Democrat-Times*, January 10, 1956, 1+; "Milam Says He May Sue Look Magazine," *Delta Democrat-Times*, January 13, 1956, 1+; "Milam Denies Story," *Jackson State Times*, January 10, 1956, 1A; "Milam Denies Ever Talking with Author," *Jackson State Times*, January 13, 1956, 1A.

53. "Places Till Article in Congress Record," *Clarion-Ledger*, January 14, 1956, 1+; "'Look' Writer Claims All Sources Authentic," *Jackson State Times*, January 13, 1956, 1A+; "Diggs Puts Look Yarn on Till Case into Congressional Record," *Delta Democrat-Times*, January 13, 1956, 1+.

54. Jay Milner, "Milam Says He's 'Not Sure' If He Has Grounds for Libel Suit," *Delta Democrat-Times*, January 15, 1956, 1+.

55. Roy Wilkins, letter to the editor, *Look*, March 6, 1955, 10. Huie published a follow-up piece which appeared in the January 22, 1957, issue of *Look*; it was titled, "What's Happened to the Emmett Till Killers?"

Chapter 8. Retrospective Prospects

1. Many scholars have made this claim about Emmett Till and the origins of the civil rights movement. See, esp., Clenora Hudson-Weems, *Emmett Till: The Sacrificial Lamb of the Civil Rights Movement*, 4th ed. (Troy, MI: Bedford, 2006) and *The Definitive Emmett Till: Passion and Battle of a Woman for Intellectual Justice* (Bloomington, IN: Authorhouse, 2006).

2. A copy of the amendment is available at http://index.ls.state.ms.us/isysnative/UzpcRGqjdW1lbnRzXDIwMDVccGRmXHNhbVxzYjIwNzZfc180Y210ZVgzdWIpX2FtZW5kXzAyLnBkZg==/sb2076_s_(cmte_sub)_amend_02.pdf#xml=http://10.240.72.35/isysquery/irla39a/27/hilite and in Jerry Mitchell and Andy Kanengiser, "Senate OKs Naming Roads for Martyrs of Civil Rights," *Clarion-Ledger*, February 11, 2005 at http://www.clarionledger.com/apps/pbcs.dll/article?AID=/20050211/NEWS010504/502110368/1205 (9 Nov. 2005).

Notes

3. For example, see John B. Hatch, "Reconciliation: Building a Bridge from Complicity to Coherence in the Rhetoric of Race Relations," *Rhetoric and Public Affairs* 6 (2003): 737–64; Mitchell and Kanengiser, "Senate OKs Naming Roads."

4. Donna Ladd, "Hush! Somebody's Calling Our Name," *Jackson Free Press*, March 9, 2005 at http://www.jacksonfreepress.com/comments.php?id=5412_0_7_0_C (10 October 2005); Edward S. Casey, "Public Memory in Place and Time," in *Framing Public Memory*, ed. Kendall R. Phillips (Tuscaloosa, AL: University of Alabama Press, 2005), 40; W. Fitzhugh Brundage, *The Southern Past: A Clash of Race and Memory* (Cambridge, MA: Belknap Press of Harvard University Press, 2005), 314.

5. Paul Hendrickson, "Mississippi Haunting," *Rhetoric and Public Affairs* 8 (2005): 177–88; Casey, "Public Memory in Place and Time," 25. Alderman contends that this transcendence of the black community is a key controversial element to understanding the highway memorial's significance as roads have hierarchies based on size, use, etc. See D. H. Alderman, "Street Names and Scaling of Memory: The Politics of Commemorating Martin Luther King, Jr. within the African American Community," *Area* 35 (2003): 163–73.

6. Mitchell and Kanengiser, "Senate OKs Naming Roads"; Robert Jackson, interview with authors, December 28, 2005. Unfortunately, we were informed by the Mississippi Legislative Archivist that the State of Mississippi does not keep a stenographic record of Senate floor deliberations. However, during our interview with Senator Jackson, significant details were revealed about the Till Memorial amendment. It was a last-minute floor amendment on a Friday afternoon when senators were ready to leave for the weekend. Jackson and several other senators were inspired to propose the amendment by a last-minute attachment of the Chaney, Goodman, Schwerner Memorial amendment. The Till Memorial amendment was so "last minute," that Senator Jackson's speech supporting the amendment was done "off the cuff" without any preparation, and Emmett Till's name was misspelled in the original amendment ("Emmitt Till"). According to Jackson, the Mississippi House of Representatives followed the lead of the Senate, as the latter is the more conservative body.

7. Brundage, *The Southern Past*, 310–11; Owen Dryer, "Location, Politics, and the Production of Civil Rights Memorial Landscapes," *Urban Geographer* 23 (2002): 31–56; Mitchell and Kanengiser, "Senate OKs Naming Roads." According to the article, Senator David Jordan is in the process of working with archive officials to purchase the former Bryant Grocery and Meat Market and turn it into a museum.

8. A spur to civil-rights tourism came from Jim Carrier's book *A Travel Guide to the Civil Rights Movement* (New York: Harcourt, 2004). In an interview with PBS's Terrence Smith, Carrier deemed the Bryant Grocery and Meat Market the "most haunting" site of all the important places he had written about. See www.pbs.org/newshour/bb/media/jan-june04/carrier_06-23.html.

9. Karen E. Till, "Places of Memory," in *A Companion for Political Geography*, ed. John Agnew, Katharyne Mitchell, Gearoid O'Tuathail (Oxford: Blackwell, 2002), 289–301.

10. "Officials Investigating Vandalism of Sign Honoring Emmett Till," *Sun Herald*, 25 June 2006 at http://www.sunherald.com/mld/sunherald/14900798.htm (26 June 2006).

Notes

11. For example, see appendix 4 of Hudson-Weems, *Emmett Till*, 3rd ed.; Hudson-Weems's title, *Emmett Till: Sacrificial Lamb of the Civil Rights Movement*; and Till-Mobley and Benson, *Death of Innocence*, xii.

12. Heribert Adam and Kanya Adam, "The Politics of Memory in Divided Societies," in *After the TRC: Reflections on Truth and Reconciliation in South Africa*, ed. Wilmot James and Linda Van de Vijver (Athens, OH: Ohio University Press, 2000), 47. For an example of language placing the Till case in the past, see Mitchell and Kanengiser, "Senate OKs Naming Roads."

13. John Herbers, "The Murder of Emmett Till and the Struggle for Civil Rights" (Roundtable Discussion, Stillman College, Tuscaloosa, AL, September 17, 2005). Herbers is a former UP reporter who covered the Till trial.

14. Al Kuettner, "After Two Years, Few Talk about Till Case," *Jackson State Times*, August 28, 1957. This article was accessed online from the Mississippi State Sovereignty Commission Papers at the Mississippi Department of Archives and History's website at http://mdah.state.ms.us/arlib/contents/er/sovcom/.

Works Cited

"About Till's Father." *Jackson Daily News*, October 15, 1955, 1.
"Accuse Men of Fostering Idea of Integration." *Meridian Star*, September 29, 1955, 1+.
"Accused White Men Plead Innocent of Murder and Kidnap; To Set Trial Date Thursday; Guard Removed." *Greenwood Morning Star*, September 7, 1955, 1.
"Acquittal." *Delta Democrat-Times*, September 25, 1955, 4.
Adam, Heribert, and Kanya Adam. "The Politics of Memory in Divided Societies." In *After TRC: Reflections on Truth and Reconciliation in South Africa*. Ed. Wilmot James and Linda Van de Vijver. Athens, OH: Ohio University Press, 2000, 32–47.
Adams, Virgil. "Bitterest Statements from Chicago." *Greenwood Morning Star*, September 20, 1955, 6.
———. Editorial. *Greenwood Morning Star*, November 6, 1955, 4.
———. "Fair Trial Was Credit to Mississippi." *Greenwood Morning Star*, September 23, 1955, 4.
———. "More Vicious Threats." *Greenwood Morning Star*, September 28, 1955, 4.
———. "A New Wrinkle in the Vilification of Mississippi." *Greenwood Morning Star*, September 27, 1955, 6.
———. "Resentment Rising against Radicals at Trial." *Greenwood Morning Star*, September 22, 1955, 6.
———. "State Granted Recess to Produce New Witnesses in Till Case; Defense to Testify Attack Tried." *Greenwood Morning Star*, September 21, 1955, 1.
———. "10 Jurors Accepted as Milam and Bryant Go on Trial at Sumner; Most Spectators Predict Acquittal." *Greenwood Morning Star*, September 20, 1955, 1.
Agnew, John, Katharyne Mitchell, and Gearoid O'Tuathail, eds. *A Companion for Political Geography*. Oxford: Blackwell, 2002.
Ainsworth, A. B. Letter to the editor. *Greenwood Commonwealth*, September 8, 1955, 8.
"Ainsworth Asks for Funds to Defend Milam and Bryant." *Greenwood Morning News*, September 9, 1955, 1.
Alderman, D. H. "Street Names and Scaling of Memory: The Politics of Commemorating Martin Luther King, Jr. within the African American Community." *Area* 35 (2003): 163–73.
Alewine, Thomas M. "Built for the NAACP." *Brandon News*, September 8, 1955, 2.
———. "They'd Better Stay Home." *Brandon News*, September 8, 1955, 2.
———. "Time Out with the Editor." *Brandon News*, September 22, 1955, 1.
———. "Time Out with the Editor." *Brandon News*, September 29, 1955, 1.
———. "Time Out with the Editor." *Brandon News*, October 6, 1955, 1.
———. "Time Out with the Editor." *Brandon News*, October 13, 1955, 1.
———. "Time Out with the Editor." *Brandon News*, October 20, 1955, 1.
"All Is Quiet at Sumner as Trial Begins." *Jackson State Times*, September 19, 1955, 8A.
Anderson, W. H. Editorial. *Southern Sentinel*, September 15, 1955.

Works Cited

———. Editorial. *Southern Sentinel*, October 20, 1955.
Arrington, Jimmy. "Random Remarks." *Collins News-Commercial*, October 21, 1955, 1.
———. "Random Remarks by Ye Editor." *Collins News-Commercial*, September 9, 1955.
"Arrival Expected at Clarksdale." *Jackson State Times*, September 18, 1955, 14A.
"Arrival of Victim's Mother Causes Stir." *Jackson State Times*, September 20, 1955, 1A.
"As It Is in Chicago." *Jackson Daily News*, September 7, 1955, 8.
"As Time Passes." *Laurel Leader-Call*, September 26, 1955, 4.
"Asks Law against Displaying Bodies to Collect Money." *Greenwood Commonwealth*, September 8, 1955, 1.
"Assault Suspect Sought." *Jackson State Times*, September 25, 1955, 1A+.
"Attempted Rape of White Woman Occurs Near Marks." *Clarion-Ledger*, September 25, 1955, 1.
"Bad News for NAACP." *Jackson Daily News*, September 8, 1955, 8.
Barloon, Marvin J. "Till Kidnapping Challenges Right of American to Defend Household." *Delta Democrat-Times*, September 9, 1995, 7.
Beauchamp, Keith. *The Untold Story of Emmett Louis Till*. DVD. New York: Till Freedom Come Productions, THINKFilm, 2005.
Big Yick. "Communists Are Stirring Strife." *Oxford Eagle*, October 6, 1955, 6.
Bradley, Norman. "The Real Loser." *Jackson State Times*, November 11, 1955, 4A.
Bready, Dave. "Sidelights at Sumner Trial." *Greenwood Commonwealth*, September 23, 1955, 1.
———. "Sidelights of Trial at Sumner." *Greenwood Commonwealth*, September 22, 1955, 1.
Breed, Warren. "Comparative Newspaper Handling of the Emmett Till Case." *Journalism Quarterly* 35 (1958): 291–98.
Breland, J. J. Letter to the editor. *Jackson Daily News*, October 20, 1955, 3.
"Broad View of the Verdict in the Till Trial." *Natchez Democrat*, September 25, 1955, 6.
Brownmiller, Susan. *Against Our Will: Men, Women and Rape*. New York: Simon and Schuster, 1975.
Brumfield, Robert H. Letter to the editor. *McComb Enterprise-Journal*, September 2, 1955, 2.
———. "Mississippians Are Urged to Stand, Be Counted in Actions Local Doctor Says 'White Trash' Is Perpetrating." *McComb Enterprise-Journal*, September 1, 1955, 1.
Brundage, W. Fitzhugh. *The Southern Past: A Clash of Race and Memory*. Cambridge, MA: Belknap Press of Harvard University Press, 2005.
"A Brutal Murder." *Clarksdale Press Register*, September 1, 1955, 4.
"A Brutal Slaying." *Delta Democrat-Times*, September 2, 1955, 4.
"Bryant and Milam Deny Giving Story." *Clarion-Ledger*, January 10, 1956, 1.
"Bryant and Milam Deny Look Story." *Greenwood Commonwealth*, January 13, 1955, 1.
"Bryant and Milan [sic] Face Murder Charge in Slaying of 15 [sic] Year Old Negro Boy." *Greenwood Morning Star*, September 1, 1955, 1.

Works Cited

"Bryant, Milam Face Leflore Kidnap Case." *Jackson State Times*, September 24, 1955, 1A.

"Bryant, Milam Get Preliminary Hearing This Week on Kidnaping Charge Arising in State's Till Case—Expected Outcries Begin to Be Heard Up North." *McComb Enterprise-Journal*, September 26, 1955, 1+.

"Bryant, Milam Indicted for Murder, Kidnaping by Jury in Tallahatchie." *West Point Daily Times Leader*, September 6, 1955, 1.

"Bryant, Milam Released under $10,000 Bonds in Emmett Till Kidnaping." *Jackson Daily News*, September 30, 1955, 1.

"Bryant's Store in Money Robbed Sat. Night; Boys Fire Guns." *Greenwood Morning Star*, September 20, 1955, 1.

Burke, Kenneth. *A Grammar of Motives*. Berkeley, CA: University of California Press, 1968.

———. *Language as Symbolic Action: Essays on Life, Literature, and Method*. Berkeley, CA: University of California Press, 1966.

Burton, Paul. "'Old Man Mose' Sells Out, He'll Move to New York." *Clarion-Ledger*, September 26, 1955, 1.

"By Striking at Till Jury's Verdict NAACP Plays in Communist Hands." *Aberdeen Examiner*, September 29, 1955, 4.

"'Cannot Condone' Killing." *Clarion-Ledger*, September 3, 1955, 4.

"A Careful Last Look." *Clarion-Ledger*, October 2, 1955, 8.

Carrier, Jim. *A Travel Guide to the Civil Rights Movement*. New York: Harcourt, 2004.

Carter, Hodding. "Justice in Leflore County." *Delta Democrat-Times*, November 10, 1955, 4.

Casey, Edward S. "Public Memory in Place and Time." In *Framing Public Memory*. Ed. Kendall R. Phillips. Tuscaloosa, AL: University of Alabama Press, 2005, 17–44.

"Cast in Impelling Court Drama Matches Movies." *Jackson Daily News*, September 20, 1955, 6.

"Charged Greenwood Storekeeper with Abducting Youth." *Delta Democrat-Times*, August 29, 1955, 2.

"Chicago Has Its Troubles." *Jackson Daily News*, September 14, 1955, 14.

"Chicago Negro Youth Abducted by Three White Men at Money." *Greenwood Commonwealth*, August 28, 1955, 1.

"Citizens Councils Are Given Unjust Criticism." *Greenwood Morning Star*, September 9, 1955, 6.

"City Watches Trial Results." *Clarksdale Press Register*, September 26, 1955, 1.

"Claim Release Boy Unharmed." *Meridian Star*, August 30, 1955, 1.

Cole, C. H. "Hardly a Column by Chance." *Picayune Item*, September 29, 1955, 1.

———. "Hardly a Column by Chance." *Picayune Item*, October 13, 1955, 1.

———. "Hardly a Column by Chance." *Picayune Item*, October 27, 1955, 1.

———. "Interference Will Injure...." *Picayune Item*, September 8, 1955, 2.

"Coleman Names Assistant to Aid Delta Prosecution." *Clarion-Ledger*, September 10, 1955, 1.

Coody, A. S. Letter to the editor. *Jackson Daily News*, October 20, 1955.

Cooper, Caryl A. "Percy Greene and the *Jackson Advocate*." In *The Press and Race:*

Works Cited

Mississippi Journalists Confront the Movement. Ed. David R. Davies. Jackson, MS: University Press of Mississippi, 2001, 54–83.

Cox, Prentiss. "Jury to Probe Boy's Murder." *Jackson State Times*, September 1, 1955, 1A+.

"Crowded Courtroom Causes Judge to Recess Sumner Trial Overnight." *Greenwood Commonwealth*, September 20, 1955, 1.

Crowe, Chris. *Getting Away with Murder: The True Story of the Emmett Till Case*. New York: Fogelman, 2003.

Cunningham, Morris. "Father of Till Hanged in Italy for Attacks on 3 Women in 1944." *Grenada Daily Sentinel-Star*, October 17, 1955, 1+.

Davies, David R., "J. Oliver Emmerich and the *McComb Enterprise-Journal*." In *The Press and Race: Mississippi Journalists Confront the Movement*. Ed. Davies. Jackson, MS: University Press of Mississippi, 2001, 111–34.

Davis, Angela. *Women, Race and Class*. New York: Random House, 1981.

"Defense Predicts State Cannot Prove Murder; Till Trial Opens Monday." *Greenwood Morning Star*, September 18, 1955, 1.

"Defense Urges Acquittal; State Asserts Defendants Guilty of Cowardly Crime." *Laurel Leader-Call*, September 23, 1955, 1+.

"Delta Veniremen Called; Mother to Attend Trial." *Clarion-Ledger*, September 16, 1955, 1.

"'A Den of Snakes' Youth's Mother Calls Mississippi." *Delta Democrat-Times*, September 1, 1955, 1.

"Denies Definite Knowledge Till Is Found Alive." *Meridian Star*, September 29, 1955, 1.

Denley, Robert H. "Southern Accent Throws Newsmen at Till Trial." *Columbus Commercial Dispatch*, September 25, 1955, 1:6.

"Designed to Inflame." *Jackson Daily News*, September 2, 1955, 8.

"Dianne Kearney Given Certificate of Merit Award." *Greenwood Commonwealth*, September 9, 1955, 1.

"Dianne Kearney to Receive Red Cross Award for Saving Nurse." *Greenwood Morning Star*, September 9, 1955, 1.

"Diggs Puts Look Yarn on Till Case into Congressional Record." *Delta Democrat-Times*, January 13, 1956, 1+.

"District Attorney Opens State's Final Arguments in Sumner Trial; Jury May Return Verdict Today." *Daily Corinthian*, September 23, 1955, 1.

Dittmer, John. *Local People: The Struggle for Civil Rights in Mississippi*. Champagne, IL: University of Illinois Press, 1994.

"Doubts Body Found in River Is Till's." *Meridian Star*, September 4, 1955, 1+.

"Dr. T.R.M. Howard in Chicago Limelight after Till Slaying." *Jackson Advocate*, September 19, 1955, 1+.

"Drawing of Jury List Begins for Two White Men at Sumner." *Vicksburg Evening Post*, September 12, 1955, 1.

"Drowsy State Delta Stirs Uneasily as 2 Governors Ask Probe in Negro Death." *Laurel Leader-Call*, September 2, 1955, 1+.

Dryer, Owen. "Location, Politics, and the Production of Civil Rights Memorial Landscapes." *Urban Geographer* 23 (2002): 31–56.

Works Cited

Durr, M. C. Letter to the editor. *Lincoln County Advertiser*, September 29, 1955.
———. "Open Forum." *Brookhaven Leader-Times*, September 14, 1955, 2.
Editorial. *Jackson Daily News*, October 25, 1955.
Editorial. *Jackson Daily News*, November 13, 1955.
Editorial. *Jackson State Times*, September 13, 1955.
"Ella Mae Shuns Willie." *Jackson Daily News*, September 30, 1955, 1.
Emmerich, Oliver. "A Trap Is Set . . . and Baited with Insults." *McComb Enterprise-Journal*, October 7, 1955, 1.
"Emmett Till Still Alive, Says Sheriff." *Biloxi Daily Herald*, September 29, 1955, 1+.
"Entire State Is Blamed by Negro Leader." *Vicksburg Evening Post*, October 8, 1955, 1.
Ethridge, Tom. "Mississippi Notebook." *Jackson Daily News*, September 9, 1955.
———. "Mississippi Notebook." *Jackson Daily News*, September 18, 1955.
"An Even Bigger Crime." *Scott County Times*, September 8, 1955, 4.
Everett, Arthur. "Defendants Admit Kidnaping Till Boy but Deny 'Murder.'" *Clarion-Ledger*, September 22, 1955, 1+.
———. "Jury Deliberations Expected to Begin Today in Till Case; Bryant's Wife Tells Incident." *Clarion-Ledger*, September 23, 1955, 1.
———. "Sumner Trial Opens Briskly." *Clarion-Ledger*, September 20, 1955, 1+.
———. "Till Case Defendants Freed by Jury on Third Ballot because of Doubt Concerning Identification of Body." *Clarion-Ledger*, September 24, 1955, 1+.
———. "Till Nearly Missed His Fatal Journey to Land of Cotton." *Clarion-Ledger*, September 19, 1955, 1+.
———. "Trial in Leflore Must Await Action by Next Grand Jury." *Clarion-Ledger*, September 24, 1955, 1+.
"Fair Trial Fairly Reported." *Clarksdale Press Register*, September 26, 1955, 4.
"Fate of Negro Accused of Raping White Woman Goes to Jury in Laurel." *Jackson Daily News*, October 8, 1955, 1.
Faulkner, William. "Faulkner Pictures Till Case as Test of Survival of White Man, America." *Jackson Daily News*, September 10, 1955, 1.
Featherston, James. "Delta Courtroom Is Packed as Murder Trial Opens; Evidence 'Circumstantial.'" *Jackson Daily News*, September 19, 1955, 1+.
———. "Dim Light Casts Some Doubt on Identity Of Till's Abductors; Slain Boy's Uncle [sic] Points Finger at Bryant, Milam but Admits Light Was Dim." *Jackson Daily News*, September 21, 1955, 1+.
———. "Mandy Bradley, Reed Boy Leave with Congressman after Testifying at Trial." *Jackson Daily News*, September 24, 1.
———. "Negro Congressman Eyes Trial—His Role Not Clear; Testimony Starts Today." *Jackson Daily News*, September 20, 1955, 1+.
———. "'Surprise' Witness Describes 'Hollering' in Sunflower Barn; Negro Youth Testifies He Saw Milam Armed at Barn, Says Till Boy Was There." *Jackson Daily News*, September 22, 1955, 1+.
———. "Two Who 'Saw Milam, Till at Barn' Flown North by Congressman Diggs." *Jackson Daily News*, September 24, 1955, 1.
———. "White Orders Investigation in Slaying of Delta Negro." *Jackson Daily News*, September 1, 1955, 1.

Works Cited

Featherston, James, and W. C. Shoemaker. "Byrant [sic], Milam Still in Custody of Law to Face Kidnap Charges in Leflore after Acquittal of Murder at Sumner." *Jackson Daily News*, September 24, 1955, 1+.

———. "Verdict Awaited in Till Trial; State Demands Conviction; Defense Says No Proof Presented, Asks Acquittal." *Jackson Daily News*, September 23, 1955, 1+.

Feldstein, Ruth. *Motherhood in Black and White: Race and Sex in American Liberalism, 1930–1965*. Ithaca, NY: Cornell University Press, 2000.

"15,000 Attend Funeral." *Biloxi Daily Herald*, September 3, 1955, 2.

"Final Arguments Underway in Till Trial; Jury May Get Case Today." *Grenada Daily Sentinel-Star*, September 23, 1955, 1.

"Find Body of Missing Boy in State River." *Meridian Star*, August 31, 1955, 1+.

"Find Missing Youth's Body; Blow on Head Killed Him." *Clarksdale Press Register*, August 31, 1955, 1.

Flournoy, John Craig. "Reporting the Movement in Black and White: The Emmett Till Lynching and the Montgomery Bus Boycott." PhD Diss., Louisiana State University, 2003.

"For a Few Extra Nickles." *Greenwood Commonwealth*, September 13, 1955, 6.

Foreman, Harold. "Reports Till Boy Alive in Detroit Bring 'Hoax' Comment from Mother." *Jackson Daily News*, September 29, 1955, 1.

"France Irate over Till Case." *Clarion-Ledger*, September 26, 1955, 2:6.

"French Protest Till Verdict in Mass Meeting." *Jackson State Times*, September 29, 1955, 11A.

"From Press Dispatches." *Clarion-Ledger*, September 25, 1955, 1.

"'Full Prosecution' Ordered in Slaying of Negro Youth." *Tupelo Daily Journal*, September 2, 1955, 1.

Gibson, Gwen. "Negroes Assured of Action If Probe Proves Violation of Civil Rights in State," *Jackson Daily News*, September 8, 1955, 2.

Goldsby, Jacqueline. "The High and Low Tech of It: The Meaning of Lynching and the Death of Emmett Till." *Yale Journal of Criticism* 9 (1996): 245–82.

Goldzwig, Steven R. "Multiculturalism, Rhetoric, and the Twenty-first Century." *Southern Communication Journal* 63 (1998): 273–90.

"Gov. Hugh White Asks Full Probe on Murder Kidnapping, Greenwood." *Delta Democrat-Times*, September 1, 1955, 1+.

"Governors Ask Probe of Slaying." *Biloxi Daily Herald*, September 2, 1955, 1+.

"Grand Jury Calls Several Witnesses in Till Murder Case; More Due to Testify; Guards at Courthouse." *Greenwood Morning Star*, September 6, 1955, 1.

"Grand Jury Now Considers Case of Two White Men." *Vicksburg Evening Post*, November 9, 1955, 1.

"Grand Jury to Call 5 More Witnesses in Kidnap-Slaying Case." *Delta Democrat-Times*, September 6, 1955, 1+.

"Grenada Pastor Speaks 'Mind' on NAACP Remarks." *Grenada Daily Sentinel-Star*, September 9, 1955.

"Guard Pair at Greenwood against Mob." *Biloxi Daily Herald*, September 5, 1955, 1+.

Haines, Carolyn. *My Mother's Witness*. Fairbanks, AK: River City Press, 2003.

Halberstam, David. *The Fifties*. New York: Villard, 1993.

Works Cited

———. "Tallahatchie County Acquits a Peckerwood." *Reporter*, April 19, 1956, 26–30.
"Half Brothers to Face Trial Later in Month." *Tupelo Daily Journal*, September 12, 1955, 1+.
"Half-Brothers Back in Jail." *West Point Daily Times Leader*, September 24, 1955, 1+.
"Half-Brothers Found Innocent of Slaying." *Biloxi Daily Herald*, September 24, 1955, 1+.
"Halt Hunt for Woman in Slaying." *Biloxi Daily Herald*, September 3, 1955, 1.
Harris, Henry. "Pencil Shavings." *West Point Daily Times Leader*, September 6, 1955, 4.
———. "Pencil Shavings." *West Point Daily Times Leader*, September 7, 1955, 6.
———. "Pencil Shavings." *West Point Daily Times Leader*, September 20, 1955, 4.
Harris, Sid R. "As Diggs Sows His Seeds of Ill Will." *Houston (MS) Times-Post*, September 22, 1955, 2.
———. "Nation Eyes Wolf-Whistle Murder Trial." *Houston (MS) Times-Post*, September 15, 1955, 2.
———. "Till's Father Executed for Rape-Murder in Italy." *Houston (MS) Times-Post*, October 20, 1955, 2.
———. "The 'Wolf Whistle' Murder Case." *Houston (MS) Times-Post*, September 8, 1955, 2.
Hatch, John B. "Reconciliation: Building a Bridge from Complicity to Coherence in the Rhetoric of Race Relations." *Rhetoric and Public Affairs* 6 (2003): 737–64.
"Hearst Newspaper in Chicago Accuses Daily News of Slanting NAACP Stories." *Jackson Daily News*, October 7, 1955, 1.
Hendrickson, Paul. "Mississippi Haunting." *Rhetoric and Public Affairs* 8 (2005): 177–88.
———. *Sons of Mississippi: A Story of Race and Its Legacy*. New York: Vintage, 2004.
Herbers, John. "'Case Closed' as Jury Fails to Indict Pair for Till Kidnapping." *Delta Democrat-Times*, November 10, 1955, 1.
———. "Contradictions Develop as Testimony in Till Trial Begins; Negro Tells How Till Was Taken from Bed." *Greenwood Morning Star*, September 22, 1955, 1.
———. "Cross-Burning at Sumner Went Almost Un-Noticed Yesterday." *Delta Democrat-Times*, September 22, 1955, 11.
———. "Defendants Confident Acquittal Will Result in Trial at Sumner." *Grenada Daily Sentinel-Star*, September 19, 1955, 1.
———. "Jury Absent as Mrs. Bryant Tells of Struggle with Till; Expect to Complete Case Today." *Greenwood Morning Star*, September 23, 1955, 1.
———. "'Mississippi Justice' Draws Critics' Fire." *Jackson State Times*, November 10, 1955, 1A.
———. "The Murder of Emmett Till and the Struggle for Civil Rights." Roundtable Discussion, Stillman College, Tuscaloosa, AL, September 17, 2005.
———. "Not Guilty Verdict in Wolf Whistle Murder." *Greenwood Morning Star*, September 24, 1955, 1.
———. "State Asks Death or Life Sentence." *Jackson State Times*, September 23, 1955, 1A+.

Works Cited

———. "Sumner Surprised by Way World Watching Pending Till Trial Today." *Delta Democrat-Times*, September 18, 1955, 1.

———. "Testimony Opens Today in Till 'Wolf-Whistle' Murder Trial." *Delta Democrat-Times*, September 20, 1955, 1+.

———. "Till Trial Bogs Down in Jury-Picking Job." *Delta Democrat-Times*, September 19, 1955, 1+.

———. "Uncle [sic] Identifies Boy's Abductors; Says One Had Gun and Light." *Jackson State Times*, September 21, 1955, 1A.

———. "Uncle [sic] of Slain Boy Appears as First Witness." *Grenada Daily Sentinel-Star*, September 21, 1955, 1.

———. "Witness Says He Saw Milam Take Lad Into. . . ." *Delta Democrat-Times*, September 22, 1955, 1+.

———. "Wolf Whistle Murder Case Goes to Jury in Sumner Circuit Court." *Delta Democrat-Times*, September 23, 1955, 1+.

———. "Wright Tells of Kidnaping of Till Boy." *Delta Democrat-Times*, September 21, 1955, 1+.

———. "Youth Testifies Saw Till Taken into Barn; Tells Jury of Hearing Screaming." *Jackson State Times*, September 22, 1955, 1A+.

Holland, Endesha Ida Mae. *From the Mississippi Delta: A Memoir*. New York: Simon and Schuster, 1997.

Houck, Davis W. "Killing Emmett." *Rhetoric and Public Affairs* 8 (2005): 225–62.

H. S. "Hal-Lucinations." *Tate County Democrat*, September 29, 1955, 1.

Hudson-Weems, Clenora. *The Definitive Emmett Till: Passion and Battle of a Woman for Intellectual Justice*. Bloomington, IN: Authorhouse, 2006.

———. *Emmett Till: The Sacrificial Lamb of the Civil Rights Movement*. 3rd ed. Troy, MI: Bedford, 2000.

———. *Emmett Till: The Sacrificial Lamb of the Civil Rights Movement*. 4th ed. Troy, MI: Bedford, 2006.

Huie, William Bradford. "The Shocking Story of Approved Killing in Mississippi." *Look*, January 24, 1956, 46–50.

Hutto, Ralph. "Dynamic Personalities Form Till Trial Cast." *Jackson State Times*, September 20, 1955, 2A.

———. "Mother, 'Surprise Witness' Give Dramatic Testimony; Mamie Bradley Says Corpse Was That of Her Slain Son." *Jackson State Times*, September 22, 1955, 2A.

———. "Now Sumner Is Just Another Sleepy Delta Town." *Jackson State Times*, September 24, 1955, 1A.

———. "Slain Boy's Uncle [sic] Identifies Bryant, Milam on Stand; But Mose Wright Admits He Never Saw Faces in Light." *Jackson State Times*, September 21, 1955, 8A.

"I Saw Them Take Emmett Till." *Inside Detective*, February 1956, 26+.

"Impose Equal Justice." *Jackson Daily News*, September 19, 1955, 10.

"Indict 2 Men Charged with Youth's Death." *Meridian Star*, September 6, 1955, 1.

"Innocent Pleas Entered by 2 Indicted in Slaying of Negro Youth; Early Trial Predicted." *Laurel Leader-Call*, September 7, 1955, 1+.

"Ironic Parallel." *Daily Corinthian*, September 14, 1955, 4.

"Irresponsible Statement." *Laurel Leader-Call*, September 2, 1955, 4.

Works Cited

"Is Emmett Till Alive?" *Clarksdale Press Register*, September 29, 1955, 1.

"It Was A Fair Trial." *The Greenwood Commonwealth*, September 24, 1955, 4.

"Jackson News Says NAACP Holds Negroes Captive." *Natchez Democrat*, October 6, 1955, 1+.

James, Wilmot, and Linda Van de Vijver, eds. *After the TRC: Reflections on Truth and Reconciliation in South Africa*. Athens, OH: Ohio University Press, 2000.

Johnson, Sam. "Bryant, Milam Freed in Till Slaying; Face Kidnap Charge." *Hattiesburg American*, September 24, 1955, 1+.

———. "Grand Jury Empaneled Today, Expect Action in Kidnapping." *Greenwood Commonwealth*, November 7, 1955, 1.

———. "Grand Jury, Not Examined Witnesses in Till Kidnaping." *Greenwood Commonwealth*, November 8, 1955, 1.

———. "Jury Completed in Sumner Trial; State Summons 13 Witnesses in Trial; Till's Mother Arrives." *Vicksburg Evening Post*, September 20, 1955, 1.

———. "Jury Hears Defense and Prosecution Arguments as Testimony Ends in Kidnap-Slaying Case." *Greenwood Commonwealth*, September 23, 1955, 1.

———. "Jury Selected, State Summons 13—Till's Mother, Now at Sumner, Is Included as One Trial Witness." *McComb Enterprise-Journal*, September 20, 1955, 1+.

———. "Mother of Till Says Body That of Her Son—Negro Youth Testifies Four White Men Took Chicago Boy into Sunflower Plantation Barn." *McComb Enterprise-Journal*, September 22, 1955, 1+.

———. "Murder Trial at Sumner Opens Monday." *Natchez Democrat*, September 18, 1955, 1+.

———. "69 Covering Murder Trial in Mississippi." *Natchez Democrat*, September 19, 1955, 1.

———. "State Is Not Seeking Death Penalty for Men as Delta Trial Opens." *McComb Enterprise-Journal*, September 19, 1955, 1+.

———. "State Tentatively Accepts Eleven Jurors in Trial of Bryant and Milam at Sumner." *Vicksburg Evening Post*, September 19, 1955, 1+.

———. "State Will Not Ask Death Penalty in Trial of White Men at Sumner." *Greenwood Commonwealth*, September 19, 1955, 1.

———. "State Won't Ask Death Penalty." *Hattiesburg American*, September 19, 1955, 1.

———. "Two White Men Go on Trial Monday for Slaying of Negro." *Clarion-Ledger*, September 18, 1955, 4.

———. "Uncle [*sic*] of Till's Identifies Pair as Men Who Abducted Chicago Negro; State Hopes to Strengthen Case by Surprise Witnesses." *Greenwood Commonwealth*, September 21, 1955, 1.

Jones, Charles C. "This Mendenhall Preacher Has the Right Ideas." *Drew Leader*, November 3, 1955, 1.

Jones, J. Morris. Letter to the editor. *McComb Enterprise-Journal*, September 6, 1955, n.p.

"Judge Limits Sketching of Murder Trial." *Jackson State Times*, September 20, 1955, 2A.

"Judge Sends Jury out of Courtroom during Testimony of Defendant Roy Bryant's Wife." *Jackson State Times*, September 23, 1955, 2A.

Works Cited

"Juror Selection Underway in Till Murder Trial." *Daily Corinthian*, September 19, 1955, 1.

"Jury Acquits Bryant, Milam of Murder Charge as Trial Ends." *Clarksdale Press Register*, September 23, 1955, 1+.

"Jury Returns Not Guilty Verdict in Till Trial, Deliberated One Hour." *Natchez Democrat*, September 24, 1955, 1+.

"A Just Appraisal." *Greenwood Commonwealth*, September 2, 1955, 1.

"Justice Is the Answer." *Jackson State Times*, September 2, 1955, 4A.

Katagiri, Yasuhiro. *The Mississippi State Sovereignty Commission: Civil Rights and States' Rights*. Jackson, MS: University Press of Mississippi, 2001.

"Kidnap Counts Face 2 Freed in Till Trial." *Meridian Star*, September 24, 1955, 1.

"Kidnap-Murder Case Grand Jury to Report Today." *Natchez Democrat*, September 6, 1955, 1+.

"Kidnap-Murder Case Will Be Transferred to Tallahatchie." *Greenwood Commonwealth*, September 1, 1955, 1.

"Kidnap-Murder Stirs Delta." *Clarksdale Press Register*, September 2, 1955, 1+.

"Kidnapping Near Columbus Brings FBI Probe; Stirs More NAACP Criticism." *Greenwood Morning Star*, September 14, 1955, 1.

Kuettner, Al. "After Two Years, Few Talk about Till Case." *Jackson State Times*, August 28, 1957.

Ladd, Donna. "Hush! Somebody's Calling Our Name." *Jackson Free Press*, March 9, 2005. http://www.jacksonfreepress.com/comments.php?id=5412_0_7_0_C (10 October 2005).

Langford, Dave. Editorial. *Lincoln County Advertiser*, September 8, 1955, 1.

Laughman, Royce. "Just Beating Around." *Simpson County News*, September 29, 1955, 1.

"Leflore Officials Delay Fixing Bond in Till Case." *Clarion-Ledger*, September 25, 1955, 1.

"Lives of Two Negroes Saved by J. W. Milam." *Vicksburg Evening Post*, September 20, 1955, 1.

"Look Says It Has 'True Story' of Emmett Till Case." *Delta Democrat-Times*, January 9, 1956, 1.

"'Look' Says Till's Boastful Defiance Spelled His Death." *Jackson State Times*, January 9, 1956, 1A.

"'Look' Writer Claims All Sources Authentic." *Jackson State Times*, January 13, 1956, 1A+.

"Lynching Post-Facto." *Delta Democrat-Times*, September 6, 1955, 4.

"Mamie Bradley Says Trial a 'Comedy'." *Clarion-Ledger*, September 26, 1955, 2:6.

"Mamie Bradley Wants NAACP to File Suit." *Jackson State Times*, November 10, 1955, 1.

"Many People Resentful over Coverage of Case." *Greenwood Morning Star*, September 9, 1955, 6.

Marsh, Harry. "Communist Writer at Trial Lauds Citizens." *Delta Democrat-Times*, September 22, 1955, 1.

———. "Editors Eye Clock in Awaiting Verdict." *Delta Democrat-Times*, September 23, 1955, 1.

Works Cited

———. "Sheriff Says He Got Little Cooperation." *Delta Democrat-Times*, November 10, 1955, 1.
Marshall, Chester, and James McBroom. "Delta Pair Indicted for Murdering Negro." *Jackson Daily News*, September 6, 1955, 1+.
McClary, Webster. "Negro Pastor Declares: Neither Race Wants Mixing." *Clarion-Ledger*, September 25, 1955, 2:7.
"A Meagre Correction." *Jackson Daily News*, November 5, 1955, 6.
"A Meddlesome Visitor." *Jackson Daily News*, September 24, 1955, 6.
"Meddling in Local Case Creates Problems." *Greenwood Morning Star*, September 6, 1955, 4.
Metress, Christopher, ed. *The Lynching of Emmett Till: A Documentary Narrative.* Charlottesville, VA: University of Virginia Press, 2002.
Middlebrooks, William. "Sheriff Says Body Thousands Viewed May Not Be Till's." *Delta Democrat-Times*, September 4, 1955, 1+.
"Milam, Bryant Face Leflore Kidnap Case." *Jackson State Times*, September 24, 1955, 1A.
"Milam Denies Ever Talking with Author." *Jackson State Times*, January 13, 1956, 1A.
"Milam Denies Look Article Quotes; May Sue Magazine." *Delta Democrat-Times*, January 10, 1956, 1+.
"Milam Denies Story." *Jackson State Times*, January 10, 1956, 1A.
"Milam Is Pictured a War Hero Who Also Snatched Negro from Drowning." *Jackson Daily News*, September 20, 1955, 6.
"Milam Is Pictured a War Hero Who Snatched a Negro from Drowning." *Jackson Advocate*, September 24, 1955, 6.
"Milam Says He May Sue Look Magazine." *Delta Democrat-Times*, January 13, 1956, 1+.
Milam, Wade. Letter to the editor. *Jackson Daily News*, October 19, 1955.
Milner, Jay. "Bryant Didn't Mind His Negro Non-Com during Korean War." *Clarion-Ledger*, September 20, 1955, 1+.
———. "Chicago Hysteria Called Hinderance [sic] in Delta Slaying; Arrest of Negroes on Speeding Charge Sets Off Wild Rumor." *Clarion-Ledger*, September 4, 1955, 1.
———. "Delta Town Welcomes Quiet Following in Wake of Sensational Murder Trial." *Clarion-Ledger*, September 25, 1955, 10.
———. "Doctor's Testimony May Alter Inquiry." *Clarion-Ledger*, September 6, 1955, 1+.
———. "Jittery News Men at Sumner Kept in a Dither by Rumors." *Clarion-Ledger*, September 22, 1955, 2.
———. "Milam Says He's 'Not Sure' If He Has Grounds for Libel Suit." *Delta Democrat-Times*, January 15, 1956, 1+.
———. "Negro's Funeral at Sumner Takes Spotlight from Trial." *Clarion-Ledger*, September 19, 1955, 1.
———. "Newsmen Disagree on Protest Rallies." *Clarion-Ledger*, September 27, 1955, 1+.
———. "Sumner Folk Already Plenty Bored with All This Ruckus." *Clarion-Ledger*, September 21, 1955, 2.

Works Cited

———. "Till Case Defendants Freed by Jury on Third Ballot because of Doubt Concerning Identification of Body." *Clarion-Ledger*, September 24, 1955, 1+.

———. "2 Accused Deny Advocacy of Integration in Holmes." *Clarion-Ledger*, September 30, 1955, 1+.

"Missing Negro's Body Discovered in River." *Tupelo Daily Journal*, September 1, 1955, 1.

"Mississippi Barbarism." *Crisis*, October 1955, 480–81.

"Mississippi Editors Unanimous in Deploring Delta Kidnap and Murder." *Laurel Leader-Call*, September 3, 1955, 5.

"Mississippi Gets New Rapping at NAACP Rallies." *Vicksburg Evening Post*, October 24, 1955, 12.

"Mississippi Hard Hit by the Slaying of Till." *Jackson Advocate*, September 10, 1955, 1+.

"Mississippi: Many Share the Guilt." *Southern Patriot*, October 1955, 1+.

"Mississippi Sheriff Voices Doubt Body Was That of Till." *Greenwood Morning Star*, September 4, 1955, 1.

Mitchell, Jerry, and Andy Kanengiser. "Senate OKs Naming Roads for Martyrs of Civil Rights." *Clarion-Ledger*, February 11, 2005. http://www.clarionledger.com/apps/pbcs.dll/article?AID=/20050211/NEWS010504/502110368/1205 (9 November 2005).

"'Money' Jars for Defense Delay Trial." *Jackson State Times*, September 20, 1955, 2A.

"Mose Wright Tells New York Paper He Fled for His Life." *Vicksburg Evening Post*, October 4, 1955, 1.

"Mother Denies Till Found Alive; Rumor in Detroit Held 'Cruel Hoax' by Mamie Bradley." *Vicksburg Evening Post*, September 29, 1955, 1.

"Mother of Accused Men Promises to Stand by Them; Dead Boy's Mother and Chicago Mayor Write President." *Grenada Daily Sentinel-Star*, September 2, 1955, 1.

"Mother of Pair Accused in Delta Slaying 'Will Stand by Them.'" *Jackson Daily News*, September 2, 1955, 14.

"Mother of Till Boy to Testify at Trial." *Clarion-Ledger*, September 11, 1955, 1+.

"Mother to Testify at Trial; May Set Date Today." *Greenwood Morning Star*, September 9, 1955, 1.

"Mother Vows to Stand by 2 Accused Sons." *Meridian Star*, September 2, 1955, 1.

"Mother Won't Attend Trial." *Jackson State Times*, September 18, 1955, 14A.

Moulder, Bob. "Radio, Newspaper, TV Overplay Till Trial." *Jackson State Times*, September 25, 1955, 9B.

"Mourners, Curious Mingle at Till Rites; Abandon Search for Woman Who Figured in Case." *Clarksdale Press Register*, September 3, 1955, 1.

"Mrs. Bryant Tells How Northern Negro Grabbed Her, 'Wolf-Whistled' in Store." *Jackson Daily News*, September 23, 1955, 9.

"Much Conflict in Newspaper Report." *Natchez Democrat*, October 8, 1955, 1+.

"Mullen Musings: "Let's Not Change." *Madison County Herald*, September 8, 1955, 3.

"Murder Charges against Deltans in Case of Slain Negro Boy, 14 Will Go Swiftly to Grand Jurors." *McComb Enterprise-Journal*, September 1, 1955, 1+.

"Murder of Four Boys." *Vicksburg Evening Post*, October 27, 1955, 4.

Works Cited

"NAACP Charges Lynch, Council Sends Regrets." *Meridian Star*, September 1, 1955, 1.

"NAACP Officials Launch Bitter Attack on State." *Clarion-Ledger*, September 1, 1955, 1+.

"NAACP Signs Rap Eastland." *Jackson State Times*, October 7, 1955, 1A.

"NAACP Sows Seeds of Hate." *Kosciusko Star-Herald*, October 13, 1955, 4.

"National Boycott of Mississippi Products Urged." *Vicksburg Evening Post*, October 11, 1955, 1.

"National Guard Called to Protect Accused Men after Outside Threats." *Greenwood Commonwealth*, September 5, 1955, 1.

"Negro Body Was in Water 10 Days, Witnesses Say." *Jackson Daily News*, September 23, 1955, 9.

"Negro Boy's Slaying to Grand Jury." *Biloxi Daily Herald*, September 1, 1955, 1+.

"Negro Editor Denies Trio Held." *Vicksburg Evening Post*, October 6, 1955, 8.

"Negro Lad's Slaying Attributed to Whistle." *Hattiesburg American*, September 1, 1955, 1.

"Negro Mass March Called Rumor; Discount Doubts of Till's Identity." *Jackson State Times*, September 4, 1955, 1A.

"Negro Pastor Favors Voluntary Segregation." *Picayune Item*, October 6, 1955, 4.

"Negro Youth's Slaying Slated for Grand Jury Monday While NAACP Pours Wrath on State." *Laurel Leader-Call*, September 1, 1955, 1+.

Nelson, Marilyn. *A Wreath for Emmett Till*. Boston: Houghton Mifflin, 2005.

"New Story on Murder of Till." *Greenwood Commonwealth*, September 21, 1955, 1.

"New Witnesses May Take Till Murder Trial to Sunflower." *Delta Democrat-Times*, September 21, 1955, 1.

N. H. C. "Just Beating Around." *Simpson County News*, September 22, 1955, 1.

"No Change in Attitude." *West Point Daily Times Leader*, October 15, 1955, 4.

"No Indictment Returned in Brookhaven Slaying." *Tupelo Daily Journal*, September 21, 1955, 1.

"Not Enough Evidence Reports Grand Jury." *Lincoln County Advertiser*, September 22, 1955, 1.

"Officer Fears Actions Build Up Resentment." *Clarion-Ledger*, September 4, 1955, 1.

"Officer Fears Actions Build Up Resentment." *Jackson Daily News*, September 4, 1955, 1.

"Officers Hunt Evidence to Support Charges of Murder." *Meridian Star*, September 3, 1955, 1+.

"Officers Offer Different Opinions in Race Slaying; Delta Sheriff Links Murder with N.A.A.C.P." *Tupelo Daily Journal*, September 5, 1955, 1.

"Officials Investigating Vandalism of Sign Honoring Emmett Till." *Sun Herald*, 25 June 2006. http://www.sunherald.com/mld/sunherald/14900798.htm (26 June 2006).

"On the Emmett Louis Till Incident." *Jackson Advocate*, September 10, 1955, 4.

"An Open Letter from the Glendora Lions Club." *Sumner Sentinel*, December 8, 1955, 1.

"Pair Indicted in Race Slaying." *Jackson State Times*, September 6, 1955, 1A.

"Panel of Jurors May Be Drawn for Till Case Today." *Daily Corinthian*, September 21, 1955, 1.

Works Cited

"Parents and Relatives Keep Silent in Case of Boy Charged with Ugly Remarks to Storekeeper[']s Wife." *Jackson Advocate*, September 3, 1955, 1+.

Patterson, Robert B. Letter to the editor. *Clarksdale Press Register*, September 14, 1955, 7.

———. Letter to the editor. *McComb Enterprise-Journal*, September 6, 1955, 1+.

Phillips, Kendall R., ed. *Framing Public Memory*. Tuscaloosa, AL: University of Alabama Press, 2005.

"Places Till Article in Congress Record." *Clarion-Ledger*, January 14, 1956, 1+.

Popham, John N. "Till Case Rocked by Many Factors." *Jackson State Times*, November 6, 1955, 5A.

Porteous, Clark. "Grand Jury to Get Case of Slain Negro Boy Monday." *Memphis Press-Scimitar*, September 1, 1955, 1+.

———. "New Till Evidence: Reporter Finds It; Officers Work All Night on Searches." *Memphis Press-Scimitar*, September 21, 1955, 1+.

"Prosecution Doesn't Say If Death Penalty Sought in Trial of White Men." *Jackson Daily News*, September 12, 1955, 1.

"Prosecution Ready for Trial of Men." *Greenwood Commonwealth*, September 12, 1955, 1.

"P. S. to NAACP." *Jackson Daily News*, September 4, 1955, 6.

"Publicity in the Big City Papers." *Greenwood Morning Star*, September 16, 1955, 4.

"Random Thoughts by the Editor." *Yazoo City Herald*, September 8, 1955, 1.

"Reed Boy, Bradley Woman Fled State for 'Safety' but Police Guard Homes." *Jackson Daily News*, September 30, 1955, 1.

"Rep. Diggs Blasts Mississippi Trial." *Clarion-Ledger*, September 26, 1955, 2:6.

"Roman Circus." *Jackson Daily News*, September 22, 1955, 12.

"Rumors Till Seen Alive Lack Basis." *Jackson State Times*, September 30, 1955, 1A.

Rutherford, Barry. "Both Races Must Reject Hot-Headed Leaders." *Tupelo Daily Journal*, September 13, 1955, 11.

———. "Need of Trained Crime Investigators Mounts." *Tupelo Daily Journal*, September 26, 1955, 11.

"Says Usual Thing for Negroes to Visit Relatives in Delta." *Jackson State Times*, September 4, 1955, 1A.

Schultz, Lois J. "Strolling—Around Clarksdale." *Clarksdale Press Register*, September 17, 1955, 1.

"Set Trial For Sept. 19 in Till Slaying." *Delta Democrat-Times*, September 9, 1955, 1.

"Sheriff Doubts Body That of Emmitt [sic] Till." *Jackson Daily News*, September 4, 1955, 1.

"Sheriff Doubts Identity of Boy." *Commercial Dispatch*, September 4, 1955, 1.

"Sheriff Repeats Belief That Till Is Still Alive." *Vicksburg Evening Post*, September, 29, 1955, 1.

"Sheriff Strider's Testimony Raises Doubt Body in River Was Till Youth." *Jackson Daily News*, September 23, 1955, 9.

Shoemaker, W. C. "Mrs. Bryant Won 2 Top Beauty Honors—Mother Loyally Stays At Trial." *Jackson Daily News*, September 22, 1955, 11.

———. "Reporter for Commies Relates How He Shifted to 'Left'—Says Trial 'Fair.'" *Jackson Daily News*, September 21, 1955, 14.

Simpson, William M. "Reflections on a Murder: The Emmett Till Case." In

Works Cited

Southern Miscellany: Essays in History in Honor of Glover Moore. Ed. Frank Allen Dennis. Jackson, MS: University Press of Mississippi, 1981, 177–200.
"Sidelights at Sumner Trial." *Greenwood Commonwealth*, September 20, 1955, 1.
Skelton, B. J. "Testimony at Bryant-Milam Trial Has Left Many Questions Unanswered." *Clarksdale Press Register*, September 23, 1955, 7.
———. "Visiting Newsmen Pack Typewriters, Head for Homes." *Clarksdale Press Register*, September 24, 1955, 1.
Skewes, James. "We Can't Condone Murder." *Meridian Star*, September 8, 1955, 4.
"Slaying, NAACP Methods Rapped by Newspapers." *Biloxi Daily Herald*, September 3, 1955.
Smith, Hazel Brannon. "Through Hazel Eyes." *Lexington Advertiser*, October 20, 1955, 1.
Smothers, David. "Killing of Boy in Mississippi Called 'Atrocity.'" *Jackson Daily News*, September 3, 1955, 1.
"Sordid Crime Has Even More Serious Aspects." *Clarion-Ledger*, September 16, 1955, 12.
"Speedy Trial Planned in Kidnap-Slaying Case." *Greenwood Commonwealth*, September 7, 1955, 1.
Spell, Bill. "Daily News Readers Offer Help to Send Willie Reed's Girl Friend to Chicago." *Jackson Daily News*, September 29, 1955, 1.
———. "Effort to Tell Mandy of Her Husband Fails as Phone Connection Was Cut." *Jackson Daily News*, October 8, 1955, 1.
———. "How the NAACP Network Operates." *Jackson Daily News*, October 7, 1955, 1+.
———. "State Negroes Held 'Captive' in Chicago." *Jackson Daily News*, October 5, 1955, 1+.
———. "Woman Witness Told to Keep Silence." *Jackson Daily News*, October 6, 1955, 1+.
———. "Would Take $77,880,783.51 to Haul All Our Good Negroes to the Nawth." *Jackson Daily News*, September 28, 1955, 5.
Spell, Bill, and W. C. Shoemaker. "'Missing' Negro Used in NAACP Propaganda Found; He's Not Able to Contact His Wife, Mandy Bradley." *Jackson Daily News*, October 6, 1955, 1.
"'Spurs Fight.'" *Delta Democrat-Times*, September 9, 1955, 1.
Stapleton, Jack. "Query Lingers: Is Till Dead?" *Clarksdale Press Register*, September 30, 1955, 1.
"State Calls Special Counsel to Assist with Prosecution." *Clarksdale Press Register*, September 10, 1955, 1.
"State Declines to Comment as to Whether It Will Ask for Death in Delta Trial." *Laurel Leader-Call*, September 12, 1955, 1.
"State Negroes Not Surprised at Till Verdict." *Jackson Advocate*, October 1, 1955, 1+.
Stewart, Mrs. Charles. Letter to the editor. *Greenwood Commonwealth*, September 13, 1955, 8.
"Strider Believes Till Is Still Alive." *Greenwood Commonwealth*, September 29, 1955, 1.
Stroupe, Phil. "Delta Residents Expected Indictments and Want Justice Done

Works Cited

in Till Case but Outside Interference Resented." *Jackson Daily News*, September 7, 1955, 2:3.
Sullens, Frederick. *Jackson Daily News*, October 2, 1955, 1.
"Sullens Praised for Till Exposure." *Greenwood Commonwealth*, October 18, 1955, 8.
Taylor, Velma. "Just Ramblin.'" *Holly Springs Southern Reporter*, September 22, 1955, 1.
"328 Attend 'Protest' of Till Killing." *Arizona Republic*, November 20, 1955, n.p.
"13 Witnesses Summoned in Murder Case." *Biloxi Daily Herald*, September 20, 1955, 1+.
Thompson, Julius E. *The Black Press in Mississippi, 1865–1985*. Gainesville, FL: University Press of Florida, 1993.
———. *Percy Greene and the Jackson Advocate: The Life and Times of a Radical Conservative Black Newspaperman, 1897–1977*. Jefferson, NC: McFarland, 1994.
"The Till Case in Retrospect." *Jackson State Times*, November 21, 1955, 4A.
"Till Case Is Still Helping to Fill Mailbox of Greenville Newspaper." *Delta Democrat-Times*, September 29, 1955, 10.
"The Till Case Verdict." *Jackson Advocate*, October 1, 1955, 4.
Till, Karen E. "Places of Memory." In *A Companion for Political Geography*. Ed. John Agnew, Katharyne Mitchell, Gearoid O'Tuathail. Oxford: Blackwell, 2002, 289–301.
"Till Murder Case Hurts US Prestige." *Natchez Democrat*, October 22, 1955, 1.
"Till Murder Trial at Sumner Got Underway Yesterday." *Natchez Democrat*, September 20, 1955, 1+.
"Till Trial Acquittal Protested by Rallies." *Delta Democrat-Times*, September 26, 1955, 1+.
"Till Witness Says Hears Beating, Cries; Claims Milam Wearing Gun; Seen with Boy." *Meridian Star*, September 22, 1955, 1.
Till-Bradley, Mamie. "I Want You to Know What They Did to My Boy." *Afro-American*, November 12, 1955, 6+.
Till-Mobley, Mamie, and Christopher Benson. *Death of Innocence: The Story of the Hate Crime That Changed America*. New York: One World, 2003.
"Till's Dad Raped 2 Women, Murdered a Third in Italy." *Jackson Daily News*, October 14, 1955, 1.
"Till's GI Dad Hanged in Italy for Women Attacks in 1944." *Winona Times*, October 28, 1955, 1.
"Till's Mother Denies Report He Is Alive." *Hattiesburg American*, September 29, 1955, 1.
"Till's Mother, 'Wary of Foes,' Keeping Her Route to Trial Secret." *Jackson Daily News*, September 16, 1955, 1.
"Time for Us to Forget the Till Murder Case." *Tupelo Daily Journal*, October 18, 1955, 11.
Tisdale, John R. "Different Assignments, Different Perspectives: How Reporters Reconstruct the Emmett Till Civil Rights Murder Trial." *Oral History Review* 29 (2002): 39–58.
"To All White Men and Women in Jackson." *Winona Times*, September 30, 1955.
"To [sic] Much Angry Shouting. . . ." *Madison County Herald*, October 18, 1955, 3.

Works Cited

Torres, Sasha. *Black, White, and In Color: Television and Black Civil Rights.* Princeton, NJ: Princeton University Press, 2003.
"Trial at Sumner Draws Attention of Entire Nation." *Coffeeville Courier*, September 22, 1955, 1.
Trimble, Elliott. "Lamentable Aspects of Racial Propaganda." *Natchez Democrat*, October 7, 1955, 4.
"Troops Guarding Pair Charged with Kidnap-Murder of Negro Lad." *Delta Democrat-Times*, September 5, 1955, 1.
"The Truth Remains." *Jackson State Times*, September 24, 1955, 1A.
"Try to Determine Spot Where Negro Was Slain." *Greenwood Morning Star*, September 3, 1955, 1.
"Two Greenwood Men Arrested Monday on Kidnapping Charges." *Grenada Daily Sentinel-Star*, August 30, 1955, 1.
"2 White Men Censured in Protest Meet." *Jackson State Times*, September 29, 1955, 1A+.
"Two White Men Charged with Kidnaping Negro." *Delta Democrat-Times*, August 30, 1955, 1.
"Two White Men Indicted for Murder; Grand Jury Takes Action in Slaying of Chicago Negro." *Vicksburg Evening Post*, September 6, 1955, 1.
"Two White Men Plead Innocent to Murder of Negro Youth." *Natchez Democrat*, September 7, 1955, 1+.
"Unable to Find Young Negro Boy." *Biloxi Daily Herald*, August 30, 1955, 17.
"Uncle of Victim Identifies Defendants as Abductors." *West Point Daily Times Leader*, September 21, 1955, 1+.
"Undertaker's Story Heard." *Jackson State Times*, September 21, 1955, 1A+.
"Unfortunate and Regretable [sic]." *Kosciusko Star-Herald*, September 8, 1955, 2:4.
"The Verdict at Sumner." *Jackson Daily News*, September 25, 1955, 8.
"Vote of Thanks Due." *Kosciusko Star-Herald*, October 20, 1955, 4.
Weir, Murphy. "Ramblins." *Weekly Democrat*, October 13, 1955, 1+.
"Where Women Do the Wolf Whistling." *Jackson State Times*, September 25, 1955.
Whitaker, Hugh Stephen. "A Case Study in Southern Justice: The Murder and Trial of Emmett Till." *Rhetoric and Public Affairs* 8 (2005): 189–224.
"White Calls Boy's Death 'Murder; Not Lynching.'" *Jackson Daily News*, September 2, 1955, 14.
"White Demands Full Probe into Murder; Mom Stands by Sons." *Delta Democrat-Times*, September 2, 1955, 1.
"White Man Held in Abduction of Negro Youth." *Hattiesburg American*, August 29, 1955, 9.
"White Man Was Hanged 65 Years Ago in Grenada for Murdering Negro." *Columbia-Progress*, September 29, 1955, 2:2.
"White Orders Boy's Death Investigated; Woman's Arrest Ordered in Tallahatchie County." *Clarksdale Press Register*, September 1, 1955, 1+.
"White Says No Lynching." *West Point Daily Times Leader*, September 2, 1955, 1.
"White Storekeeper Held in Abduction of Negro Youth." *Jackson Daily News*, August 29, 1955, 1.

Works Cited

Whitten, Ellen. "Injustice Unearthed: Revisiting the Murder of Emmett Till." Honors Thesis. Rhodes College, 2005.

"Why Didn't They Get the Same Publicity?" *Greenwood Morning Star*, September 7, 1955, 4.

Wilkins, Roy. Letter to the editor. *Look*, March 6, 1956, 10.

"Will the NAACP Accept Blame?" *Delta Democrat-Times*, September 21, 1955, 4.

"Willie Reed, Negro Youth, Testifis [sic] about Seeing Pick-Up Truck and Hearing Hollering from Barn." *Jackson Daily News*, September 22, 1955, 8.

Wold, Felix B. "Mose Tells of Sleeping in Cemetery but 'Middle Man' Attended Interview." *Jackson Daily News*, October 8, 1955, 1.

Wright, Moses. "I Saw Them Take Emmett Till." *Inside Detective*, February 1956, 26+.

"Youth's Killing Labeled Murder by Governor; Full Investigation Called For in State, Elsewhere." *McComb Enterprise-Journal*, September 2, 1955, 1.

Index

Aberdeen News, 7, 115
Abrams, Jimmie, 55, 134
Adams, Virgil, 77, 87, 88, 107–8, 113, 114, 135, 141, 164
Ainsworth, A. B., 53, 71
Alewine, Thomas M., 51, 93, 115, 132, 134, 142, 164
American Jewish Committee, 139
Anderson, Dillon, 64
Anderson, W. H., 67, 139
AP (Associated Press), 8, 18, 20, 26, 33, 39, 43, 44, 58, 60, 70, 71, 75, 92, 129, 142, 143
Arrington, Jimmy, 52, 139
Attala County (Miss.), 48, 49

Baier Lustgarten Farms and Nurseries, 117
"Ballot or the Bullet, The," 7
Baltimore (Md.), 92, 121, 122
Barloon, Marvin J., 56, 57
Barlow, E. C., 87
Beauchamp, Keith, 5–6, 151, 156
Beckwith, Byron de la, 164
Behall, John, 121
Belzoni (Miss.), 17, 47, 151
Belzoni Banner, 17, 48, 63
Big Black River, 156
Billingsley, Walter, 91
Biloxi (Miss.), 8, 18
Biloxi Daily Herald, 19, 32, 40
Birmingham (Ala.), 7
Black Codes, 153
Boyce, L. W., 102
Bradley, Alonzo, 128
Bradley, Amanda (Mandy), 91, 96, 117, 126, 127, 128, 129, 130, 132
Bradley, Norman, 146, 147
Brady, Mozella, 124
Brandon (Miss.), 139, 147
Brandon News, 51, 93, 115, 132
Bready, David, 93, 95, 101, 164
Breland, J. J., 58, 60, 61, 62, 86, 90, 91, 92, 94, 101, 137, 138
Brett, Vernon, 43
Broadway, June, 144
Brookhaven (Miss.), 17, 49, 87, 110, 119

Brookhaven Leader-Times, 81
Brotherhood of Sleeping Car Porters, 122
Brown, Earl, 122, 124
Brown vs. Board of Education, 6, 7, 16, 17, 59, 110, 114, 137, 138, 150, 153, 155, 163
Brownell, Herbert, 19, 122
Brumfield, Dr. Robert H., 20–21, 22, 23, 29, 42, 49
Bryant, Carolyn, 5, 8, 10, 13, 19, 25, 33, 47, 60, 70, 71, 80, 81, 82, 83, 99, 105, 106, 113, 114, 116, 121, 135, 136, 145, 162; looks of, 9, 26, 27, 44, 60, 74, 75, 78, 79, 95; photographs of, 40, 44, 56, 69–70, 76, 84; store encounter with Emmett Till, 14; trial testimony of, 14, 86, 87, 96–98, 104; warrant issued for, 22, 30
Bryant, Eula Lee, 29–30, 99
Bryant, Roy, 8, 10, 14, 15, 18, 19, 23, 30, 32, 34, 35, 38, 39, 40, 41, 43, 46, 47, 50, 57, 60, 62, 63, 64, 67, 68, 71, 74, 75, 77, 80, 81, 82, 83, 85, 87, 88, 89, 90, 95, 99, 101, 102, 103, 104, 105, 106, 107, 109, 115, 116, 117, 123, 125, 128, 129, 138, 143, 145, 149, 150, 152, 153, 157; confession of, 11; grand jury indictment of, 39; patriotism of, 29, 33, 80; photographs of, 29, 44, 84; physical appearance of, 79; trial of, 58, 73–106
Bryant Grocery and Meat Market, 5, 13, 23, 27, 43, 48, 70, 80, 95, 113, 135, 157, 165
Bunn, F., 134
Burke, Kenneth, 9
Burr Oak Cemetery (Alsip, Ill.), 43, 45, 94, 156

Caldwell, James Hamilton, 58, 74, 84, 101, 109, 149
Campbell, Mrs. Louise, 79
Carlton, C. Sidney, 8, 43, 46, 58, 60, 71, 80, 87, 91, 96, 97, 101, 104, 105
Carter, Hodding, 18, 39, 146, 147, 149
Carthan, John, 59, 78, 99
Chaney, Goodman, and Schwerner Memorial Highway, 158

Index

Chaney, James, 156
Charleston (Miss.), 61, 62, 79, 117, 148
Charlottesville (Va.), 131
Chatham, Gerald, 8, 25, 35, 38, 58, 59, 74, 76, 84, 100, 102, 103, 109, 116
Cheatham, J. J., 121
Chicago (Ill.), 4, 5, 9, 13, 14, 15, 18, 19, 21, 22, 23, 29, 30, 32, 35, 36, 38, 39, 40, 41, 44, 45, 46, 47, 48, 49, 50, 52, 56, 60, 62, 63, 64, 66, 76, 88, 93, 94, 98, 100, 101, 103, 108, 111, 115, 117, 119, 124, 127, 128, 129, 130, 131, 132, 134, 137, 144, 150, 151, 157, 165
Chicago American, 129, 131
Chicago Defender, 17, 31, 83, 132
Chicago Tribune, 45
Chickasaw County, 50
Citizens' Councils, 6, 16, 21, 22, 23, 28, 42, 49, 55, 59, 63, 65, 66, 118, 126, 134
Civil War, 146
civil-rights movement, 6, 7, 16, 25, 154
Civitavecchia, Italy, 134
Clarion-Ledger, 18, 22, 23, 24, 30, 31, 34, 35, 36, 40, 44, 45, 68, 70, 72, 74, 75, 79, 80, 82, 84, 87, 89, 90, 99, 116, 117, 118, 119, 120, 123, 150, 164
Clarksdale (Miss.), 69, 148
Clarksdale Press Register, 19, 20, 32, 56, 65, 88, 101, 102, 112, 120, 121, 124, 134
Clay County, 83
Cleveland (Miss.), 17, 101, 121
Cleveland (Ohio), 56, 69, 76
Clutts, W. V., 43
Cochran, Edward, 37
Coffeeville (Miss.), 93
Coffeeville Courier, 93–94
cold war, 6, 42, 139, 154
Cole, C. H., 51–52, 140, 141, 164
Coleman, J. P., 24, 58
Collins (Miss.), 139
Collins, Leroy "Too Tight," 8, 85, 102, 117, 122, 132
Collins News-Commercial, 52
Columbia Progress, 121
Columbus Commercial Dispatch, 35, 120
Communism (Communists), 6, 32, 51, 64, 65, 76, 80, 87, 112, 115, 116, 119, 123, 132, 139, 143
Congressional Record, 150
Coody, A. S., 138, 139
CORE (Congress of Racial Equality), 52

corpus delicti, 35, 41, 49, 61, 80, 82, 85, 91, 94, 99, 101, 102, 145, 149
Cothran, John Ed, 15, 34, 35, 36, 81, 84, 86, 89, 90, 91, 105, 124, 144
Cox, A. E., 119
Crawford, Johnny, 16
Crawford, Rutha Mae, 14
Crisis, The, 31

Daily Corinthian, 65, 67
Daily Worker, 64, 87, 112, 122
Daley, Richard, 29
Deacons for Defense, 154
Death in the Delta, A, 5
Dee, Henry, 156
Delta Democrat-Times, 18, 24, 28, 34, 38, 39, 41, 56, 57, 71, 74, 82, 85, 87, 88, 100, 101, 111, 112, 121, 145, 149
Denley, Robert H., 120
Denver (Colo.), 157
Des Moines (Iowa), 142
Detroit (Mich.), 103, 121, 122, 124
Devils and Dust, 3
Diggs, Charles C., 8, 78, 89, 93, 99, 105, 108, 109, 111, 115, 117, 118, 121, 122, 128, 142, 150
Dittmer, John, 7, 17
Dogan, Harry, 152
D'Orlando, Albert, 120–21
Douglass, Frederick, 154
Drew (Miss.), 92, 128
Drew Leader, 141
DuBois, W. E. B., 154
Duke, Grover, 102
Durr, M. C., 66, 81, 118–19

Eastland, James O., 52, 126, 134, 138, 139
Eisenhower, Dwight David, 29, 64, 65, 122, 134
Emmerich, Oliver, 21, 134, 147
Emmett Till Bridge, 157
Emmett Till Math and Science Academy, 157
Emmett Till Memorial Highway, 4, 157, 158, 159, 160, 161
Emmett Till Road, 157
Ethridge, Tom, 54, 71
Everett, Arthur, 82, 90, 98, 99
Evers, Medgar, 104, 148
Eyes on the Prize, 5

Index

Faulkner, William, 57, 58
FBI (Federal Bureau of Investigation), 5, 19, 58, 64, 151, 160
Featherston, James, 21, 76, 78, 93
Ford, Fulton, 69
Ford, Louis Henry, 59, 69, 78
Foreman, Harold, 123
Fountain, Carolyn, 135
Fraiser, John, Jr., 36, 116
Frank, Anne, 4
Freedom Rides, 7
Freedom Summer, 7
Freeman, Curtis, 120

Garvey, Marcus, 154
Glendora (Miss.), 14, 30, 125, 147, 148
Goldzwig, Steven, 7
Goodman, Andrew, 156
Greene, Percy, 8, 37, 59, 73, 114, 115
Greenville (Miss.), 8, 33, 39, 44, 112, 121, 124
Greenville Delta Leader, 8
Greenwood (Miss.), 4, 8, 18, 24, 33, 35, 37, 40, 44, 45, 46, 48, 51, 53, 55, 62, 64, 65, 68, 83, 86, 100, 116, 119, 121, 126, 132, 143, 145, 147, 148, 160
Greenwood Commonwealth, 18, 28, 43, 45, 52, 53, 55, 62, 63, 67, 77, 82, 85, 93, 111, 139, 164
Greenwood Morning Star, 33, 34, 35, 36, 42, 44, 45, 54, 55, 62, 65, 68, 71, 77, 82, 83, 87, 88, 99, 103, 107, 113, 141, 143, 145
Grenada (Miss.), 18, 55, 121
Grenada Daily Sentinel-Star, 29, 55, 56, 136

H. C. "Clarence" Strider Highway, 4
Halberstam, David, 83
Hall, Rob, 87, 89, 101, 122
Harding, John F., 150
Harlem (N.Y.), 115, 134
Harrell, E. E., 121
Harris, Henry, 40–41, 46, 47, 83
Harris, Sid R., 50, 66, 67, 88–89, 139
Hattiesburg (Miss.), 8, 17, 18, 33, 101, 165
Hattiesburg American, 25, 44, 76
Hawkins, Armis E., 66
Heard, Joe, 36
Henderson, Harvey, 58, 101, 104
Hendrickson, Paul, 5, 159
Herbers, John, 82, 88, 92, 93, 95, 99

Hernando (Miss.), 111
Hicks, James, 78
High, Arrington H., 8
Hinant, G. W., 120
Hodges, Floyd, 16
Holloway, Mrs. Frances, 95
Holly Springs Southern Reporter, 88
Holmes, Marguerite, 140, 141
Hoover, J. Edgar, 64
Houston (Miss.), 50, 66
Houston Times-Post, 50, 67, 88, 139
Howard, T. R. M. (Theodore Roosevelt Mason), 8, 17, 37, 58, 59, 72, 76, 85, 86, 91, 99, 102, 104, 105, 109, 111, 116, 117, 118, 121, 122, 142
Huff, William Henry, 19, 21, 77, 136
Huie, William Bradford, 11, 149, 150, 151, 154
Hurley, Ruby, 66
Hutto, Ralph, 79, 90, 107, 120

"I Have a Dream," 7
Illinois Central railroad, 4, 12, 17, 22, 82
Indianola (Miss.), 13, 16, 22, 95
Indianola Enterprise-Tocsin, 26
integration, 7, 37, 43, 48, 59, 68, 114, 119, 120, 137
International League against Racialism and Anti-Semitism, 122
interracial sex, 16, 18, 114
Itta Bena (Miss.), 125
"I've Been to the Mountaintop," 7

Jackson (Miss.), 8, 33, 36, 48, 53, 70, 71, 83, 89, 103, 110, 115, 124, 126, 137, 138, 147, 152, 164
Jackson, Jesse, 160
Jackson Advocate, 8, 19, 37, 59, 73, 80, 114
Jackson Daily News, 10, 18, 19, 21, 23, 27–28, 29, 32, 34, 35, 36, 38, 39, 43, 45, 46, 48, 50, 53, 54, 57, 66, 67, 68, 71, 74, 76, 77, 78, 79, 80, 84, 88, 93, 95, 98, 99, 101, 105, 108, 109, 111, 112, 121, 123, 124, 125, 126, 127, 128, 129, 130, 131, 133, 134, 135, 136, 137, 138, 139, 141, 142, 145, 164
Jackson Eagle Eye, 8
Jackson Enterprise, 8
Jackson State Times, 24, 64, 68, 69, 72, 76, 78, 79, 86, 90, 94, 97, 107, 117, 119, 120, 123, 143, 145, 146, 149, 164

Index

Jim Crow, 16, 25, 27, 29, 38, 51, 53, 71, 72, 80, 109, 129, 153, 157, 159, 160, 163
Johnson, James Weldon, 154
Johnson, Sam, 70, 71, 75, 78, 92
Jones, Charles C., 141
Jones, J. Morris, 42
Jordan, Arthur, 116, 144
Justice Department, 19, 108, 156

Kalich, Tim, 164
Kansas City (Mo.), 65
Kansas City Times, 65
Kearney, Dianne, 10, 29, 45, 54, 55, 65, 67, 73, 88, 134
Kearney, John, 45
Kellum, J. W., 44, 58, 105, 149
Kempton, Murray, 117
Kennard, Clyde, 164
Killen, Edgar Ray, 164
Kimball, Elmer, 11, 83, 147, 149
King, Martin Luther, Jr., 4, 7, 157, 163
Kingstree (S.C.), 118
Korean War, 68, 80
Kosciusko (Miss.), 48, 49
Kosciusko Star-Herald, 48, 132, 139
Ku Klux Klan, 64, 88, 104, 156, 160
Kuettner, Al, 164

Landrum, Dr. John W., 55–56
Langford, Dave, 49, 50, 51
Laurel (Miss.), 33, 110, 118, 132
Laurel Leader-Call, 28, 33, 69, 110, 118
Lee, Rev. George W., 17, 21, 48, 49, 151
Leflore County (Miss.), 4, 5, 10, 11, 16, 21, 22, 29, 30, 33, 34, 36, 38, 45, 52, 62, 63, 81, 84, 93, 116, 125, 143, 144, 145, 146, 157, 164
Leggett, Ed, 152
Leghorn, Italy, 134
Leland High School, 95
"Letter from Birmingham Jail," 7
Lexington Advertiser, 138
Life magazine, 138, 139, 142
Lin, Maya, 157, 163
Lincoln County, 49, 87, 119
Lincoln County Advertiser, 118
Little Rock (Ark.), 7
Loggins, Henry Lee, 85, 102, 117, 122, 132
Look magazine, 5, 149, 150, 154, 164
Love, J. T., 119

Lucretzia, Benni, 134
Lucy, Autherine, 154
lynching, 23, 27, 28, 31, 36, 41, 42, 44, 48, 49, 50, 51, 122, 132, 134, 156

Madison County Herald, 49, 137
Malone, H. B., 101, 116
March on Washington, 7
Mari, Frieda, 134
Marsh, Harry, 101
Marshall, Chester, 39
Matamoros Banks, 3
Matthews, Henry, 46
McBroom, James, 39
McClary, Webster, 118, 134
McComb (Miss.), 20, 42, 49, 133, 146
McComb Enterprise-Journal, 20, 26, 29, 56, 120
McGarrh, Lee, 147, 149
McGraa, Pete, 102
Melton, Beulah, 148, 149
Melton, Clinton, 11, 147, 148, 149, 152
Melton, Wilson, 118
Memphis (Tenn.), 79, 85, 87, 117
Memphis Commercial Appeal, 120, 139
Memphis Press-Scimitar, 12, 85
Mendenhall (Miss.), 141
Menter, Willard, 27, 28
Meredith, James, 48, 164
Meridian (Miss.), 8, 18
Meridian Star, 18, 19, 29, 30, 32, 35, 42, 50, 88, 119
Michael Reece Hospital, 127
Milam, Bill, 80
Milam, Ed, 125
Milam, Harvey, 80
Milam, James, 37
Milam, John (J. W.), 8, 14, 15, 18, 32, 34, 37, 38, 40, 41, 43, 46, 47, 50, 57, 60, 61, 62, 63, 64, 66, 68, 70, 71, 74, 75, 76, 77, 81, 82, 83, 84, 85, 87, 88, 89, 90, 91, 92, 96, 99, 101, 102, 103, 104, 105, 106, 109, 115, 116, 117, 121, 123, 125, 127, 128, 129, 132, 138, 141, 143, 145, 147, 149, 150, 151, 152, 153, 157; confession of, 11; grand jury indictment of, 39; patriotism of, 29, 33; photographs of, 29, 44; physical appearance of, 79; trial of, 58, 73–106
Milam, Juanita, 14, 71, 97, 98, 99, 106, 107; looks of, 75, 79; photographs of, 69–70

Index

Milam, Leslie, 85, 92, 128
Milam, Wade, 138
Milam and Bryant Defense Fund, 53
Miller, Chester A., 86
Milner, Jay, 36, 40, 80, 82, 84, 87, 89, 119, 122, 123, 150, 151
Minter, D. R., 119
Minter City (Miss.), 163
Mississippi: A Story of Race and Its Legacy, 5
Mississippi Delta, 4, 11, 18, 22, 26, 40, 41, 45, 47, 48, 49, 51, 61, 68, 69, 71, 72, 74, 75, 76, 83, 88, 95, 99, 108, 120, 124, 125, 132, 149, 153, 158, 162
Mississippi Department of Archives and History, 152, 164–65
Mississippi State Sovereignty Commission, 114, 138, 152, 165
Mitchell, Jerry, 164
Mobile (Ala.), 142
Money (Miss.), 4, 5, 9, 12, 15, 18, 21, 22, 23, 29, 39, 45, 47, 54, 73, 96, 98, 103, 114, 120, 125, 159, 165
Montgomery (Ala.), 157, 163
Montgomery bus boycott, 7
Moore, Charles, 156
Mooty, Rayfield, 64
Moulder, Bob, 120
Mound Bayou (Miss.), 17, 37, 58, 72, 76, 91, 103, 105, 116
MPVL (Mississippi Progressive Voters' League), 17
MSDO (Mississippi State Democratic Organization), 17
Muhammad, Elijah, 154

NAACP (National Association for the Advancement of Colored People), 5, 6, 7, 10, 19, 21, 23, 24, 28, 29, 31, 33, 40, 42, 43, 46, 47, 49, 51, 52, 53, 54, 55, 58, 63, 65, 66, 68, 69, 71, 72, 76, 77, 87, 88, 95, 101, 103, 104, 107, 109, 111, 114, 115, 116, 118, 119, 121, 126, 127, 129, 130, 131, 132, 133, 134, 136, 138, 139, 140, 144, 146, 147, 148, 149, 156; alleged conspiracy planned by, 37, 39, 41
Natchez (Miss.), 8, 71, 110, 124, 134, 156
Natchez Democrat, 71, 75, 110, 131
National Baptist Convention, 56
National Guard, 10, 44, 131
National Urban League, 42, 53
Nelms, Mrs. Mozell, 63
New Albany Community Citizen, 8

New Orleans (La.), 115, 120, 132
New York (N.Y.), 23, 24, 48, 64, 88, 101, 121, 122, 124, 144
New York Amsterdam News, 31
New York Times, 32, 64, 68, 143

Olney, Warren, 54
Orsby, Hubert, 156
Otken, Dr. L. B., 39, 40, 61, 82, 94; trial testimony of, 100–1, 116
Outlaw, Clara Mae, 152
Oxford (Miss.), 164
Oxford Eagle, 132

Parchman State Penitentiary, 124
Paris, France, 122
Parker, Mack Charles, 132, 156
Parker, Wheeler, 15
Parks, Rosa, 7, 25, 163
Parsons, J. A., 56, 63
Pascagoula (Miss.), 87, 101
Patterson, Robert B. (Tut), 22, 42, 65
Pecan Point, 16
Pennington, Jim, 116
Perry, Harold, 102
Philipp (Miss.), 16
Picayune (Miss.), 51, 133, 140, 147
Picayune Item, 51, 115, 132
Pittsburgh (Pa.), 142
Pittsburgh Courier, 31, 120
Plessy, Homer, 153
Popham, John, 143
Poplarville (Miss.), 132, 156
Porteous, Clark, 12, 13, 85, 86, 121
Powell, Adam Clayton, 134
Providence Farms, 11, 119
Pueblo (Colo.), 157
Pushis, Joanne, 46

Randolph, A. Philip, 154
Rayner, A. A., 22, 31, 32, 41
RCNL (Regional Council of Negro Leadership), 17, 37
Reed, Add, 91
Reed, Mrs. O. R., 121
Reed, Willie, 11, 89, 91, 102, 117, 121, 123, 124, 126, 127, 129, 130, 132, 141; trial testimony of, 92, 93, 94, 116, 144
Revelation 21:8, 56
Ripley (Miss.), 58
Ripley Southern Sentinel, 139
Rutherford, Barry, 63, 112–13

Index

Sanders, James, 102
Sanders, Stanny, 30, 85, 116, 143, 144, 147
Schultz, Lois J., 69, 88
Schwerner, Mickey, 156
SCLC (Southern Christian Leadership Conference), 52
Scott County Times, 50, 68
segregation, 6, 16, 22, 28, 38, 45, 63, 64, 78, 103, 113, 118, 119, 123, 126, 129, 133, 141, 153, 164
Selma (Ala.), 7
Shanks, A. W., 30
Sharkey (Miss.), 29
Shaw, J. A., 105, 116
Sheridan plantation (Sunflower County, Miss.), 85, 96, 102
Shoemaker, W. C., 95, 101, 128
Simpson County (Miss.), 89
Simpson County News, 89, 115
sit-ins, 7
Skelton, B. J., 102
Skewes, James, 50, 51
Smith, Crosby, 15, 22
Smith, Franklin, 102
Smith, George, 15, 18, 19, 22, 28, 34, 35, 36, 38, 80, 84, 85, 86, 89, 116, 125, 143, 144, 164; trial testimony of, 90–91, 105, 144
Smith, Lamar, 17, 49, 66, 87, 110
Smith, Robert B., 58, 66, 74, 84, 86, 92, 94, 96, 100, 103, 109, 116
Smithdale (Miss.), 42
SNCC (Student Nonviolent Coordinating Committee), 52
South Deering Bulletin, 66, 82
Southern Poverty Law Center, 163
Southern Sentinel, 67
Soviet Union, 123
Spearman, Alma, 128
Spell, Bill, 124, 127, 128, 129, 130, 131, 132, 134, 135, 164
Spingarn, Arthur, 138
Springsteen, Bruce, 3-4
Stennis, John, 134
Stewart, Mrs. Charles, 63
Stowers, Ernest, 125
Stratton, William, 29
Strider, Sheriff H. C., 7, 11, 21, 22, 23, 25, 29, 30, 31, 33, 61, 73, 78, 80, 94, 101, 111, 116, 123, 124, 143, 149, 152, 163; and change of mind about identity of corpse, 10, 34–35; and identity of corpse, 82; and NAACP conspiracy, 37, 38, 39, 41, 46, 49, 53, 112; trial testimony of, 99–100
Stroupe, Phil, 46
Stubbs, Ella Mae, 124, 127
Sullens, Major Fred, 50, 53, 127, 139, 164
Sumner (Miss.), 4, 5, 39, 43, 54, 58, 60, 69, 71, 72, 78, 87, 88, 89, 93, 101, 103, 105, 108, 110, 112, 113, 114, 117, 118, 119, 120, 122, 123, 126, 135, 143, 145, 148
Sumner Sentinel, 105, 148
Sunflower County (Miss.), 13, 85
Swango, Curtis, 11, 43, 61, 73, 84, 85, 86, 90, 91, 93, 96, 102, 104, 105, 107, 111, 116, 121, 122, 143, 149

Tallahatchie County, 4, 5, 10, 16, 21, 22, 33, 35, 38, 39, 51, 52, 58, 61, 65, 66, 70, 71, 72, 77, 80, 116, 117, 124, 149, 152, 157
Tallahatchie River, 3, 16, 19, 21, 29, 33, 34, 35, 38–39, 45, 55, 60, 80, 83, 94, 100, 133, 143, 150, 154, 159, 163
Tate County Democrat, 115
Taylor, Velma, 88
Tchula (Miss.), 11, 119, 126, 132
"Ten Feet Tall," 132
Till, Emmett, 3, 4, 5, 6, 7, 8, 11, 12, 16, 17, 18, 19, 20, 22, 23, 24, 26, 27, 29, 32, 33, 35, 36, 37, 38, 41, 42, 44, 45, 47, 48, 49, 50, 51, 52, 54, 55, 56, 57, 58, 63, 64, 66, 67, 68, 71, 72, 74, 76, 80, 81, 83, 85, 86, 87, 88, 89, 91, 92, 93, 94, 95, 96, 99, 100, 101, 102, 103, 105, 109, 114, 118, 119, 120, 123, 124, 125, 126, 128, 132, 135, 136, 138, 139, 141, 142, 143, 146, 148, 150, 151, 152, 153, 154, 156, 157, 158, 159, 160, 161, 163, 164, 165; alleged assault of Carolyn Bryant, 82, 84; alleged castration of, 31, 91; alleged handicaps of, 28, 30, 79; burial of, 43, 45; and postmortem photograph of, 8, 31; and civil rights historiography, 155; condition of corpse, 21; encounter with Carolyn Bryant, 14; kidnapping of, 14–15; memorialization of, 155–65; photographs of, 20, 44, 56, 60, 70, 75;

Index

positive news coverage of, 18–23; press characterizations of, 9; public viewing of, 31, 33; ring worn by, 3, 13, 16, 34, 35, 41, 83, 86, 94, 101, 123, 134

Till, Louis, 11, 34, 41, 134, 135, 136, 137, 138, 139, 140, 141, 142, 143

Till, Mamie (Till-Bradley and Till-Mobley), 4, 6, 7, 11, 12, 15, 17, 19, 21, 22, 23, 26, 29, 31, 35, 45, 47, 58, 61, 63, 64, 65, 67, 69, 71, 72, 73, 80, 85, 92, 93, 94, 98, 100, 105, 109, 115, 121, 122, 124, 128, 134, 135, 140, 142, 144, 147, 155; appearance of, 27, 78, 79, 84; identification of son's body, 31; photographs of, 20, 30, 56, 75, 76, 99; press characterizations of, 9; and statement of September 1, 1955, 10, 24, 25; trial testimony of, 94–95, 116

Tillman, Jim, 121

Tobias, Channing H., 116

Townsend, Kid, 72–73

Trimble, Elliott, 133

Truth and Reconciliation Committee, 162

Tupelo (Miss.), 8, 63

Tupelo Daily Journal, 32, 38, 63, 112, 137

Tupman, Johnny, 80

Tutwiler (Miss.), 4, 101

United States Supreme Court, 6, 16, 17, 48, 110, 114, 133, 137, 138, 153

University of Alabama, 154

University of Mississippi (Ole Miss), 7, 48, 164

University of Southern Mississippi (Mississippi Southern College), 164

Untold Story of Emmett Louis Till, The, 5, 156

UP (United Press), 8, 18, 30, 34, 36, 38, 43, 56, 58, 65, 69, 92

Vaiden (Miss.), 63

Vicksburg (Miss.), 8, 33, 44, 103

Vicksburg Evening Post, 20, 75–76, 131, 142

Washington, Booker T., 154

Washington, D.C., 64, 68

Webb (Miss.), 4, 163

Weekly Democrat, 132

Wells, Ida, 154

West Point (Miss.), 133

West Point Daily Times Leader, 29, 40, 46, 83

Whitaker, Hugh Stephen, 24, 61, 71, 77, 97, 117

White, Gov. Hugh, 21, 28, 34, 36, 44, 58, 59, 66, 122, 131

Whitfield, Stephen J., 5

Whitten, John W., 58, 99, 100, 101, 103, 104, 150

Wilkins, Roy, 7, 8, 23, 24, 25, 27, 28, 33, 37, 42, 46, 47, 50, 54, 55, 56, 59, 64, 66, 95, 103, 109, 116, 122, 131, 132, 134, 144, 147, 151; and statement of September 1, 1955, 10, 23–25, 29, 31, 41, 53, 68, 71

William Winter Institute for Racial Reconciliation, 164

Williams, Esther, 75

Winona (Miss.), 42, 65

Winona Times, 140

Withers, Ernest, 83

Wold, Felix B., 130

World War II, 17, 29, 30, 33, 34, 79, 80, 94, 134, 136, 140, 150

Wright, Elizabeth, 12, 14, 15, 38, 47, 60, 144

Wright, Maurice, 12, 13, 14, 20

Wright, Moses, 3, 9, 11, 12, 13, 14, 15, 16, 18, 19, 21, 30, 34, 37, 38, 47, 57, 60, 70, 75, 76, 85, 87, 91, 105, 117, 121, 125, 126, 127, 129, 130, 132, 151; as prosecution witness, 73, 96; trial testimony of, 83, 84, 86, 89, 90, 102, 104, 144

Wright, Simeon, 14, 15, 156

X, Malcolm, 7, 154

Yazoo City Herald, 7, 48

Young, Frank, 91, 102

Zanchi, Anna, 134

www.ingramcontent.com/pod-product-compliance
Lightning Source LLC
Chambersburg PA
CBHW050442240426
43661CB00055B/2480